Taste*of*Home

all-new MOST REQUESTED *recipes*

TASTE OF HOME BOOKS • RDA ENTHUSIAST BRANDS, LLC • MILWAUKEE, WI

Visit us at **tasteofhome.com** for other Taste of Home
books and products.

International Standard Book Number:
978-1-62145-967-5

Chief Content Officer, Home & Garden: Jeanne Sidner
Content Director: Mark Hagen
Creative Director: Raeann Thompson
Senior Designer: Jazmin Delgado
Deputy Editor, Copy Desk: Dulcie Shoener
Senior Copy Editor: Ann Walter

Cover Photography: Taste of Home Photo Studio

Pictured on front cover:
Bacon Cheeseburger Slider Bake, p. 34

Pictured on back cover:
Juicy Watermelon Salad, p. 126; Citrus-Herb Roast
Chicken, p. 135; Refreshing Berry Wine, p. 43;
Sheet-Pan New England Clambake, p. 195; Pumpkin
Chocolate Chip Cookies, p. 235; Tra Vigne Green
Beans, p. 108; Banh Mi Baby Back Ribs, p. 168;
Maple Pumpkin Pie, p. 249; Spicy Roasted Carrot
Hummus, p. 43

> The flavor is over-the-top delish! My guests loved it and asked for the recipe. I can hardly wait to make again.
> —NUTS4COOKING
> TASTEOFHOME.COM

DOUBLE CHOCOLATE ESPRESSO
CHEESECAKE, PAGE 266

Savor the Most Requested Recipes of All Time!

The greatest thing about working at *Taste of Home* is learning what family cooks serve at their own tables. We're amazed by all the recipes readers send us, but there are always a few that rise to the top of the taste test.

These are the specialties home cooks prepare when they want to impress, the favorites that receive 5-star reviews, and the contest winners everyone clamors for. Now those cooks are sharing their secrets in this brand-new must-have cookbook, *Taste of Home All-New Most Requested Recipes.*

Inside you'll discover ...

• 268 cherished recipes for everything from entrees and desserts to snacks and sides

• At-a-glance icons that highlight dishes made in the slow cooker 🍲, air fryer 🍳 and even the Instant Pot 🍲

• 62 contest winners 🏆 in addition to dozens of must-try main courses, appetizers, soups, salads and breakfasts ready in 30 minutes

• Inspiring stories from today's family cooks as well as easy-to-follow how-to photos and timesaving tips

Deemed best-of-the-best by the *Taste of Home* Test Kitchen pros, these are the dishes that lead to guaranteed success each and every time. Cook with confidence when you turn to any of the much-loved specialties found here. With *All-New Most Requested Recipes* at your side, you've got an "in" on the best recipes in the country!

TABLE OF CONTENTS

CAST-IRON
LOADED BREAKFAST
BISCUITS, PAGE 20

"
I like to bake these biscuits on weekends and freeze them for busy weekday breakfasts.
—COURTNEY STULZ
WEIR, KS

CHAPTER 1

FAVORITE BREAKFASTS

Everyone wants the secrets behind rise-and-shine recipes. You'll find nothing but best-of-the-best dishes here, from quick fixes on hectic mornings to brunch specialties that satisfy a crowd.

BUTTERMILK PANCAKES

You just can't beat a basic buttermilk pancake for a down-home country breakfast.
Paired with sausage and fresh fruit, this pancake is just like the ones you get at Cracker Barrel.
—*Betty Abrey, Imperial, SK*

PREP: 10 MIN. • COOK: 5 MIN./BATCH • MAKES: 2½ DOZEN

4   cups all-purpose flour
¼   cup sugar
2   tsp. baking soda
2   tsp. salt
1½ tsp. baking powder
4   large eggs, room temperature
4   cups buttermilk

1. In a large bowl, combine the flour, sugar, baking soda, salt and baking powder. In another bowl, whisk the eggs and buttermilk until blended; stir into dry ingredients just until moistened.

2. Pour batter by ¼ cupfuls onto a lightly greased hot griddle; turn when bubbles form on top. Cook until second side is golden brown.

Freeze Option: Freeze cooled pancakes between layers of waxed paper in a freezer container. To use, place pancakes on an ungreased baking sheet, cover with foil and reheat in a preheated 375° oven 6-10 minutes. Or place a stack of 3 pancakes on a microwave-safe plate and microwave on high until heated through, 45-90 seconds.

3 pancakes: 270 cal., 3g fat (1g sat. fat), 89mg chol., 913mg sod., 48g carb. (11g sugars, 1g fiber), 11g pro.

Pecan Apple Pancakes: To flour mixture, stir in 1¾ tsp. ground cinnamon, ¾ tsp. ground ginger, ¾ tsp. ground mace and ¾ tsp. ground cloves. To batter, fold in 2½ cups shredded peeled apples and ¾ cup chopped pecans.

Blueberry Pancakes: Fold in 1 cup fresh or frozen blueberries.

Banana Walnut Pancakes: Fold in 2 finely chopped ripe bananas and ⅔ cups finely chopped walnuts.

DID YOU KNOW?

It's easy to make your own buttermilk. For each cup of buttermilk simply put 1 Tbsp. white vinegar in a measuring cup. Add enough milk to measure 1 cup. Stir, then let stand for 5 minutes.

BUTTERMILK
PANCAKES

"

I will never use
boxed pancake
mix again after
having these!
Great recipe!
—LAWANDAJALLEN
TASTEOFHOME.COM

CORNFLAKE-COATED CRISPY BACON

I've loved my aunt's crispy-coated bacon ever since I was a child. Now I've shared the super simple recipe with my own children. We still enjoy a big panful every Christmas morning—and on many other days throughout the year!
—*Brenda Severson, Norman, OK*

PREP: 20 MIN. • **BAKE:** 25 MIN. • **MAKES:** 9 SERVINGS

½ cup evaporated milk
2 Tbsp. ketchup
1 Tbsp. Worcestershire sauce
  Dash pepper
18 bacon strips (1 lb.)
3 cups crushed cornflakes

Preheat oven to 375°. In a large bowl, combine milk, ketchup, Worcestershire sauce and pepper. Add bacon strips, turning to coat. Dip strips in crushed cornflakes, patting to help coating adhere. Place bacon on 2 racks; place each rack on an ungreased 15x10x1-in. baking pan. Bake until golden and crisp, 25-30 minutes, rotating pans halfway through baking.

2 bacon strips: 198 cal., 7g fat (3g sat. fat), 20mg chol., 547mg sod., 26g carb. (4g sugars, 0 fiber), 8g pro.

CRANBERRY-WALNUT OATMEAL

My family loves cranberries but we can only get them fresh during the winter. This recipe lets us enjoy the tartness of cranberry with the comfort of oatmeal all year long.
—*Teena Petrus, Johnstown, PA*

TAKES: 15 MIN. • **MAKES:** 4 SERVINGS

3½ cups water
¼ tsp. salt
2 cups quick-cooking oats
3 Tbsp. sugar
1 tsp. vanilla extract
2 tsp. cinnamon sugar
½ cup whole-berry cranberry sauce
¼ cup chopped walnuts, toasted

1. In a large saucepan, bring water and salt to a boil. Stir in oats. Cook 1 minute over medium heat, stirring occasionally.

2. Remove from heat; stir in sugar and vanilla. Top servings with cinnamon sugar, cranberry sauce and walnuts.

Note: To toast nuts, bake in a shallow pan in a 350°; oven for 5-10 minutes or cook in a skillet over low heat until lightly browned, stirring occasionally.

1 cup: 293 cal., 8g fat (1g sat. fat), 0 chol., 156mg sod., 53g carb. (21g sugars, 5g fiber), 7g pro.

CAST-IRON APPLE NUTMEG COFFEE CAKE

In an effort to practice my baking, I used up the morning's
last bit of coffee to make a coffee cake—literally. It is super moist and crumbly
and tastes as if you dunked your cake right into a cup of hot joe.
You can add pecans to the apples if you want some crunch.
—Darla Andrews, Boerne, TX

PREP: 25 MIN. • BAKE: 20 MIN. + COOLING • MAKES: 8 SERVINGS

- 3 Tbsp. butter, cubed
- 2 cups chopped peeled Gala apple
- ½ cup packed brown sugar, divided
- ¼ cup brewed coffee
- ⅔ cup canola oil
- ½ cup sugar
- 1 large egg plus 1 large egg white,
     room temperature
- 2 tsp. vanilla extract
- 1½ cups all-purpose flour
- 2 tsp. ground cinnamon
- ½ tsp. salt
- ½ tsp. baking soda
- ¼ tsp. ground nutmeg

DRIZZLE
- ⅓ cup brewed coffee
- ¼ cup heavy whipping cream
- 1½ cups confectioners' sugar

1. Preheat oven to 375°. In a 10-in. cast-iron or other ovenproof skillet melt butter over low heat. Add apple and ¼ cup brown sugar. Cook and stir until crisp-tender, about 5 minutes. Stir in coffee; remove from heat.

2. In a large bowl, beat oil, sugar, egg, egg white, vanilla and remaining ¼ cup brown sugar until well blended. In another bowl, whisk flour, cinnamon, salt, baking soda and nutmeg; gradually beat into oil mixture. Gently spread over apple mixture.

3. Bake until a toothpick inserted in center comes out clean, 18-22 minutes. Cool on a wire rack 10 minutes.

4. Meanwhile, for drizzle, in a small saucepan, bring coffee and cream to a boil; cook until liquid is reduced to ¼ cup, 10-12 minutes. Remove from heat; stir in confectioners' sugar. Let stand 10 minutes. Drizzle over cake.

1 piece: 532 cal., 27g fat (6g sat. fat), 43mg chol., 284mg sod., 71g carb. (51g sugars, 1g fiber), 4g pro.

TEST KITCHEN TIP

*For an indulgent after-dinner dessert, serve this coffee cake with
ice cream and then top with the coffee drizzle.*

COCONUT COLD-BREW LATTE

Cold-brew lattes are all the rage at coffee shops,
but they're so easy to make at home. This coconut cold-brew
latte is ridiculously refreshing—and it's even vegan!
—*Natalie Larsen, Grand Prairie, TX*

PREP: 20 MIN. + CHILLING • MAKES: 4 SERVINGS

½ cup coarsely ground medium-roast coffee
½ cup hot water (205°)
3½ cups cold water

COCONUT SIMPLE SYRUP
1 cup water
½ cup sugar
½ cup sweetened shredded coconut

EACH SERVING
Ice cubes
2 Tbsp. coconut milk

1. Place ground coffee in a clean glass container. Pour hot water over coffee; let stand 10 minutes. Stir in the cold water. Cover and refrigerate for 12-24 hours. (The longer the coffee sits, the stronger the flavor.)

2. Meanwhile, for coconut simple syrup, in a small saucepan, bring water, sugar and coconut to a boil. Reduce heat; simmer 10 minutes. Strain and discard coconut. Cool completely.

3. Strain coffee through a fine-mesh sieve; discard grounds. Strain coffee again through a coffee filter; discard grounds. Store coffee in the refrigerator for up to 2 weeks. For each serving, fill a large glass with ice. Add 1 cup cold-brewed coffee and 4 Tbsp. coconut syrup; stir. Top with 2 Tbsp. coconut milk.

1 cup: 145 cal., 5g fat (5g sat. fat), 0 chol., 12mg sod., 26g carb. (26g sugars, 0 fiber), 1g pro.

HAM & AVOCADO SCRAMBLE

Hearty ham, creamy avocado and a hint of garlic give this dish all it needs
to be a winning breakfast, lunch or even dinner!
—*Elisabeth Larsen, Pleasant Grove, UT*

TAKES: 15 MIN. • MAKES: 4 SERVINGS

8 large eggs
¼ cup 2% milk
1 tsp. garlic powder
¼ tsp. pepper
1 cup cubed fully cooked ham
1 Tbsp. butter
1 medium ripe avocado, peeled and cubed
1 cup shredded Colby-Monterey Jack cheese

1. In a large bowl, whisk the eggs, milk, garlic powder and pepper; stir in ham. In a large skillet, melt butter over medium-high heat. Add egg mixture; cook and stir until almost set. Stir in avocado and cheese. Cook and stir until completely set.

1 cup: 407 cal., 31g fat (13g sat. fat), 475mg chol., 789mg sod., 8g carb. (2g sugars, 3g fiber), 26g pro.

EASY BREAKFAST STRATA

We start this breakfast casserole the night before so it's ready for the oven the next day. That way, we don't have to deal with the prep and dirty dishes first thing in the morning!
—*Debbie Johnson, Centertown, MO*

PREP: 25 MIN. + CHILLING • **BAKE:** 30 MIN. • **MAKES:** 12 SERVINGS

1 loaf (1 lb.) herb or cheese bakery bread, cubed
1 lb. bulk pork sausage
1 medium green pepper, chopped
1 medium onion, chopped
1 cup shredded cheddar cheese
6 large eggs
1 tsp. ground mustard
2 cups 2% milk

1. Place bread cubes in a greased 13x9-in. baking dish. In a large skillet, cook and crumble sausage with pepper and onion over medium-high heat until no longer pink, 5-7 minutes. With a slotted spoon, place sausage mixture over bread. Sprinkle with cheese.

2. In a large bowl, whisk together eggs, mustard and milk; pour over top. Refrigerate, covered, overnight.

3. Preheat oven to 350°. Remove strata from refrigerator while oven heats.

4. Bake, uncovered, until a knife inserted in center comes out clean, 30-35 minutes. Let stand 5 minutes before cutting.

Freeze option: Cover and freeze unbaked casserole. To use, partially thaw in refrigerator overnight. Remove from refrigerator 30 minutes before baking. Preheat oven to 350°. Bake casserole as directed, increasing time as necessary to heat through and for a thermometer inserted in center to read 165°.

1 piece: 295 cal., 16g fat (6g sat. fat), 126mg chol., 555mg sod., 23g carb. (4g sugars, 2g fiber), 14g pro.

TEST KITCHEN TIP

Easily adjust this recipe to your family's likes and dislikes by replacing the pork sausage with turkey or spicy chorizo. Substitute mozzarella or pepper jack for the cheddar, then add veggies to your heart's content.
—MAGGIE KNOEBEL, *TASTE OF HOME* RECIPE EDITOR/TESTER

RASPBERRY-BANANA BREAKFAST TACOS

My sweet take on breakfast tacos uses pancakes
in place of tortillas! They're so easy and absolutely delicious. Choose
fruits and berries depending on what's in season.
—Joan Hallford, North Richland Hills, TX

PREP: 25 MIN. • COOK: 5 MIN./BATCH • MAKES: 4 SERVINGS

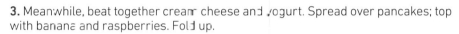

¾ cup all-purpose flour
¾ cup whole wheat flour
3 Tbsp. sugar
2 tsp. baking powder
¾ tsp. ground cinnamon
½ tsp. salt
1 large egg
1 cup 2% milk
2 Tbsp. canola oil
1 tsp. vanilla extract
⅓ cup cream cheese, softened
3 Tbsp. vanilla yogurt
1 small banana, sliced
1 cup fresh raspberries

1. Whisk together flours, sugar, baking powder, cinnamon and salt. Combine egg, milk, canola oil and vanilla; stir into dry ingredients just until moistened.

2. Preheat a griddle over medium heat Lightly grease griddle. Pour batter by ½ cupfuls onto the griddle; cook until bubbles on top begin to pop and the bottoms are golden brown. Turn; cook until second side is golden brown

3. Meanwhile, beat together cream cheese and yogurt. Spread over pancakes; top with banana and raspberries. Fold up.

1 taco: 429 cal., 17g fat (6g sat. fat) 71mg chol., 651mg sod., 59g carb. (19g sugars, 6g fiber), 11g pro.

HAWAIIAN BREAKFAST HASH

Breakfast is our favorite meal, and we love a good variety of dishes. This hash brown recipe
is full of flavor and possibilities. Top with some eggs or spinach for an extra twist!
—Courtney Stultz, Weir, KS

PREP: 10 MIN. • COOK: 30 MIN. • MAKES: 6 SERVINGS

4 bacon strips, chopped
1 Tbsp. canola or coconut oil
2 large sweet potatoes (about 1½ lbs.),
  peeled and cut into ½-in. pieces
½ tsp. salt
¼ tsp. chili powder
¼ tsp. paprika
¼ tsp. pepper
⅛ tsp. ground cinnamon
2 cups cubed fresh pineapple
  (½-in. cubes)

1. In a large skillet, cook bacon over medium heat until crisp, stirring occasionally. Remove with a slotted spoon; drain on paper towels. Discard drippings.

2. In same pan, heat oil over medium heat. Add potatoes and seasonings; cook and stir 15 minutes. Add pineapple; cook and stir until potatoes are tender and browned, 8-10 minutes. Sprinkle with bacon.

⅔ cup: 194 cal., 5g fat (1g sat. fat), 6mg chol., 309mg sod., 35g carb. (17g sugars, 4g fiber), 4g pro. **Diabetic exchanges:** 2 starch 1 fat.

AIR-FRYER APPLE DANISH

I came up with this quick and tasty treat when my daughter had a sleepover.
I whipped these together in no time and the girls devoured them!
—Jennifer Stowell, Deep River, IA

PREP: 20 MIN. • **COOK:** 10 MIN./BATCH • **MAKES:** 8 SERVINGS

1 tube (8 oz.) refrigerated crescent rolls
½ cup chunky applesauce
4 tsp. apple cider or juice, divided
1½ tsp. sugar
½ tsp. ground cinnamon
½ cup confectioners' sugar

1. Preheat air fryer to 300°. Unroll crescent dough; separate into 8 triangles. Place 1 Tbsp. applesauce at the wide end of each triangle; carefully roll up. Brush tops with 2 tsp. cider. Combine sugar and cinnamon; sprinkle over rolls.

2. In batches, arrange rolls, point side down, in a single layer in greased air fryer. Curve to form crescents. Cook until golden brown, 7-9 minutes. Cool slightly. Combine confectioners' sugar and remaining 2 tsp. cider; drizzle over rolls. Serve warm.

1 roll: 146 cal., 5g fat (2g sat. fat), 0 chol., 213mg sod., 24g carb. (14g sugars, 0 fiber), 2g pro.

CHEDDAR-HAM OVEN OMELET

We had a family reunion for 50 relatives from the U.S. and Canada, and it took four pans of this hearty five-ingredient omelet to feed the crowd. Fresh fruit and an assortment of muffins helped round out our brunch menu.
—Betty Abrey, Imperial, SK

PREP: 15 MIN. • **BAKE:** 40 MIN. + STANDING • **MAKES:** 12 SERVINGS

16 large eggs
2 cups 2% milk
2 cups shredded cheddar cheese
¾ cup cubed fully cooked ham
6 green onions, chopped

1. Preheat oven to 350°. In a large bowl, whisk eggs and milk. Stir in cheese, ham and onions. Pour into a greased 13x9-in. baking dish.

2. Bake, uncovered, until a knife inserted in the center comes out clean, 40-45 minutes. Let stand at least 10 minutes before cutting.

1 piece: 208 cal., 14g fat (7g sat. fat), 314mg chol., 330mg sod., 4g carb. (3g sugars, 0 fiber), 15g pro.

> 66
> Our grandkids loved rolling up the little triangles and sprinkling on the cinnamon sugar. Everyone thought they were delicious!
> —SGRONHOLZ
> TASTEOFHOME.COM

AIR-FRYER
APPLE DANISH

GINGERBREAD-SPICED SYRUP

Here's a wonderful treat for the winter months. Stir a tablespoon
of this syrup into coffee, tea or cider. Drizzle it over pancakes,
hot cereal or yogurt. Or use it as a glaze for roasted chicken or chops!
—*Darlene Brenden, Salem, OR*

PREP: 20 MIN. • COOK: 35 MIN. + COOLING • MAKES: 2 CUPS

2 cinnamon sticks (3 in.), broken
   into pieces
16 whole cloves
3 Tbsp. coarsely chopped fresh
   gingerroot
1 tsp. whole allspice
1 tsp. whole peppercorns
2 cups sugar
2 cups water
2 Tbsp. honey
1 tsp. ground nutmeg

1. Place the first 5 ingredients on a double thickness of cheesecloth; bring up corners of cloth and tie with string to form a bag.

2. In a large saucepan, combine the sugar, water, honey, nutmeg and spice bag; bring to a boil. Reduce heat; simmer, uncovered, until syrup reaches desired consistency, 30-45 minutes.

3. Remove from the heat; cool to room temperature. Discard spice bag; transfer syrup to airtight containers. Store in the refrigerator for up to 1 month.

2 Tbsp.: 108 cal., 0 fat (0 sat. fat), 0 chol., 0 sod., 28g carb. (27g sugars, 0 fiber), 0 pro.

TEST KITCHEN TIP

Gingerbread syrup can be as thick or as thin as you'd like. I suggest cooking it until it coats the back of a spoon. I wouldn't suggest reducing by more than half, however, or you risk crystallizing your syrup. If it does crystallize, simply warm it back up with a little water and cook it until the crystals melt again.
—SHANNON NORRIS, *TASTE OF HOME* SENIOR FOOD STYLIST

TAHITIAN BREAKFAST TREATS

In Tahiti, you'll often be served *firi firi* for breakfast. They are delicious, light and airy breakfast breads that are similar to doughnuts. Instead of deep-frying them, I tried making them in my air fryer. They come out just as delicious!
—*Susan Falk, Sterling Heights, MI*

PREP: 35 MIN. + RISING • **COOK:** 10 MIN./BATCH • **MAKES:** 8 SERVINGS

1   pkg. (¼ oz.) active dry yeast
¼   cup warm water (110° to 115°)
½   cup warm coconut milk (110° to 115°)
½   cup sweetened shredded coconut
⅓   cup sugar
½   tsp. salt
2   to 2½ cups all-purpose flour

SPICED SUGAR

½   cup sugar
1   tsp. ground cinnamon
½   tsp. ground ginger
½   vanilla bean
¼   cup butter, melted

1. Add yeast to warm water and stir to dissolve; allow to sit until yeast has bubbled, 5-7 minutes. Add yeast mixture to warm coconut milk. In a large bowl, combine coconut, sugar, salt, yeast mixture and 1 cup flour. Beat on medium speed until smooth. Stir in enough remaining flour to form a stiff dough (dough will be sticky). Turn the dough onto a floured surface; knead until smooth and elastic, 6-8 minutes. Place in a greased bowl, turning once to grease the top. Cover and let rise in a warm place until doubled, about 1½ hours.

2. Punch down dough. Turn onto a lightly floured surface; divide into 8 portions. Roll each into a 12-in. rope. Curl ends in opposite directions to form a figure 8. Tuck each end under where it meets center of roll and pinch lightly to seal. Place 2 in. apart on a parchment-lined baking sheet. Cover with a kitchen towel; let rise in a warm place until almost doubled, about 30 minutes.

3. Preheat air fryer to 325°. In batches, arrange in a single layer on greased tray in air-fryer basket. Cook until light brown, 7-10 minutes. Meanwhile, place sugar, cinnamon and ginger in a shallow bowl. Split vanilla bean lengthwise. Using the tip of a sharp knife, scrape seeds from the center; stir into sugar mixture. Brush warm pastries with melted butter, roll in sugar mixture to coat.

Note: In our testing, we find cook times vary dramatically between brands of air fryers. As a result, we give wider than normal ranges on suggested cook times. Begin checking at the first time listed and adjust as needed.

1 pastry: 251 cal., 8g fat (6g sat. fat), 8mg chol., 191mg sod., 42g carb. (18g sugars, 1g fiber), 4g pro.

GIANT CINNAMON
ROLLS

GIANT CINNAMON ROLLS

As a young newlywed, I took it upon myself to make cinnamon rolls because I thought that was the hallmark of a good baker. The rolls were dense like hockey pucks and somewhat flavorless. Our dear black Lab Annie wouldn't even eat one. I practiced for a couple of months and entered a contest at the Iowa State Fair—and I won!
—*Cristen Clark, Runnells, IA*

PREP: 45 MIN. + RISING • **BAKE:** 25 MIN. + COOLING • **MAKES:** 1 DOZEN

2 pkg. (¼ oz. each) quick-rise yeast
½ cup warm water (110° to 115°)
2 tsp. honey
1½ cups warm 2% milk (110° to 115°)
½ cup sugar
½ cup butter, softened
½ cup mashed potatoes
3 large eggs, room temperature, lightly beaten
2 tsp. salt
7½ to 8 cups all-purpose flour

FILLING
1 cup packed brown sugar
2 Tbsp. ground cinnamon
1½ tsp. all-purpose flour
Dash salt
½ cup butter, softened

VANILLA ICING
3 cups confectioners' sugar
¼ cup 2% milk
1 tsp. vanilla bean paste or vanilla extract
Dash salt

1. In a small bowl, dissolve yeast in warm water and honey. In a large bowl, combine milk, sugar, butter, potatoes, eggs, salt, yeast mixture and 4 cups flour; beat on medium speed until smooth. Stir in enough remaining flour to form a soft dough (dough will be sticky). Turn dough onto a floured surface; knead until smooth and elastic, 6-8 minutes. Place in a greased large bowl, turning once to grease the top. Cover and let rise in a warm place until doubled, about 1 hour.

2. For filling, combine brown sugar, cinnamon, flour and salt. Punch down the dough. Turn onto a lightly floured surface; roll into a 24x12-in. rectangle. Spread butter to within ½ in. of edges; sprinkle with brown sugar mixture. Roll up jelly-roll style, starting with a long side; pinch seam to seal. Cut into 12 slices. Place in 2 greased 13x9-in. baking pans (6 slices per pan), cut side down. Cover with kitchen towels; let rise in a warm place until doubled, about 30 minutes.

3. Preheat oven to 350°. Bake until lightly browned, 25-30 minutes, covering loosely with foil during the last 10 minutes of baking. Cool in pan 30 minutes. In a small bowl, mix icing ingredients; drizzle over rolls.

1 roll: 695 cal., 18g fat (11g sat. fat), 90mg chol., 588mg sod., 122g carb. (59g sugars, 3g fiber), 11g pro.

Best In Show

When not working on her farm, this mom is mixing up blue-ribbon recipes.

Cristen Clark
Runnells, IA

What's your favorite state-fair category?
I have three stand mixers, and when the Iowa State Fair kicks off, all three are busy kneading batches of dough. There are 15 classes of yeast rolls, and I like to compete in all of them. That said, yeast rolls are kind of my jam.

When was your first competition?
I started competing in 2010, and I won for my Giant Cinnamon Rolls. With the money I won, I bought a red female pig and named her Cinnamon. This led to our family business; a purebred-pig farm. Those animals are raised primarily for breeding and fair showing, but my husband I also manage a larger commercial pig farm.

What are some of the staples in your kitchen?
I get home around 7 p.m. often after watching my 14-year-old daughter, Halle, and 11-year-old son, Barrett, play sports. I was an athlete in high school and college, and once that's in your blood, it's always there. I need quick, easy meals, so I'm a big fan of skillet meals. The kids love pork chops smothered in sauce so those are standbys in my home too. Halle also loves to bake anything she can dream up. I enjoy helping her, so from-scratch bakes are a welcomed staple in our home.

COMFORTING COFFEE MILK

This recipe is special to me because the delicious ingredients and flavors speak for themselves without those extra preservatives. Now that's refreshing!
—*Brenda Schrag, Farmington, NM*

TAKES: 20 MIN. • **MAKES:** 6 SERVINGS

4 cups whole milk
1⅓ cups strong brewed coffee
½ cup maple syrup
2 Tbsp. molasses
2 tsp. baking cocoa

WHIPPED CREAM
1 cup heavy whipping cream
1 Tbsp. maple syrup
1 tsp. vanilla extract
  Additional baking cocoa

1. In a large saucepan, combine first 5 ingredients over medium heat to just simmering (do not boil), stirring occasionally.

2. Meanwhile, in a small bowl, beat cream until it begins to thicken. Add maple syrup and vanilla; beat until soft peaks form. Serve with coffee milk. Dust with additional cocoa.

1 cup coffee milk with ⅓ cup whipped cream: 338 cal., 20g fat (12g sat. fat), 71mg chol., 91mg sod., 34g carb. (32g sugars, 0 fiber), 6g pro.

CAST-IRON LOADED BREAKFAST BISCUITS

SHOWN ON PAGE 4

These biscuits are full of hearty breakfast ingredients like eggs, bacon, mushrooms and cheese! A gluten-free flour blend can be substituted for the all-purpose flour.
—*Courtney Stultz, Weir, KS*

PREP: 35 MIN. • **BAKE:** 20 MIN. • **MAKES:** 8 SERVINGS

4 bacon strips, chopped
1 cup chopped fresh mushrooms
⅓ cup chopped onion
1 garlic clove, minced
4 large eggs
2 cups all-purpose flour
3 tsp. baking powder
½ tsp. salt
½ cup cold butter, cubed
1 cup buttermilk
½ cup shredded cheddar cheese

Preheat oven to 400°. In a 10-in. cast-iron or other ovenproof skillet, cook bacon over medium heat until crisp, stirring occasionally. Remove with a slotted spoon; drain on paper towels. Cook and stir mushrooms, onion and garlic in bacon drippings until tender, 4-5 minutes. Remove from pan. In a small bowl, whisk eggs until blended. Pour eggs into same pan; cook and stir over medium heat until eggs are thickened and no liquid egg remains. Remove from pan. In a large bowl, whisk the flour, baking powder and salt. Cut in butter until mixture resembles coarse crumbs. Add the buttermilk; stir just until moistened. Gently stir in mushroom mixture, eggs, bacon and cheese. Drop dough by ½ cupfuls 1 in. apart into the same skillet. Bake until bottoms are golden brown, 20-25 minutes.

1 biscuit: 356 cal., 22g fat (11g sat. fat), 141mg chol., 653mg sod., 27g carb. (2g sugars, 1g fiber), 11g pro.

ROASTED TOMATO QUICHE

This cheesy quiche comes together quickly enough that I don't have to wake up really early to get it on the table, and that's a bonus.
—*Elisabeth Larsen, Pleasant Grove, UT*

PREP: 45 MIN. • BAKE: 40 MIN. + STANDING • MAKES: 6 SERVINGS

1 sheet refrigerated pie crust
1 cup grape tomatoes
1 Tbsp. olive oil
⅛ tsp. plus ½ tsp. salt, divided
⅛ tsp. plus ¼ tsp. pepper, divided
½ lb. bulk Italian sausage
1 small onion, chopped
1 pkg. (6 oz.) fresh baby spinach, chopped
1 cup shredded part-skim mozzarella cheese
3 large eggs
1 cup half-and-half cream
½ tsp. garlic powder

1. Unroll crust into a 9-in. pie plate; flute edge. Line unpricked crust with a double thickness of heavy-duty foil. Fill with dried beans, uncooked rice or pie weights.

2. Bake at 450° for 8 minutes. Remove foil and weights; bake 5 minutes longer. Cool on a wire rack.

3. Place tomatoes in a 15x10x1-in. baking pan. Drizzle with oil; sprinkle with ⅛ tsp. each salt and pepper. Bake at 450° until skins blister, 8-10 minutes.

4. In a large skillet, cook sausage and onion over medium heat until sausage is no longer pink; drain. Remove sausage. In the same skillet, cook spinach until wilted, 4-5 minutes.

5. Combine sausage, tomatoes, spinach and cheese; transfer to crust. Whisk eggs, cream, garlic powder and remaining salt and pepper; pour over top.

6. Bake at 375° until a knife inserted in center comes out clean, 40-45 minutes. Cover edge with foil during the last 15 minutes to prevent overbrowning if necessary. Let stand 10 minutes before serving.

Note: Let pie weights cool before storing. Beans and rice may be reused for pie weights, but not for cooking.

1 piece: 397 cal., 26g fat (11g sat. fat), 158mg chol., 725mg sod., 23g carb. (5g sugars, 1g fiber), 15g pro.

PUMPKIN CHEESE COFFEE CAKE

This is one of my favorite recipes, especially in autumn. It is much easier to
make than a traditional pumpkin roll—and it's always a crowd-pleaser!
—*Carlene Jessop, Hildale, UT*

PREP: 15 MIN. • BAKE: 35 MIN. • MAKES: 15 SERVINGS

2 cups sugar
2 large eggs, room temperature
1¼ cups canned pumpkin
¼ cup vegetable oil
½ tsp. vanilla extract
2¼ cups all-purpose flour
2 tsp. ground cinnamon
1 tsp. baking soda
½ tsp. salt

FILLING
1 pkg. (8 oz.) cream cheese, softened
1 large egg
1 Tbsp. sugar

TOPPING
¾ cup sweetened shredded coconut
½ cup chopped pecans
¼ cup packed brown sugar
¼ tsp. ground cinnamon

1. In a large bowl, beat sugar, eggs, pumpkin, oil and vanilla. Combine the flour, cinnamon, baking soda and salt; add to egg mixture and mix well. Pour into a greased 13x9-in. baking dish.

2. In a small bowl, beat cream cheese, egg and sugar until smooth. Drop tablespoons of cream cheese mixture over batter; cut through batter with a knife to swirl. Combine topping ingredients; sprinkle over top. Bake at 350° for 35-40 minutes or until a toothpick comes out clean. Cool on a wire rack.

1 piece: 344 cal., 15g fat (6g sat. fat), 59mg chol., 234mg sod., 50g carb. (33g sugars, 2g fiber), 5g pro.

DID YOU KNOW?

You can add a bit of homey spice by mixing a little nutmeg or pumpkin pie spice into the flour mixture.

HOMEMADE SAGE SAUSAGE PATTIES

Oregano, garlic and sage add savory flavor to these easy ground pork patties.
I've had this Pennsylvania Dutch recipe for years, and it always brings compliments.
—*Diane Hixon, Niceville, FL*

PREP: 10 MIN. + CHILLING • COOK: 15 MIN. • MAKES: 8 SERVINGS

1 lb. ground pork
¾ cup shredded cheddar cheese
¼ cup buttermilk
1 Tbsp. finely chopped onion
2 tsp. rubbed sage
¾ tsp. salt
¾ tsp. pepper
⅛ tsp. garlic powder
⅛ tsp. dried oregano

1. In a bowl, combine all ingredients, mixing lightly but thoroughly. Shape into eight ½-in.-thick patties. Refrigerate 1 hour.

2. In a large cast-iron or other heavy skillet, cook patties over medium heat until a thermometer reads 160°, 6-8 minutes on each side.

1 patty: 162 cal., 11g fat (5g sat. fat), 49mg chol., 323mg sod., 1g carb. (0 sugars, 0 fiber), 13g pro.

PUMPKIN CHEESE
COFFEE CAKE

"
This is one of
my absolute
go-to recipes.
Everyone
always loves it!
—DFAUSNACHT
TASTEOFHOME.COM

SPICY ROASTED CARROT
HUMMUS, PAGE 43

"People who say they don't like hummus love this version. I share the recipe often."
—ANNE ORMOND
DOVER, NH

CHAPTER 2

SNACKS & APPETIZERS

Turn here when the munchies come calling! These are the nibbles, appetizers, drinks and hors d'oeuvres hosts and hostesses rely on most. Whip up any of these recipes with confidence, knowing they'll turn out deliciously every time.

SOUTHERN DEVILED EGGS

There is nothing more simple, or delicious, than these deviled eggs.
I make them for every BBQ, tailgate or picnic, and they're always a hit.
—*Ellen Riley, Murfreesboro, TN*

TAKES: 20 MIN. • **MAKES:** 1 DOZEN

6 hard-boiled large eggs
2 Tbsp. mayonnaise
2 Tbsp. sweet pickle relish, drained
½ tsp. prepared mustard
¼ tsp. salt
⅛ tsp. pepper
Optional: Paprika and fresh dill

1. Slice eggs in half lengthwise. Remove yolks; set whites aside. In a small bowl, mash yolks. Stir in the mayonnaise, relish, mustard, salt and pepper.

2. Pipe or spoon into egg whites. Refrigerate until serving. If desired, sprinkle with paprika before serving.

1 stuffed egg half: 57 cal., 4g fat (1g sat. fat), 94mg chol., 114mg sod., 1g carb. (1g sugars, 0 fiber), 3g pro.

TEST KITCHEN TIP

You can make deviled eggs up to 2 days in advance. To optimize their freshness, wait to add the yolk filling to the egg whites until you're just about ready to serve. Store the egg whites in an airtight container, and keep the egg yolk filling in a resealable plastic bag, making sure to press out all the air. When it's time to serve, simply snip off a corner of the bag, and the filling is conveniently ready to be piped into the egg whites.
—ELLIE CROWLEY, *TASTE OF HOME* CULINARY ASSISTANT

SOUTHERN
DEVILED EGGS

WATERMELON MARGARITAS

Summer's best flavors get frosty in the cocktail we serve at all our backyard shindigs. We mix sun-ripened watermelon and our favorite tequila with just the right amount of ice for a thick sipper that's perfect when we're grilling and chilling.
—*Alicia Cummings, Marshalltown, IA*

TAKES: 20 MIN. • **MAKES:** 12 SERVINGS

2 medium limes
⅓ cup sugar, optional
8 cups cubed seedless watermelon (1 in.)
2 cups ice cubes
2 cups tequila
1 cup Triple Sec
¼ cup lime juice

1. Cut 1 lime into 12 wedges; reserve for garnishes. If desired, coat the rim of each glass with sugar: Cut remaining lime into wedges. Using these wedges, moisten the rims of 12 margarita or cocktail glasses. Sprinkle sugar on a plate; hold each glass upside down and dip rim into sugar. Discard remaining sugar.

2. Place half the watermelon in a blender; cover and process until pureed (this should yield 3 cups). Add half each of the following: ice cubes, tequila, Triple Sec and lime juice. If desired, add sugar to taste. Cover and process until blended.

3. Serve in prepared glasses. Repeat with remaining ingredients. Garnish with reserved lime wedges.

¾ cup: 188 cal., 0 fat (0 sat. fat), 0 chol., 5mg sod., 19g carb. (17g sugars, 1g fiber), 0 pro.

GUAVA JAM BAKED BRIE EN CROUTE WITH PISTACHIOS

There's a ton of buzz around baked Brie. I decided to make it my own with guava paste and chopped pistachios. It's the same beloved app—but with a seriously tasty Cuban spin!

—Marisel Salazar, New York, NY

PREP: 10 MIN. • BAKE: 25 MIN. • MAKES: 8 SERVINGS

1 sheet frozen puff pastry, thawed
1 round Brie cheese (8 oz.)
⅔ cup guava paste or guava jelly, divided
⅔ cup chopped pistachios, divided

1. Preheat oven to 375°. Roll puff pastry into a 12-in. square. Place round of Brie in center of pastry; spread ⅓ cup guava paste over cheese; sprinkle with ⅓ cup pistachios. Fold pastry around cheese; trim excess dough. Pinch edges to seal. Place seam side down on ungreased baking sheet. Heat remaining ⅓ cup guava paste until mostly melted; pour over pastry.

2. Bake for 15 minutes. Top with remaining ⅓ cup pistachios; bake until puffed and golden brown, about 10 minutes longer. Serve warm.

1 piece: 370 cal., 21g fat (7g sat. fat), 28mg chol., 323mg sod., 38g carb. (17g sugars, 3g fiber), 10g pro.

A World of Flavor

A love of Latin foods and a desire to wake the senses drives this cook's creativity in the kitchen.

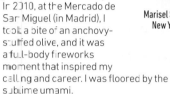

Marisel Salazar
New York, NY

What's your fondest food-related memory?
In 2010, at the Mercado de San Miguel (in Madrid), I took a bite of an anchovy-stuffed olive, and it was a full-body fireworks moment that inspired my calling and career. I was floored by the sublime umami.

What is your all-time favorite thing about cooking—the "why" of why you cook?
The best thing about cooking is that it is edible art—and multisensory enjoyment. You can enjoy seeing, smelling and tasting it; you can even enjoy listening to the sounds of cooking. What other art form lets you do that?

You do a lot of incredible Latin cooking. How might one respectfully pay homage to the myriad Latinx food traditions?
This is my take on how to show respect: If you are making a recipe from a Latinx cook, take a photo of your meal, tag the person and share it on social media. When dining out, try visiting a restaurant owned by Hispanics and send your compliments to the staff. We love to see others enjoying our food and recipes, and recognizing us.

AIR-FRYER
CALAMARI

AIR-FRYER CALAMARI

You can make crispy calamari just like your favorite Italian restaurant's thanks to the air fryer! A quick coat in crunchy panko bread crumbs and a few minutes in the air fryer are all it takes to make this special appetizer.

—Peggy Woodward. Taste of Home Senior Food Editor

PREP: 20 MIN. COOK: 10 MIN./BATCH • MAKES: 5 DOZEN

½ cup all-purpose flour
½ tsp. salt
1 large egg, lightly beaten
½ cup 2% milk
1 cup panko bread crumbs
½ tsp. seasoned salt
¼ tsp. pepper
8 oz. cleaned fresh or frozen calamari (squid), thawed and cut into ½-in. rings
Cooking spray

1. Preheat air fryer to 400°. In a shallow bowl, combine flour and salt. In another shallow bowl, whisk egg and milk. In a third shallow bowl, combine bread crumbs, seasoned salt and pepper. Coat the calamari with flour mixture, then dip in egg mixture and coat with bread crumb mixture.

2. In batches, place calamari in a single layer on greased tray in air-fryer basket; spritz with cooking spray. Cook 4 minutes. Turn; spritz with cooking spray. Cook until golden brown, 3-5 minutes longer.

Note: In our testing, we find cook times vary dramatically between brands of air fryers. As a result, we give wider than normal ranges on suggested cook times. Begin checking at the first time listed and adjust as needed.

1 piece: 11 cal., 0 fat (0 sat. fat), 10mg chol., 28mg sod., 1g carb. (0 sugars, 0 fiber), 1g pro.

TEST KITCHEN TIP

To clean calamari, first pull the skin off to reveal the white, slightly translucent flesh underneath. Rinse the tube of squid under cold water. Slice the tube into ½-in. pieces as directed in the recipe.

—SARAH TRAMONTE, *TASTE OF HOME* ASSOCIATE CULINARY PRODUCER

BACON, ONION & APPLE STRUDEL

This is such a fun recipe—an appetizer twist on a traditional dessert. It can be served hot out of the oven, warm or cold. Different types of cheese, such as goat, feta or jack, can be used in this strudel.
—*DonnaMarie Ryan, Topsfield, MA*

PREP: 30 MIN. • **BAKE:** 25 MIN. • **MAKES:** 10 SERVINGS

- 2 Tbsp. butter
- 2 large sweet onions, halved and sliced
- 2 medium Granny Smith apples, peeled and thinly sliced
- ½ cup chopped walnuts, toasted
- 2 Tbsp. honey Dijon mustard
- 2 Tbsp. honey
- 1 tsp. salt
- ½ tsp. pepper
- 1 pkg. (17.3 oz.) frozen puff pastry, thawed
- 2 cups shredded sharp cheddar cheese
- 4 bacon strips, cooked and crumbled
- 1 large egg
- 1 Tbsp. water

1. Preheat oven to 400°. In a large skillet, heat the butter over medium-high heat. Add the onions and apples; cook and stir 12-15 minutes or until tender. Stir in walnuts, mustard, honey, salt and pepper. Remove from heat; cool slightly.

2. On 2 parchment-lined baking sheets, roll out each pastry into a 14x12-in. rectangle. Place half the onion mixture down the center of each rectangle; top with cheese and bacon.

3. On each long side, cut eight 1¾-in.-wide strips. Starting at 1 end, fold alternating strips at an angle across filling; pinch ends to seal. Whisk egg with water; brush over braids. Bake until golden brown, 25-28 minutes. Let stand 5 minutes before cutting.

1 piece: 463 cal., 29g fat (10g sat. fat), 41mg chol., 656mg sod., 42g carb. (11g sugars, 5g fiber), 12g pro.

CHEESY VEGETABLE GARDEN TART

Flower focaccia has been the rage recently, so I took this beautiful trend and applied it to a simple, savory vegetarian tart. I topped it with herbaceous Boursin and Parmesan, then decorated it with a medley of veggies.

—Juls Palmer, Lebanon, NJ

PREP: 30 MIN. • BAKE: 15 MIN. + COOLING • MAKES: 12 SERVINGS

1 pkg. (5.2 oz.) Boursin garlic and fine herbs cheese
2 Tbsp. grated Parmesan cheese
2 Tbsp. sour cream
1 tsp. grated lemon zest
1 sheet frozen puff pastry, thawed
   Assorted fresh vegetables and herbs such as olives, sliced red onion, sliced miniature sweet peppers and rosemary
1 Tbsp. olive oil
1 large egg, beaten
   Sesame seeds, optional

1. Preheat oven to 400°. In a large bowl, mash Boursin cheese with a fork. Add Parmesan, sour cream and zest; beat until smooth and creamy.

2. On a lightly floured surface, unfold the puff pastry. Roll into a 13x11-in. rectangle. Transfer to a parchment-lined baking sheet. Prick pastry several times with a fork. Using a sharp knife, score a ½ in. border around edges of pastry sheets (do not cut through). Spread Boursin mixture evenly over center of pastry.

3. Arrange the vegetables and herbs over cheese mixture as desired. Brush vegetables with olive oil. Brush edges of pastry with egg; sprinkle with sesame seeds, if desired. Bake until pastry is puffed and golden brown, 15-20 minutes. Cool 10 minutes before serving. Refrigerate leftovers.

1 piece: 171 cal., 13g fat (5g sat. fat) 20mg chol., 161mg sod., 12g carb. (1g sugars, 2g fiber), 3g pro.

ADD HOLIDAY FLAIR

Create a stunning tree scene by layering sliced yellow and green bell peppers, rosemary sprigs, sweety drops and red onion atop the tart.

BACON CHEESEBURGER SLIDER BAKE

I created this dish to fill two pans because these sliders disappear fast.
Just cut the recipe in half if you only want to make one batch.

—Nick Iverson, Denver, CO

PREP: 20 MIN. • BAKE: 20 MIN. • MAKES: 2 DOZEN

2   pkg. (17 oz. each) Hawaiian sweet rolls
22   slices American or cheddar cheese, divided
2   lbs. ground beef
1   cup chopped onion
1   can (14½ oz.) diced tomatoes with garlic and onion, drained
1   Tbsp. Dijon mustard
1   Tbsp. Worcestershire sauce
¾   tsp. salt
¾   tsp. pepper
24   bacon strips, cooked and broken into 1-in. pieces

GLAZE
1   cup butter, cubed
¼   cup packed brown sugar
4   tsp. Worcestershire sauce
2   Tbsp. Dijon mustard
2   Tbsp. sesame seeds

1. Preheat oven to 350°. Without separating rolls, cut each package of rolls horizontally in half; arrange bottom halves in 2 greased 13x9-in. baking pans. In each pan, place 5 slices of cheese on bottom halves of rolls. Bake until cheese is melted, 3-5 minutes.

2. In a large skillet, cook beef and onion over medium heat until beef is no longer pink and onion is tender, breaking beef into crumbles, 6-8 minutes; drain. Stir in tomatoes, mustard, Worcestershire sauce, salt and pepper. Cook and stir until combined, 1-2 minutes.

3. Spoon beef mixture evenly over rolls; top with bacon and remaining cheese. Replace tops. For glaze, in a microwave-safe bowl, combine butter, brown sugar, Worcestershire sauce and mustard. Microwave, covered, on high until butter is melted, stirring occasionally. Pour over rolls; sprinkle with sesame seeds. Bake, uncovered, until golden brown and heated through, 20-25 minutes.

1 slider: 380 cal., 24g fat (13g sat. fat), 86mg chol., 628mg sod., 21g carb. (9g sugars, 2g fiber), 18g pro.

TEST KITCHEN TIP

Here in our Test Kitchen, we adored this sweet and savory combination. If you want a more classic burger flavor, just use a package of dinner rolls in place of the Hawaiian rolls. Use ground turkey instead of ground beef and halve the glaze if you want to lighten things up a bit.

—MAGGIE KNOEBEL, *TASTE OF HOME* ASSOCIATE RECIPE EDITOR/TEST COOK

BACON
CHEESEBURGER
SLIDER BAKE

MOROCCAN-SPICED CHICKEN SLIDERS

This recipe is fantastic for both entertaining and fast, easy weeknight dinners. Ras el hanout is a mixture of ground spices that typically includes various peppers, cardamom, ginger, cinnamon, nutmeg, turmeric and mace. It can be found in the spice section of well-stocked supermarkets. For a more peppery slider, substitute baby arugula for the leaf lettuce.
—*Kathi Jones-DelMonte, Rochester, NY*

PREP: 25 MIN. • COOK: 10 MIN. • MAKES: 8 SERVINGS

1   container (6 oz.) plain yogurt, divided
2   Tbsp. Dijon mustard
2   tsp. grated lemon zest
1   tsp. grated orange zest

CHICKEN SLIDERS
3   Tbsp. chopped fresh mint
4   tsp. minced garlic
2   tsp. ras el hanout (Moroccan seasoning)
1½ tsp. coarsely ground pepper
1   tsp. ground cumin
1   tsp. kosher salt
1   lb. ground chicken
2   Tbsp. canola oil
4   miniature pita pockets, halved and warmed
8   red leaf lettuce leaves
8   slices tomato

1. In a small bowl, stir together ⅔ cup yogurt, mustard and zests. Refrigerate until serving.

2. In a large bowl, combine remaining 2 Tbsp. yogurt, mint, garlic, ras el hanout, pepper, cumin and salt. Crumble chicken into bowl; mix lightly but thoroughly. Shape into 8 ½-in.-thick patties; press small indention in middle of each patty.

3. In a large nonstick skillet, heat oil over medium heat. Add patties; cook until golden brown and no longer pink, 4-5 minutes on each side. Serve patties inside pita pocket with sauce, lettuce and tomato.

1 slider: 173 cal., 9g fat (2g sat. fat), 40mg chol., 456mg sod., 11g carb. (2g sugars, 1g fiber), 12g pro.

GARLIC MOZZARELLA BREAD BITES

These little balls of deliciousness are ridiculously easy to make and insanely tasty! They are the perfect low-carb, keto-friendly, gluten-free appetizer, snack or side dish. To make them extra cheesy, sprinkle the tops with more mozzarella cheese after taking them out of the oven the second time, and then return them to the oven until the cheese is melted. Serve with your favorite low-carb dipping sauce.
—*Anna Bowden, Littleton, CO*

TAKES: 30 MIN. • MAKES: 1 DOZEN

1½ cups shredded part-skim
    mozzarella cheese
3   oz. cream cheese, softened
1   large egg, room temperature
1   cup almond flour
½   tsp. onion powder
½   tsp. garlic powder
½   tsp. salt
½   tsp. pepper

TOPPING
2   Tbsp. unsalted butter, melted
1½ tsp. minced garlic
    Prepared pesto, optional

1. Preheat oven to 400°. In a microwave-safe bowl, combine mozzarella cheese and cream cheese; microwave, covered, on high until melted, 30-60 seconds. Stir until smooth. Stir in egg. In another bowl, mix almond flour and seasonings; stir into cheese mixture until combined (mixture will be thick).

2. With wet hands, shape into 12 balls. Place 1 in. apart on a parchment-lined baking sheet. Bake for 12 minutes. Combine butter and garlic; brush over rolls. Bake until light brown, 2-4 minutes longer. Let cool 5 minutes before serving. If desired, serve with prepared pesto.

1 appetizer: 144 cal., 12g fat (5g sat. fat), 37mg chol., 224mg sod., 4g carb. (1g sugars, 1g fiber), 6g pro.

SIDECAR

Welcome the weekend with this tart citrus delight.
Treat yourself to this sunny drink any time of year.
—Taste of Home *Test Kitchen*

TAKES: 5 MIN. • MAKES: 1 SERVING

    Ice cubes
1   oz. brandy
⅔   oz. (4 tsp.) Triple Sec
1½ to 3 tsp. lemon juice

OPTIONAL GARNISH
    Lemon twist

1. Fill a shaker three-fourths full with ice. Add the brandy, Triple Sec and lemon juice. Cover and shake for 15-20 seconds or until condensation forms on outside of shaker.

2. Strain into a chilled cocktail glass. Garnish as desired.

1 serving: 137 cal., 0 fat (0 sat. fat), 0 chol., 2mg sod., 10g carb. (8g sugars, 0 fiber), 0 pro.

OYSTERS
ROCKEFELLER
EGG ROLLS

OYSTERS ROCKEFELLER EGG ROLLS

Oysters Rockefeller is a classic appetizer from New Orleans that is so elegant and timeless.
I love the flavor but wanted to try it in another of my favorite appetizers: egg rolls. I think the combination is a winner.
—*Renee Murby, Johnston, RI*

PREP: 35 MIN. • COOK: 5 MIN./BATCH • MAKES: 10 SERVINGS

6 bacon strips, chopped
¼ cup all-purpose flour
2 cans (8 oz.) whole oysters, drained and patted dry
¼ tsp. salt
⅛ tsp. cayenne pepper
1 shallot, minced
1 Tbsp. minced garlic
1 tsp. dried parsley flakes
1 Tbsp. canola oil
1 pkg. (10 oz.) frozen chopped spinach, thawed and squeezed dry
½ tsp. grated lemon zest
1 large egg
10 egg roll wrappers
   Oil for deep-fat frying
   Optional: Seafood cocktail sauce and lemon wedges

1. In a large skillet, cook bacon over medium-high heat, stirring often, until crisp, about 5 minutes; remove bacon, reserving drippings in skillet. Place flour in a shallow dish. Sprinkle oysters with salt and cayenne pepper; toss oysters in flour. Cook in reserved drippings until golden brown, 3–4 minutes; drain.

2. Wipe out skillet. In same skillet, cook shallot, garlic and parsley in canola oil over medium heat until shallot is tender, 2-3 minutes. Add spinach and lemon zest; cook, stirring occasionally, until heated through, 2-3 minutes. Transfer spinach mixture to a bowl; stir in oysters and bacon.

3. In a small bowl, whisk egg and 1 tsp. water. Brush edges of an egg roll wrapper. Place ¼ cup oyster mixture in the center; fold bottom corner over filling. Fold sides over filling toward center; roll up tightly to seal. Repeat with remaining wrappers and filling.

4. In an electric skillet, heat ½ in. canola oil to 375°. Fry egg rolls until golden brown, about 2 minutes on each side. Drain on paper towels. If desired, serve with cocktail sauce and lemon wedges.

1 egg roll: 299 cal., 18g fat (3g sat. fat), 43mg chol., 427mg sod., 25g carb. (1g sugars, 2g fiber), 10g pro.

PEACHY-KEEN HALLOUMI FRITTERS

How are you doing? Well, I'm peachy keen, and so are
these Halloumi fritters! Gooey Halloumi and sweet onion in a
honey-scented corn fritter is the perfect foil for summer's juicy peaches. The
addition of prosciutto makes these feel fancy with little effort. Serve them as a
quick and easy party snack, or top salads with them to jazz up your routine.
—*Chainey Kuykendall, Richmond, VA*

PREP: 25 MIN. + STANDING • COOK: 5 MIN./BATCH • MAKES: 2½ DOZEN

1¼ cups cornmeal
 2   Tbsp. minced fresh basil
 1   tsp. baking powder
 1   tsp. salt
 ½   tsp. pepper
 1   large egg plus 1 large egg white,
     room temperature
 ¾   cup 2% milk
 2   Tbsp. honey
 1   cup finely chopped sweet onion
 ½   cup diced Halloumi cheese
     Oil for deep-fat frying
 1   medium peach, chopped
 4   thin slices prosciutto, cut into
     thin strips

1. In a large bowl, whisk the first
5 ingredients. In another bowl, whisk
egg, egg white, milk and honey until
blended. Add to dry ingredients, stirring
just until moistened. Fold in onion and
cheese; let stand 10 minutes.

2. In an electric skillet or deep fryer,
heat oil to 375°. Stir batter. Drop batter
by tablespoonfuls, a few at a time,
into hot oil. Fry until golden brown,
2-3 minutes on each side. Drain on
paper towels. (Keep cooked fritters
warm on a baking sheet in a 200° oven until all fritters are made.)

3. Serve the fritters with chopped peach and prosciutto; sprinkle with
additional pepper.

1 fritter: 71 cal., 4g fat (1g sat. fat), 10mg chol., 159mg sod., 8g carb. (2g sugars,
0 fiber), 2g pro.

PROSCIUTTO SHRIMP WITH TROPICAL MANGO SALSA

Prosciutto and melon are a quintessential pairing. I took things a few steps further by adding an assortment of other fresh ingredients, including mango, pineapple and papaya. Finally, add shrimp, and you've got yourself one tasty starter.
—*Jane Whittaker, Pensacola, FL*

TAKES: 30 MIN. • MAKES: 24 SERVINGS

24 peeled and deveined cooked shrimp (16-20 per lb.)
5 Tbsp. lime juice

MANGO SALSA
2 medium ripe mangoes, peeled and chopped
¾ cup cubed fresh pineapple
¾ cup chopped peeled papaya
½ cup finely chopped red onion
½ cup finely chopped sweet red pepper
2 jalapeno peppers, seeded and minced
2 Tbsp. minced fresh cilantro
2 Tbsp. lime juice
24 thin slices cantaloupe
12 thin slices prosciutto, halved lengthwise

1. Place shrimp and lime juice in a large shallow bowl. Refrigerate, covered, while making salsa, turning once. In a large bowl, combine the mangoes, pineapple, papaya, red onion, red pepper, jalapenos, cilantro and lime juice. Refrigerate, covered, until serving.

2. Drain shrimp, discarding lime juice. Place 1 cantaloupe slice on each prosciutto slice; top each with 1 shrimp. Fold both sides to close. If desired, secure with toothpicks. Serve with mango salsa.

1 wrapped shrimp with 1 Tbsp. salsa: 65 cal., 1g fat (0 sat. fat), 37mg chol., 170mg sod., 7g carb. (6g sugars, 1g fiber), 7g pro.

SPICY ROASTED
CARROT HUMMUS

> 66
> The best
> hummus I've
> ever had. It was
> so quick and
> easy! I will be
> making this
> hummus again
> and again!
> —SMJRKS
> TASTEOFHOME.COM

SPICY ROASTED CARROT HUMMUS

This is a wonderful appetizer for Easter, Mother's Day or any spring gathering.
The roasted carrots give this hummus such a bright, fresh flavor.
—Anne Ormond, Dover, NH

PREP: 20 MIN. ROAST: 15 MIN. + COOLING • MAKES: 2 CUPS

1 cup chopped carrots
3 garlic cloves
3 Tbsp. olive oil, divided
1 can (15 oz.) garbanzo beans or chickpeas, rinsed and drained
2 Tbsp. lemon juice
2 Tbsp. tahini
1 Tbsp. water
1 tsp. hot pepper sauce, such as Tabasco
¼ tsp. sea salt
¼ tsp. ground turmeric
¼ tsp. ground cumin
⅛ tsp. cayenne pepper
¼ cup sunflower kernels
Assorted fresh vegetables and pita wedges

1. Preheat oven to 400°. Place carrots and garlic in a rimmed baking sheet. Drizzle with 2 Tbsp. oil; toss to coat. Roast until carrots are soft, 15-20 minutes. Cool on a wire rack.

2. Transfer carrot mixture to a food processor. Add garbanzo beans, lemon juice, tahini, water, hot sauce, salt and spices. While processing, add remaining 1 Tbsp. oil. Process until desired consistency. Transfer to a serving dish. If desired, drizzle with additional oil and hot sauce. Top with the sunflower kernels. Serve warm or chilled with vegetables and pita wedges.

¼ cup: 155 cal., 11g fat (1g sat. fat), 0 chol., 175mg sod., 12g carb. (2g sugars, 3g fiber), 4g pro. **Diabetic exchanges:** 2 fat, 1 starch.

REFRESHING BERRY WINE

This is an easy way to dress up wine for a party. Other fruit, like watermelon balls or sliced peaches, can be used in place of the strawberry slices.
—Laura Wilhelm, West Hollywood, CA

PREP: 35 MIN. + CHILLING • MAKES: 8 SERVINGS

1¼ cups frozen unsweetened raspberries
1 cup white grape juice
1 bottle (750 ml) dry rosé wine
2 cups sliced fresh strawberries
Ice cubes
Fresh mint or rosemary sprigs

In a small saucepan, combine the raspberries and juice. Bring to a boil; reduce heat. Cook and stir over medium heat until liquid is almost evaporated, about 30 minutes. Remove from the heat. Press through a fine-mesh strainer into a bowl; discard seeds. Transfer puree to a pitcher. Stir in the wine and strawberries. Refrigerate, covered, until chilled. Serve with ice; garnish with mint.

¾ cup: 122 cal., 0 fat (0 sat. fat), 0 chol., 3mg sod., 14g carb. (7g sugars, 1g fiber), 0 pro.

FIVE CHEESE BAKED FONDUTA

If melted cheese isn't one of the most mouthwatering foods of all time, I don't know what is! Replace any cheese you don't like with your favorites.
—*Cheri Gilmore, Festus, MO*

TAKES: 30 MIN. • **MAKES:** 3 CUPS

3 Tbsp. melted butter, divided
1 pkg. (8 oz.) cream cheese, softened
2 cups shredded part-skim mozzarella cheese
1 cup shredded fontina cheese
1 cup shredded cheddar cheese
½ cup grated Parmesan cheese
4 garlic cloves, thinly sliced
1 tsp. dried rosemary, crushed
1 tsp. dried thyme
½ tsp. pepper
Optional: Toasted French bread baguette slices, baked pita chips or assorted fresh vegetables

Preheat oven to 450°. Brush an 8-in. cast-iron or other ovenproof skillet with 1 Tbsp. butter; set aside. In a large bowl, beat cream cheese and mozzarella, fontina, cheddar and Parmesan cheeses with garlic, rosemary, thyme, pepper and remaining 2 Tbsp. butter until combined. Spread into prepared skillet. Bake until bubbly and golden brown, 15-20 minutes. Serve with baguette slices, pita chips or vegetables as desired.

¼ cup: 237 cal., 20g fat (12g sat. fat), 61mg chol., 402mg sod., 4g carb. (1g sugars, 0 fiber), 11g pro.

PANCETTA-WRAPPED SHRIMP WITH HONEY-LIME GLAZE

These shrimp appetizers are requested by my family regularly. We're all familiar with bacon-wrapped shrimp bites, but this version uses pancetta and a honey-lime cilantro glaze.
—*Jenn Tidwell, Fair Oaks, CA*

TAKES: 25 MIN. • **MAKES:** 1½ DOZEN

6 thin slices pancetta
18 uncooked large shrimp, peeled and deveined
¼ cup honey
2 Tbsp. lime juice
1 tsp. hot water
1 Tbsp. minced fresh cilantro

1. Preheat oven to 375°. Cut each slice of pancetta into 3 strips. Wrap 1 strip around each shrimp; secure with a toothpick. Place in a foil-lined 15x10x1-in. baking pan. In a small bowl, whisk honey, lime juice and water until blended; reserve 2 Tbsp. for brushing cooked shrimp.

2. Brush half the remaining honey mixture over shrimp. Bake 5 minutes. Turn shrimp; brush with remaining half of the honey mixture. Bake 4-6 minutes longer or until pancetta is crisp and shrimp turns pink.

3. Remove from oven; brush with reserved 2 Tbsp. honey mixture. Sprinkle with cilantro.

1 pancetta-wrapped shrimp: 55 cal., 3g fat (1g sat. fat), 26mg chol., 160mg sod., 4g carb. (4g sugars, 0 fiber), 4g pro.

PRESSURE-COOKER CHERRY BOURBON HAM BALLS

My family loves meatballs and cherries so I decided to try
to combine the two. This quick and easy dish
is the result, and my family couldn't be happier.
—*Joyce Moynihan, Lakeville, MN*

PREP: 45 MIN. • **COOK:** 15 MIN. + RELEASING • **MAKES:** 5 DOZEN

1   fully cooked boneless ham steak
    (1¼ lbs.)
1   lb. ground pork
1   cup soft marble rye bread crumbs
2   large eggs, lightly beaten
2   tsp. dried minced onion
2   tsp. ground mustard
½   tsp. pepper
1   can (14½ oz.) pitted tart cherries,
    undrained
¼   cup sugar
¼   cup yellow mustard
½   tsp. Worcestershire sauce
1   Tbsp. cornstarch
¼   cup bourbon

1. Cut ham into 2-in. pieces; place in a food processor. Process until ground; transfer to a large bowl. Add ground pork, bread crumbs, eggs, onion, ground mustard and pepper; mix lightly but thoroughly. Shape into 1½-in. balls.

2. Place trivet insert in a 6-qt. electric pressure cooker. Place meatballs on trivet, overlapping as needed. Combine undrained cherries, sugar, mustard and Worcestershire sauce; pour over meatballs. Lock lid; close pressure-release valve. Adjust to pressure-cook on high for 15 minutes. Allow pressure to release naturally. Remove meatballs; keep warm. Remove trivet.

3. In a small bowl, mix cornstarch and bourbon until smooth; add to cooking juices in cooker. Select saute setting and adjust for low heat. Simmer, stirring constantly, until thickened, 1-2 minutes. Press cancel. Serve sauce with meatballs.

Note: To make soft bread crumbs, tear bread into pieces and place in a food processor or blender. Cover and pulse until crumbs form. One slice of bread yields ½-¾ cup crumbs.

1 meatball with about 1 tsp. sauce: 39 cal., 2g fat (1 g sat. fat), 16mg chol., 120mg sod., 2g carb. (1g sugars 0 fiber), 4g pro.

CHEESY CARAMELIZED ONION SKILLET BREAD

This appetizer is perfect for a football game or informal party, but it came about because I have two sons who are always hungry. I needed time to get dinner on the table after coming home from work. They love the skillet bread for the flavor, and I love it because it keeps them in the kitchen to chat while I prepare the rest of dinner! If you'd like, you can use homemade biscuits instead of prepared.
—*Mary Leverette, Columbia, SC*

PREP: 45 MIN. • **BAKE:** 20 MIN. • **MAKES:** 8 SERVINGS

2 tsp. caraway seeds
1 Tbsp. olive oil
1 large onion, chopped
¼ tsp. salt
1 cup shredded sharp cheddar cheese
½ cup butter, melted
1 tube (16.3 oz.) large refrigerated buttermilk biscuits
1 Tbsp. minced fresh thyme, optional

Preheat oven to 350°. In a 10-in. cast-iron or other ovenproof skillet, toast caraway seeds until fragrant, about 1 minute. Remove and set aside. In the same skillet, heat oil over medium heat. Add onion; cook and stir until softened, 5-6 minutes. Reduce heat to medium-low; cook until deep golden brown, 30-40 minutes, stirring occasionally. Stir in salt; remove from the heat and cool slightly. Sprinkle cheese over onions in skillet. Place melted butter and caraway seeds in a shallow bowl. Cut each biscuit into fourths. Dip biscuit pieces in butter mixture; place in a single layer over onion mixture in skillet. Bake until puffed and golden brown, 20-25 minutes. Cool in skillet 5 minutes before inverting onto a serving plate. If desired, sprinkle with thyme. Serve warm.

1 serving: 352 cal., 25g fat (13g sat. fat), 45mg chol., 874mg sod., 27g carb. (4g sugars, 1g fiber), 7g pro.

AIR-FRIED AVOCADO

Avocado just got even more exciting! These juicy, flavorful, easy and healthy appetizers are for those who are huge fans of avocado. They even go well on tacos!
—*Julie Peterson, Crofton, MD*

PREP: 10 MIN. • **COOK:** 10 MIN./BATCH • **MAKES:** 28 SERVINGS

1 large egg, beaten
¼ cup cornmeal
½ tsp. salt
½ tsp. garlic powder
½ tsp. ground chipotle pepper
2 medium avocados, peeled and sliced
   Cooking spray
   Optional: Lime wedges, salsa, pico de gallo or spicy ranch dressing

1. Preheat air fryer to 400°. Place egg in a shallow bowl. In another shallow bowl, mix cornmeal, salt, garlic powder and chipotle pepper. Dip avocado slices in egg, then into cornmeal mixture, gently patting to help adhere.

2. In batches, place avocado slices in a single layer on greased tray in air-fryer basket; spritz with cooking spray. Cook until golden brown, about 4 minutes. Turn; spritz with cooking spray. Cook until golden brown, 3-4 minutes longer. If desired, serve avocado slices with lime wedges, salsa, pico del gallo or ranch dressing.

1 piece: 22 cal., 2g fat (0 sat. fat), 5mg chol., 25mg sod., 1g carb. (0 sugars, 1g fiber), 0 pro.

CHEESY CARAMELIZED
ONION SKILLET BREAD

GLUTEN-FREE FLUFFY DINNER
ROLLS, PAGE 53

66
These rolls
are the perfect
addition to any
meal, and you
can customize
them with
herbs to match
your entree.
—PEGGY WOODWARD
TASTE OF HOME
SENIOR FOOD EDITOR

CHAPTER 3

BEST-SHARED BREADS

Few things turn a house into a home like the aroma of freshly baked bread wafting about. These popular biscuits, rolls, muffins and loaves not only round out menus but make heartwarming gifts for neighbors, friends and loved ones. Bake up a surprise today!

AIR-FRYER PUMPKIN BISCUITS WITH SPICED APPLE BUTTER

A couple of years ago, one of my friend's parents made pumpkin biscuits for Thanksgiving.
I was inspired by the innovative idea but wanted to add my own spin by topping the biscuits with apple butter.
I have been experimenting with the air fryer recently and wanted to try to make bread in the machine. What a success!
—*Jessica Burke, Chandler, AZ*

PREP: 15 MIN. • COOK: 10 MIN./BATCH • MAKES: 1 DOZEN

2 cups all-purpose flour
¼ cup packed brown sugar
1 Tbsp. pumpkin pie spice
2½ tsp. baking powder
¾ tsp. salt
½ cup cold unsalted butter
¾ cup canned pumpkin
Apple butter, optional

1. Preheat air fryer to 370°. In a large bowl, whisk the first 5 ingredients. Cut in butter until mixture resembles coarse crumbs. Add the pumpkin; stir just until moistened.

2. Turn onto a lightly floured surface; knead gently 8-10 times. Pat or roll dough to ½-in. thickness; cut with a floured 2½-in. biscuit cutter. In batches, place in a single layer 1 in. apart in greased air fryer. Cook until golden brown, 7-9 minutes. If desired, serve with apple butter.

Note: This recipe was tested with commercially prepared apple butter. In our testing, we find cook times vary dramatically between brands of air fryers. As a result, we give wider than normal ranges on suggested cook times. Begin checking at the first time listed and adjust as needed.

1 biscuit: 168 cal., 8g fat (5g sat. fat), 20mg chol., 251mg sod., 22g carb. (5g sugars, 1g fiber), 2g pro.

GARLIC-CHEESE CRESCENT ROLLS

Here's a recipe that just couldn't be much quicker or easier and is sure to add a nice touch to any dinner. The garlic and Parmesan flavors really come through.
—*Lori Abad, East Haven, CT*

TAKES: 20 MIN. • MAKES: 8 SERVINGS

1 tube (8 oz.) refrigerated crescent rolls
3 Tbsp. butter, melted
1½ tsp. garlic powder
1 tsp. dried oregano
2 Tbsp. grated Parmesan cheese

1. Preheat oven to 375°. Separate crescent dough into 8 triangles. Roll up from the wide end and place point side down 2 in. apart on an ungreased baking sheet. Curve ends to form a crescent.

2. Combine the butter, garlic powder and oregano; brush over rolls. Sprinkle with the cheese.

3. Bake until golden brown, 10-12 minutes. Serve warm.

1 roll: 157 cal., 11g fat (4g sat. fat), 12mg chol., 290mg sod., 12g carb. (2g sugars, 0 fiber), 3g pro.

AIR-FRYER PUMPKIN
BISCUITS WITH SPICED
APPLE BUTTER

EASY CAST-IRON PEACH BISCUIT ROLLS

I used to love going to the local coffee shop and enjoying fresh peach cinnamon rolls, but being a busy mom of three, I don't have the time anymore. To re-create it at home, I developed this no-yeast recipe that is quick and easy to make.
—*Heather Karow, Burnett, WI*

PREP: 25 MIN. • **BAKE:** 25 MIN. + COOLING • **MAKES:** 1 DOZEN

1 cup packed brown sugar
¼ cup butter, softened
3 tsp. ground cinnamon

DOUGH
2 cups all-purpose flour
2 Tbsp. sugar
1 Tbsp. baking powder
1 tsp. salt
3 Tbsp. butter
¾ cup 2% milk
1 can (15 oz.) sliced peaches in juice, undrained
1 cup confectioners' sugar

1. Preheat oven to 350°. In a small bowl, mix brown sugar, butter and cinnamon until crumbly. Reserve half for topping. Sprinkle remaining crumb mixture onto bottom of a 10-in. cast-iron or other ovenproof skillet.

2. For dough, in a large bowl, mix flour, sugar, baking powder and salt. Cut in butter until crumbly. Add the milk; stir to form a soft dough (dough will be sticky). Roll into an 18x12-in. rectangle. Sprinkle reserved topping to within ½ in. of edges.

3. Drain peaches, reserving 2 Tbsp. juice for glaze. Chop peaches; place over topping. Roll up jelly-roll style, starting with a long side; pinch seam to seal. Cut into 12 slices. Place in prepared skillet, cut side down.

4. Bake until lightly browned, 25-30 minutes. Cool on a wire rack 10 minutes. For glaze, combine confectioners' sugar and 1-2 Tbsp. reserved peach juice to reach desired consistency. Drizzle over warm rolls.

1 roll: 279 cal., 7g fat (4g sat. fat), 19mg chol., 746mg sod., 52g carb. (35g sugars, 1g fiber), 3g pro.

GLUTEN-FREE FLUFFY DINNER ROLLS
SHOWN ON PAGE 48

The dough for these gluten-free dinner rolls is stickier than traditional yeast bread,
but if you keep beating for two to three minutes in the mixer, it becomes workable. The dough balls
fit in the pan nicely with seven rolls on the perimeter and two in the middle.

—Doris Kinney, Merrimack, NH

PREP: 20 MIN. + RISING • BAKE: 20 MIN. + COOLING • MAKES: 9 ROLLS

1 Tbsp. active dry yeast
2 Tbsp. sugar
1 cup warm fat-free milk (110° to 115°)
2 large eggs, room temperature
3 Tbsp. canola oil
1 tsp. cider vinegar
2½ cups gluten-free all-purpose baking
flour (without xanthan gum)
2½ tsp. xanthan gum
1 tsp. unflavored gelatin
½ tsp. salt

1. Grease a 9-in. round baking pan and sprinkle with gluten-free flour; set aside.

2. In a small bowl, dissolve yeast and sugar in warm milk. In a stand mixer with a paddle attachment, combine the eggs, oil, vinegar and yeast mixture. Gradually beat in the flour, xanthan gum, gelatin and salt. Beat on low speed for 1 minute. Beat on medium for 2 minutes. (Dough will be sticky.)

3. Drop batter by ⅓ cupfuls into prepared pan. Smooth the tops with a wet spatula. Cover and let rise in a warm place until dough reaches the top of pan and rolls are touching, about 25 minutes. Preheat oven to 375°.

4. Bake until golden brown, 20-25 minutes. Cool in pan on a wire rack.

1 roll: 196 cal., 7g fat (1g sat. fat), 42mg chol., 163mg sod., 30g carb. (5g sugars, 4g fiber), 6g pro.

TEST KITCHEN TIP

When you are doing any kind of gluten-free baking, it's important to spoon the flour into the measuring cup, then level with the flat side of a butter knife. Avoid scooping the flour with the measuring cup because you'll get too much flour.

—PEGGY WOODWARD, *TASTE OF HOME* SENIOR FOOD EDITOR

> " This is the easiest and best bread recipe. It was loved by my family and friends. They even asked for the recipe.
>
> —STEPHANIE F.
> TASTEOFHOME.COM

WHOLE WHEAT BREAD

I'm 12 years old and make this bread with my mother, who got the recipe from her mother. I usually prepare the dough, and my mom bakes it.
—Freida Stutman, Fillmore, NY

PREP: 20 MIN. + RISING • BAKE: 40 MIN. • MAKES: 2 LOAVES (16 PIECES EACH)

1 pkg. (¼ oz.) active dry yeast
3 cups warm water (110° to 115°), divided
¾ cup canola oil
¼ cup sugar
¼ cup molasses
1 Tbsp. salt
7 to 7½ cups all-purpose flour
3 cups whole wheat flour

1. In a large bowl, dissolve yeast in ¾ cup warm water. Add oil, sugar, molasses, salt and remaining water. Combine flours; add 4-5 cups flour to mixture. Beat until smooth. Add enough remaining flour to form a firm dough.

2. Turn onto a lightly floured surface; knead until smooth and elastic, 6-8 minutes. Place in a greased bowl, turning once to grease top. Cover and let rise in a warm place until doubled, about 1 hour.

3. Punch down dough. Turn onto a lightly floured surface; divide in half. Shape each portion into a loaf. Place in 2 greased 9x5-in. loaf pans. Cover and let rise until doubled, about 30 minutes.

4. Preheat oven to 350°. Bake until golden brown 40-45 minutes. Remove from pans to cool on wire racks.

1 piece: 168 cal., 6g fat (1g sat. fat), 0 chol., 223mg sod., 26g carb. (4g sugars, 2g fiber), 4g pro.

A Pinch of Care

Valerie Chamberlain finds baking as a family has many sweet rewards.

Molly Chamberlain
Renfrew, ON

How old were your kids when they started helping in the kitchen?
It doesn't seem so long ago that my daughter, Molly, was 3 years old, tugging on my shirt and asking to help. I knew it would take me twice as long, but I tied aprons on my kids when they were tall enough to stand on chairs and peer into the big mixing bowls on the kitchen counter. The process took longer, but many sweet conversations took place while we made delicious treats.

What are some of the challenges you faced when baking with children?
I admit I sometimes lost patience and sent the cherubs on their way. Cookies burned while I was busy wiping sticky fingers, and muffins weren't always light and fluffy. Yet each time we gathered at the counter, I shared my love and gave them the gift of time, slowness and care.

As they grew older, did their love of baking continue?
These days, my kids are baking it all! They make chocolate chip cookies, brownies and gingersnaps, to name a few things. Molly, in particular, has grown fond of baking bread.

What is it about bread baking that Molly enjoys?
She adores the whole process, from measuring and mixing straight through to lifting the golden loaves from the oven. She loves the feeling of the flour in her hands and the smooth stretch of dough when she's kneading it. One of her favorite parts is punching the dough down after it has risen. We enjoy the end result when she offers slices of fresh, warm bread. Pass the butter, please!

PARMESAN SWEET CREAM BISCUITS

Sweet cream biscuits were the first kind I mastered. Since the ingredients are so simple, I can scale the recipe up or down. In fact, I've actually memorized it!
—*Helen Nelander, Boulder Creek, CA*

TAKES: 25 MIN. • MAKES: ABOUT 1 DOZEN

2 cups all-purpose flour
⅓ cup grated Parmesan cheese
2 tsp. baking powder
½ tsp. salt
1½ cups heavy whipping cream

1. Preheat oven to 400°. Whisk together the first 4 ingredients. Add cream; stir just until moistened.

2. Turn dough onto a lightly floured surface; knead gently 6-8 times. Roll or pat dough to ½-in. thickness; cut with a floured 2¾-in. biscuit cutter. Place 1 in. apart on an ungreased baking sheet.

3. Bake until light golden brown, 12-15 minutes. Serve warm.

1 biscuit: 187 cal., 12g fat (7g sat. fat), 36mg chol., 227mg sod., 17g carb. (1g sugars, 1g fiber), 4g pro.

TENDER WHOLE WHEAT MUFFINS

Want oven-baked treats but need something light? Simple whole wheat muffins are wonderful paired with soup or spread with a little jam for breakfast.
—*Kristine Chayes, Smithtown, NY*

TAKES: 30 MIN. • MAKES: 10 MUFFINS

1 cup all-purpose flour
1 cup whole wheat flour
2 Tbsp. sugar
2½ tsp. baking powder
1 tsp. salt
1 large egg, room temperature
1¼ cups whole milk
3 Tbsp. butter, melted

1. Preheat oven to 400°. In a large bowl, whisk flours, sugar, baking powder and salt. In another bowl, whisk egg, milk and melted butter until blended. Add to flour mixture; stir just until moistened.

2. Fill greased muffin cups three-fourths full. Bake 15-17 minutes or until a toothpick inserted in center comes out clean. Cool 5 minutes before removing from pan to a wire rack. Serve warm.

1 muffin: 152 cal., 5g fat (3g sat. fat), 35mg chol., 393mg sod., 22g carb. (4g sugars, 2g fiber), 5g pro. **Diabetic exchanges:** 1½ starch, 1 fat.

PESTO STAR BREAD

I was excited to work with the *Taste of Home* Test Kitchen to make a savory version of my Christmas Star Twisted Bread. It's perfect for the holidays (but it's a showstopper at any time of the year).

—Darlene Brenden, Salem, OR

PREP: 45 MIN. + RISING • BAKE: 20 MIN. + COOLING • MAKES: 16 SERVINGS

1 pkg. (¼ oz.) active dry yeast
¼ cup warm water (110° to 115°)
¾ cup warm 2% milk (110° to 115°)
1 large egg, room temperature
¼ cup butter, softened
2 Tbsp. sugar
1 tsp. salt
3¼ to 3¾ cups all-purpose flour
½ cup prepared basil pesto
6 Tbsp. grated Parmesan cheese, divided
¼ cup sun-dried tomato pesto
2 Tbsp. butter, melted
Optional: Additional grated Parmesan cheese, basil pesto, torn fresh basil and marinara sauce

1. In a small bowl, dissolve yeast in warm water. In a large bowl, combine milk, egg, butter, sugar, salt, yeast mixture and 2 cups flour; beat on medium speed until smooth. Stir in enough remaining flour to form a soft dough (dough will be sticky).

2. Turn dough onto a floured surface; knead 6-8 minutes or until smooth and elastic. Place in a greased bowl, turning once to grease the top. Cover and let rise in a warm place until doubled, about 1 hour.

3. Punch down dough. Turn onto a lightly floured surface; divide into 4 portions. Roll each into a 12-in. circle. Place 1 circle on a greased 14-in. pizza pan. Spread with half the basil pesto to within ½ in. of edge; sprinkle with 2 Tbsp. Parmesan. Place second circle of dough on top; spread with sun-dried tomato pesto and sprinkle with 2 Tbsp. Parmesan. Top with third circle of dough, remaining basil pesto and remaining 2 Tbsp. Parmesan; top with final portion of dough.

4. Place a 2½-in. round cutter on top of the dough in center of circle (do not press down). With a sharp knife, make 16 evenly spaced cuts from round cutter to edge of dough, forming a starburst. Remove cutter; grasp 2 adjacent strips and rotate twice outward. Pinch ends together. Repeat with remaining strips.

5. Cover with a kitchen towel; let rise in a warm place until almost doubled, about 30 minutes. Preheat oven to 375°. Bake until golden brown, 18-22 minutes. Remove from oven; brush with melted butter, avoiding areas where pesto is visible. Cool completely on a wire rack. If desired, sprinkle with additional cheese and basil before serving; serve with pesto or marinara.

1 piece: 192 cal., 9g fat (4g sat. fat), 26mg chol., 355mg sod., 23g carb. (3g sugars, 1g fiber), 5g pro.

TRAINING WHEEL

A round cookie cutter gently set in the middle of the dough makes it easy to create perfectly spaced cuts for an impressive starburst shape.

LAVENDER POPPY SEED MUFFINS

These muffins are so easy to put together. The lavender flavor really works well with lemon.
If you've never baked with lavender before, start with just 1 or 2 teaspoons for a more subtle flavor.
—*Elisabeth Larsen, Pleasant Grove, UT*

PREP: 15 MIN. • BAKE: 20 MIN. • MAKES: 1 DOZEN

2 cups all-purpose flour
½ cup sugar
4 tsp. poppy seeds
1 Tbsp. dried lavender flowers
3 tsp. baking powder
2 tsp. grated lemon zest
½ tsp. salt
¾ cup 2% milk
½ cup butter, melted
1 large egg, room temperature
2 Tbsp. coarse sugar

1. Preheat oven to 400°. In a large bowl, whisk the first 7 ingredients. In another bowl, whisk milk, melted butter and egg until blended. Add to flour mixture; stir just until moistened.

2. Fill 12 paper-lined muffin cups three-fourths full; sprinkle with coarse sugar. Bake until a toothpick inserted in center comes out clean, 20-25 minutes. Cool 5 minutes before removing from pan to a wire rack. Serve warm.

Note: Look for dried lavender flowers in spice shops. If using lavender from the garden, make sure it hasn't been treated with chemicals.

1 muffin: 203 cal., 9g fat (5g sat. fat), 37mg chol., 293mg sod., 27g carb. (11g sugars, 1g fiber), 3g pro.

EASY CHEESY BISCUITS

I'm a big fan of homemade biscuits, but not the rolling and cutting
that goes into making them. The drop biscuit method solves everything!
—*Christy Addison, Clarksville, OH*

TAKES: 30 MIN. • MAKES: 1 DOZEN

3 cups all-purpose flour
3 tsp. baking powder
1 Tbsp. sugar
1 tsp. salt
¾ tsp. cream of tartar
½ cup cold butter
1 cup shredded sharp cheddar cheese
1 garlic clove, minced
¼ to ½ tsp. crushed red pepper flakes
1¼ cups 2% milk

1. Preheat oven to 450°. In a large bowl, whisk flour, baking powder, sugar, salt and cream of tartar. Cut in butter until mixture resembles coarse crumbs. Stir in cheese, garlic and pepper flakes. Add milk; stir just until moistened.

2. Drop dough by heaping ¼ cupfuls 2 in. apart onto a greased baking sheet. Bake 18-20 minutes or until golden brown. Serve warm.

1 biscuit: 237 cal., 12g fat (7g sat. fat), 32mg chol., 429mg sod., 26g carb. (2g sugars, 1g fiber), 7g pro.

GLAZED GRAPEFRUIT BREAD

This grapefruit bread recipe was inspired by lime, orange and lemon nut loaves I've made in the past. Try this new variation.
—*Dawn Lowenstein, Huntingdon Valley, PA*

PREP: 20 MIN. • **BAKE:** 1 HOUR + COOLING • **MAKES:** 2 LOAVES (12 PIECES EACH)

- 1 cup butter-flavored shortening
- 2 cups sugar
- 4 large eggs, room temperature
- 3 cups all-purpose flour
- 3 tsp. baking powder
- 1 tsp. salt
- 1 cup 2% milk
- 1 cup finely chopped walnuts
- 2 Tbsp. grated grapefruit zest

GLAZE
- ½ cup sugar
- ½ cup grapefruit juice

1. Preheat oven to 350°. Grease and flour two 9x5-in. loaf pans.

2. In a large bowl, beat shortening and sugar until crumbly. Add eggs, 1 at a time, beating well after each addition. In another bowl, whisk flour, baking powder and salt; add to creamed mixture alternately with milk, beating well after each addition. Fold in walnuts and zest.

3. Transfer to prepared pans. Bake until a toothpick inserted in center comes out clean, 60-65 minutes. Meanwhile, whisk glaze ingredients. Remove pans from oven; immediately brush with glaze. Cool in pan 10 minutes before removing to a wire rack to cool completely.

Freeze option: Securely wrap cooled loaves in foil, then freeze. To use, thaw at room temperature.

1 piece: 263 cal., 12g fat (3g sat. fat), 32mg chol., 176mg sod., 35g carb. (22g sugars, 1g fiber), 4g pro.

MINI SWEET POTATO SCONES WITH ROSEMARY & BACON

I grow my own sweet potatoes, so I'm always trying to think of new ways to use them. I created this recipe on a whim and am thrilled with the results ... everyone who tries these scones thinks they're delicious! To save a little time in the morning, I like to combine the dry ingredients and cut in the butter the night before. I usually stir in the crumbled bacon at that time too. I cover and refrigerate overnight, proceeding with the recipe the next morning. In addition to saving time, this also allows the rosemary and bacon to flavor through, and chilling the butter (in the mix) results in tender scones.
—Sue Gronholz, Beaver Dam, WI

PREP: 30 MIN. • BAKE: 15 MIN. • MAKES: 16 SCONES

2½ cups all-purpose flour
½ cup sugar
2½ tsp. baking powder
1½ tsp. pumpkin pie spice or ground cinnamon
1½ tsp. minced fresh rosemary or ½ tsp. dried rosemary, crushed
½ tsp. salt
¼ tsp. baking soda
½ cup cold butter
4 bacon strips, cooked and crumbled
½ cup mashed sweet potatoes
¼ cup plain Greek yogurt
1 large egg, room temperature
2 Tbsp. maple syrup

TOPPING
1 Tbsp. 2% milk
1 Tbsp. sugar

1. Preheat oven to 425°. In a large bowl, whisk the first 7 ingredients. Cut in the butter until mixture resembles coarse crumbs. Stir in bacon. In another bowl, whisk sweet potatoes, yogurt, egg and maple syrup until blended; stir into crumb mixture just until combined.

2. Turn onto a floured surface; knead gently 10 times. Divide dough in half. Pat each half into a 6-in. circle. Cut each into 8 wedges. Place wedges on a greased baking sheet. Brush with milk; sprinkle with sugar. Bake until golden brown, 12-14 minutes. Serve warm.

Freeze option: Freeze cooled scones in freezer containers. To use, thaw before serving or, if desired, reheat on a baking sheet in a preheated 350° oven until warmed, 3-4 minutes.

1 scone: 184 cal., 7g fat (4g sat. fat), 30mg chol., 261mg sod., 26g carb. (9g sugars, 1g fiber), 3g pro.

PUMPKIN SWIRL BREAD

PUMPKIN SWIRL BREAD

This combination of pumpkin, nuts and dates makes a delicious, golden bread.
The surprise inside—a rich creamy swirl—is like a luscious layer of cheesecake in each slice.
—Cindy May, Troy, MI

PREP: 25 MIN. • BAKE: 65 MIN. + COOLING • MAKES: 3 LOAVES (16 PIECES EACH)

2 pkg. (8 oz. each) cream cheese, softened
¼ cup sugar
¼ cup 2% milk
1 large egg, room temperature

PUMPKIN BREAD

3 cups sugar
1 can (15 oz.) solid-pack pumpkin
4 large eggs, room temperature
1 cup canola oil
1 cup water
4 cups all-purpose flour
4 tsp. pumpkin pie spice
2 tsp. baking soda
1½ tsp. ground cinnamon
1 tsp. salt
1 tsp. baking powder
1 tsp. ground nutmeg
½ tsp. ground cloves
1 cup chopped walnuts
1 cup raisins
½ cup chopped dates

OPTIONAL TOPPINGS

1 cup confectioners' sugar
¼ tsp. vanilla extract
2 to 3 Tbsp. 2% milk
    Additional chopped walnuts

1. Preheat oven to 350°. Grease and flour three 8x4-in. loaf pans. Line the bottom of each pan with parchment; grease paper. In a small bowl, beat filling ingredients until smooth.

2. In a large bowl, beat sugar, pumpkin, eggs, oil and water until well blended. In another bowl, whisk flour, pie spice, baking soda, cinnamon, salt, baking powder, nutmeg and cloves; gradually beat into pumpkin mixture. Stir in walnuts, raisins and dates.

3. Pour half of the batter into prepared pans, dividing evenly. Spoon the filling over batter to within ½-in. of sides of pans; cut through filling with a knife to swirl. Cover filling completely with remaining batter; cut through batter again to swirl.

4. Bake until a toothpick inserted in bread portion comes out clean, 65-70 minutes. Cool 10 minutes before removing from pans to wire racks to cool completely before slicing. Refrigerate leftovers.

5. Just before serving, if desired, in a small bowl, mix the confectioners' sugar, vanilla and enough milk to reach a drizzling consistency. Drizzle over bread; sprinkle with walnuts.

1 piece: 189 cal., 8g fat (2g sat. fat), 27mg chol., 132mg sod., 27g carb. (17g sugars, 1g fiber), 3g pro.

TEST KITCHEN TIP

These loaves freeze very well. Make sure the bread is completely cool before wrapping it up to freeze. You don't want to trap in any excess moisture from steam. When you're certain it's cool, wrap it in plastic wrap (two layers doesn't hurt) or store in resealable plastic freezer bags. You can keep the unglazed bread in the freezer for 2 months. When you're ready to eat, defrost it in the fridge until thawed.

GREEK BREADSTICKS

Get ready for rave reviews with these crispy
Greek-inspired bites. They're best served hot and fresh
from the oven with your favorite tzatziki sauce.
—*Jane Whittaker, Pensacola, FL*

PREP: 20 MIN. • **BAKE:** 15 MIN. • **MAKES:** 32 BREADSTICKS

¼ cup marinated quartered artichoke
    hearts, drained
2 Tbsp. pitted Greek olives
1 pkg. (17.3 oz.) frozen puff pastry,
    thawed
1 carton (6½ oz.) spreadable spinach
    and artichoke cream cheese, divided
2 Tbsp. grated Parmesan cheese,
    divided
1 large egg
1 Tbsp. water
2 tsp. sesame seeds
    Refrigerated tzatziki sauce, optional

1. Place artichokes and olives in a food
processor; cover and pulse until finely
chopped. Unfold 1 pastry sheet on a
lightly floured surface; spread half of
the cream cheese over half of pastry.
Top with half of the artichoke mixture.
Sprinkle with half of the Parmesan
cheese. Fold plain half over filling;
press gently to seal.

2. Repeat with the remaining pastry,
cream cheese, artichoke mixture and
Parmesan cheese. Whisk egg and
water; brush over tops. Sprinkle with
sesame seeds. Cut each rectangle into sixteen ¾-in.-wide strips. Twist strips
several times; place 2 in. apart on greased baking sheets.

3. Bake at 400° for 12-14 minutes or until golden brown. Serve warm, with tzatziki
sauce if desired.

1 breadstick: 101 cal., 6g fat (2g sat. fat), 11mg chol., 104mg sod., 9g carb. (0 sugars,
1g fiber), 2g pro.

TRIPLE MUSTARD & GRUYERE BREAD THINS

I'm a bread baker, so the perfect sandwich in my home is more about the bread. I'm always experimenting with new combinations and I created this winning bread last year. It's become my favorite go-to for delicious sandwiches. The bread itself is so savory it elevates every sandwich to gourmet status. Though I have also made this into hamburger buns and baguettes, my preferred way is sandwich rounds. I love to use smoked Gruyere cheese but if you have a hard time finding it, you can also substitute regular Gruyere or even Swiss.
—*Veronica Fay, Knoxville, TN*

PREP: 30 MIN. + RISING • **BAKE:** 15 MIN. + COOLING • **MAKES:** 1½ DOZEN

1 Tbsp. active dry yeast
1 cup warm water (110° to 115°)
1 large egg, room temperature
⅓ cup canola oil
3 Tbsp. dried minced onion
3 Tbsp. stone-ground mustard
1 Tbsp. ground mustard
2 tsp. onion powder
1½ tsp. salt
3½ to 4 cups bread flour
8 oz. smoked Gruyere cheese, shredded
¼ cup Dijon mustard
  Optional: 1 Tbsp. each sesame seeds, poppy seeds and mustard seeds

1. In a small bowl, dissolve yeast in warm water. In a large bowl, combine egg, oil, minced onion, stone-ground mustard, ground mustard, onion powder, salt, yeast mixture and 2 cups flour; beat on medium speed until smooth. Stir in enough remaining flour to form a soft dough (dough will be sticky). Stir in the cheese.

2. Turn dough onto a floured surface; knead until smooth and elastic, 6-8 minutes. Place in a greased bowl, turning once to grease the top. Cover and let rise in a warm place until almost doubled, about 1½ hours.

3. Punch down dough. Turn onto a lightly floured surface; divide and shape into 18 balls, about 2 oz. each. Flatten each ball to a 4-in. circle. Place 2 in. apart on greased baking sheets. Cover with kitchen towels; let rise in a warm place until slightly puffed, about 30 minutes.

4. Preheat oven to 375°. Brush rolls with Dijon mustard; if desired, sprinkle with seeds. Bake until lightly browned, 15-18 minutes. Remove from pans to wire racks to cool completely.

Freeze option: Freeze cooled rolls in freezer containers. To use, thaw at room temperature or, if desired, microwave each roll on high until heated through, 10-15 seconds.

1 roll: 204 cal., 9g fat (3g sat. fat), 24mg chol., 423mg sod., 21g carb. (1g sugars, 1g fiber), 8g pro.

JALAPENO CORNBREAD FILLED WITH BLUEBERRY QUICK JAM

Fresh jalapenos and blueberry quick jam make the perfect blend of sweet and spicy in this special cornbread. Once you eat one piece, you won't be able to resist going back for another.

—Colleen Delawder, Herndon, VA

PREP: 20 MIN. + CHILLING • **BAKE:** 30 MIN. + COOLING • **MAKES:** 12 SERVINGS

2 cups fresh blueberries
1 cup sugar
1 Tbsp. cider vinegar
¼ tsp. kosher salt

CORNBREAD
½ cup 2% milk
1 Tbsp. lemon juice
1½ cups all-purpose flour
½ cup yellow cornmeal
½ cup sugar
3 tsp. baking powder
½ tsp. kosher salt
2 Tbsp. unsalted butter
1 Tbsp. honey
2 large eggs, room temperature
⅓ cup canola oil
2 jalapeno peppers, seeded and minced

1. In a large heavy saucepan, combine blueberries, sugar, vinegar and kosher salt. Bring to a boil over high heat. Cook, stirring constantly, 5 minutes. Cool completely. Refrigerate, covered, overnight.

2. For cornbread, preheat oven to 350°. Combine milk and lemon juice; let stand briefly. In another bowl, whisk next 5 ingredients. In a small bowl, microwave butter and honey on high for 30 seconds; cool slightly. Whisk eggs and oil into milk mixture (mixture may appear curdled). Add butter mixture; whisk until well combined. Add flour mixture; whisk just until combined. Fold in jalapenos.

3. Pour 2 cups batter into a well-buttered 10-in. fluted tube pan. Spoon half to three-fourths of blueberry quick jam over batter. Cover with remaining batter. Bake until a toothpick inserted in center comes out clean, 30-35 minutes. Cool 10 minutes; invert onto a cake plate or serving platter. Drizzle with remaining blueberry quick jam.

1 piece: 289 cal., 10g fat (2g sat. fat), 37mg chol., 258mg sod., 48g carb. (30g sugars, 1g fiber), 4g pro.

TEST KITCHEN TIP

Make the jam a day ahead, giving it plenty of time to cool, and wear disposable gloves when cutting hot peppers; the oils can burn skin. Avoid touching your face.

JALAPENO
CORNBREAD FILLED
WITH BLUEBERRY
QUICK JAM

66
As soon as
I saw this
recipe, I knew
we would just
love it. Great
combination
of both sweet
and spicy!
—LPHJKITCHEN
TASTEOFHOME.COM

CHERRY TOMATO & BASIL FOCACCIA

When I had 80 pounds of tomatoes, I got creative incorporating them into meals. Sometimes I slice this loaf into squares to make sandwiches with fresh mozzarella cheese and deli meats.
—*Katie Ferrier, Houston, TX*

PREP: 45 MIN. + RISING • BAKE: 15 MIN. • MAKES: 2 LOAVES (20 PIECES EACH)

1   pkg. (¼ oz.) active dry yeast
2   cups warm 2% milk (110° to 115°)
¼   cup canola oil
4½ tsp. sugar
1   tsp. salt
5   to 5½ cups all-purpose flour
2   cups cherry tomatoes
⅓   cup olive oil
2   Tbsp. cornmeal
3   Tbsp. thinly sliced fresh basil
1   tsp. coarse salt
⅛   tsp. pepper

1. In a small bowl, dissolve yeast in warm milk. In a large bowl, combine canola oil, sugar, salt, yeast mixture and 2 cups flour; beat on medium speed until smooth. Stir in enough remaining flour to form a stiff dough (dough will be sticky).

2. Turn dough onto a floured surface; knead 6-8 minutes or until smooth and elastic. Place in a greased bowl, turning once to grease the top. Cover and let rise in a warm place until doubled, about 45 minutes.

3. Meanwhile, fill a large saucepan two-thirds with water; bring to a boil. Cut a shallow "X" on the bottom of each tomato. Using a slotted spoon, place tomatoes, a cup at a time, in boiling water for 30 seconds or just until skin at the "X" begins to loosen.

4. Remove tomatoes and immediately drop into ice water. Pull off and discard skins. Place tomatoes in a small bowl; drizzle with oil.

5. Preheat oven to 425°. Sprinkle 2 greased baking sheets with cornmeal; set aside. Punch down dough. Turn onto a lightly floured surface. Cover; let rest 10 minutes. Divide dough in half. Shape each into a 12x8-in. rectangle and place on prepared baking sheets.

6. Using fingertips, press several dimples into dough. Pour tomato mixture over dough; sprinkle with basil, coarse salt and pepper. Let rise in a warm place until doubled, about 30 minutes.

7. Bake until golden brown, 15-18 minutes.

1 piece: 97 cal., 4g fat (1g sat. fat), 1mg chol., 125mg sod., 14g carb. (1g sugars, 1g fiber), 2g pro.

GLUTEN- & DAIRY-FREE CINNAMON RAISIN BREAD

After learning of gluten and dairy sensitivities in our family, I knew
I had to re-create our favorite sweet bread. This gluten-free bread can be made
using a premixed gluten-free flour or your own homemade blend. We use
coconut milk to make it dairy-free, but any type of milk works.
—Courtney Stultz, Weir, KS

PREP: 25 MIN. • BAKE: 45 MIN. + COOLING • MAKES 12 SERVINGS

2 cups plus 1 Tbsp. gluten-free
all-purpose baking flour (without
xanthan gum)
1 cup sugar, divided
1½ tsp. baking powder
½ tsp. baking soda
¼ tsp. salt
2 large eggs
1 cup coconut milk
½ cup canola oil
1 tsp. vanilla extract
1 cup raisins
3 tsp. ground cinnamon
Dairy-free spreadable margarine,
optional

1. Preheat oven to 350°. In a large
bowl, whisk flour, ¾ cup sugar, baking
powder baking soda and salt. In
another bowl, whisk eggs, coconut
milk, oil and vanilla until blended.
Add to flour mixture; stir just until
moistened. Toss the raisins with
remaining flour; fold into batter.

2. Transfer half of the batter to a
greased 9x5-in. loaf pan. Combine the cinnamon and remaining sugar. Sprinkle
half over batter. Repeat layers. Cut through batter with a knife to swirl.

3. Bake until a toothpick inserted in center comes out clean, 45-50 minutes. Cool
in pans 10 minutes before removing to a wire rack to cool completely. If desired,
serve with dairy-free margarine.

1 piece: 295 cal., 14g fat (4g sat. fat), 31mg chol., 180mg sod., 42g carb. (25g sugars,
3g fiber), 4g pro.

PARMESAN-RANCH
PAN ROLLS

PARMESAN-RANCH PAN ROLLS

Mom taught me this easy recipe, which is perfect for feeding a crowd. There is never a crumb left over. Mom used her own bread dough, but using frozen dough is my shortcut.
—*Trisha Kruse, Eagle, ID*

PREP: 30 MIN. + RISING • BAKE: 20 MIN. • MAKES: 1½ DOZEN

2 loaves (1 lb. each) frozen bread dough, thawed
1 cup grated Parmesan cheese
½ cup butter, melted
1 envelope buttermilk ranch salad dressing mix
1 small onion, finely chopped

1. On a lightly floured surface, divide dough into 18 portions; shape each into a ball. In a small bowl, combine the cheese, butter and ranch dressing mix.

2. Roll balls in cheese mixture; arrange in 2 greased 9-in. square baking pans. Sprinkle with onion. Cover and let rise in a warm place until doubled, about 45 minutes.

3. Meanwhile, preheat oven to 350°. Bake until golden brown, 20-25 minutes. Remove from pans to wire racks.

1 roll: 210 cal., 8g fat (4g sat. fat), 17mg chol., 512mg sod., 26g carb. (2g sugars, 2g fiber), 7g pro.

CORN PONE

My husband's grandmother gave me this corn pone recipe years ago. She always made it with bacon drippings—which is heavenly—but if you're trying to be a little more health-conscious, you can use canola oil or a combination of the two. I cook it until it's crisp almost all the way through. It's delicious hot, warm or cold.
—*Tina Quiggle, LaGrange, GA*

PREP: 10 MIN. • BAKE: 35 MIN. • MAKES: 10 SERVINGS

½ to ¾ cup canola oil or bacon drippings
2 cups yellow or white cornmeal
1 tsp. salt
1¼ cups water
Optional: Butter and honey

Preheat oven to 375°. Add oil to a 12-in. cast-iron or other ovenproof skillet; place in oven. In a large bowl, whisk together all cornmeal, salt and water. Mixture will be thick. Remove skillet from oven. Carefully spread mixture evenly in preheated skillet, spooning some of the oil on top of batter. Bake until edge starts to brown, about 35 minutes. To serve, break into pieces and serve with butter and honey if desired.

1 serving: 215 cal., 12g fat (1g sat. fat), 0 chol., 238mg sod., 25g carb. (1g sugars, 1g fiber), 2g pro.

66

This recipe was terrific! My entire family loved this soup, and the house smelled amazing while it cooked.

—XXCSKIER
TASTEOFHOME.COM

THAI MEATBALL SOUP, PAGE 84

CHAPTER 4

SOUPS & SAMMIES

For easy menu planning, turn to the classic combo of soup and sandwich! Quick, easy and oh, so comforting, these most-requested specialties always fill the bill. This chapter has you covered whenever you need a fast fix, from soups and sliders to chowders and chili.

GRILLED VEGETABLE PESTO SANDWICHES

I wanted to create something that was easy, but also delicious and healthy. I came up with this recipe because sandwiches are always a hit, and they're perfect during the summer months when it's hot outside. Most of my family is vegetarian, so I found a way to make a sandwich they could enjoy without sacrificing flavor. A lot of the ingredients can be altered based on availability or likes and dislikes. For example, you can use another type of cheese or different vegetables. You can also use Italian bread instead of ciabatta.

—*Tanya Mehta, Philadelphia, PA*

PREP: 25 MIN. • **GRILL:** 10 MIN. • **MAKES:** 2 SERVINGS

1 medium zucchini
1 yellow summer squash
1 medium sweet red pepper, quartered
1 medium onion, cut into ½-in. slices
1 Tbsp. olive oil
2 tsp. paprika
1 tsp. garlic powder
1 tsp. balsamic vinegar
½ tsp. salt
½ tsp. pepper
2 Tbsp. butter, softened
2 ciabatta rolls, split
2 Tbsp. prepared pesto
4 slices Asiago cheese
½ cup spring mix salad greens
6 large fresh basil leaves

1. Slice zucchini and summer squash lengthwise into ¼-in.-thick slices. Place in a large bowl with red pepper, onion, oil, paprika, garlic powder, vinegar, salt and pepper; toss to coat.

2. Grill vegetables on an oiled rack, covered, over medium heat, until crisp-tender, 3-4 minutes on each side. Remove and keep warm. Spread softened butter over cut sides of the rolls. Grill rolls, cut side down, over medium heat until toasted, 30-60 seconds.

3. To assemble, spread pesto over roll bottoms. Layer with zucchini, squash, red pepper and onion. Top with the cheese. Grill, covered, 1-2 minutes or until cheese is melted. Remove from heat; top with salad mix and basil. Replace roll top. Serve immediately.

1 sandwich: 748 cal., 37g fat (15g sat. fat), 58mg chol., 1476mg sod., 91g carb. (15g sugars, 9g fiber), 23g pro.

GRILLED VEGETABLE
PESTO SANDWICHES

EASY POT STICKER SOUP

Because my husband and I have soup often, I'm always coming up with something new. I saw pot stickers in the freezer and decided to feature them in an Asian soup. The results were delicious. Rice vinegar adds just the right tang, and the green onions and carrots act as a garnish. Stir in chopped cabbage or bok choy if you'd like. A little sesame oil goes a long way, but you can always add a bit more.
—*Darlene Brenden, Salem, OR*

PREP: 15 MIN. • COOK: 5¼ HOURS • MAKES: 6 SERVINGS (ABOUT 2 QT.)

½ lb. Chinese or napa cabbage, thinly sliced
2 celery ribs, thinly sliced
2 medium carrots, cut into matchsticks
⅓ cup thinly sliced green onions
2 to 3 Tbsp. soy sauce
2 Tbsp. rice vinegar
3 garlic cloves, minced
2 tsp. minced fresh gingerroot or ½ tsp. ground ginger
½ tsp. sesame oil
6 cups reduced-sodium chicken broth
1 pkg. (16 oz.) frozen chicken pot stickers
   Crispy chow mein noodles, optional

In a 4-qt. slow cooker, combine the first 9 ingredients. Stir in broth. Cook, covered, on low until vegetables are tender, 5-6 hours. Add pot stickers; cook, covered, on high until heated through, 15-20 minutes. If desired, sprinkle with chow mein noodles before serving.

1⅓ cups: 198 cal., 6g fat (2g sat. fat), 28mg chol., 1302mg sod., 23g carb. (5g sugars, 2g fiber), 13g pro.

CRISPY BUFFALO CHICKEN WRAPS

I'm big on wraps, even when I go out to eat. As a busy stay-at-home mom, I flip to this family favorite a lot. It's so good with chips and salsa on the side.
—*Christy Addison, Clarksville, OH*

TAKES: 30 MIN. • MAKES: 4 SERVINGS

1 pkg. (12 oz.) frozen popcorn chicken
1 pkg. (8 oz.) shredded lettuce
2 medium tomatoes, finely chopped
1 cup shredded cheddar cheese
⅓ cup Buffalo wing sauce
4 flour tortillas (10 in.), warmed
   Optional: Ranch or chipotle ranch salad dressing

1. Cook chicken according to package directions; coarsely chop. In a bowl, mix chicken, lettuce, tomatoes and cheese. Drizzle with wing sauce; toss to coat.

2. Spoon 1½ cups chicken mixture down center of each tortilla. Fold bottom of tortilla over filling; fold both sides to close. Serve immediately, with salad dressing if desired.

1 wrap: 570 cal., 26g fat (9g sat. fat), 55mg chol., 1895mg sod., 62g carb. (7g sugars, 4g fiber), 23g pro.

SLOPPY JOE MEATBALL SUBS

A mashup of two favorite recipes, these meatball subs are unique because of the sloppy joe-flavored sauce. I love to make them on a lazy afternoon and freeze leftovers for an easy weeknight meal.
—Susan Seymour, Valatie, NY

PREP: 1 HOUR • BAKE: 20 MIN./BATCH • MAKES: 12 SERVINGS

2 large eggs, lightly beaten
¼ cup canola oil, divided
2 medium onions, finely chopped, divided
½ cup dry bread crumbs
1 tsp. dried oregano
2 lbs. ground beef
1 medium green pepper, chopped
2 cans (15 oz. each) tomato sauce
¼ cup packed brown sugar
2 Tbsp. prepared mustard
2½ tsp. chili powder
¾ tsp. salt
¾ tsp. garlic powder
½ tsp. pepper
Dash Louisiana-style hot sauce

ADDITIONAL INGREDIENTS (FOR EACH SERVING)
1 hoagie bun, split and toasted
2 Tbsp. shredded cheddar cheese

1. In a large bowl, combine the eggs, 2 Tbsp. oil, ½ cup onion, bread crumbs and oregano. Crumble the beef over mixture and mix lightly but thoroughly. With wet hands, shape into 1½-in. balls.

2. Place the meatballs on greased racks in shallow baking pans. Bake, uncovered, at 400° until no longer pink, 20-25 minutes.

3. Meanwhile, in a Dutch oven, sauté green pepper and remaining onion in remaining oil until tender. Stir in the tomato sauce, brown sugar, mustard, chili powder, salt, garlic powder, pepper and hot sauce. Bring to a boil. Reduce heat; simmer, uncovered, for 5 minutes. Drain meatballs on paper towels; add to sauce and stir to coat.

4. To serve immediately, for each sandwich, place 4 meatballs on a bun and sprinkle with cheese. Cool remaining meatballs; transfer to freezer containers. Cover and freeze for up to 3 months.

To use frozen meatballs: Thaw in the refrigerator. Place in an ungreased shallow microwave-safe dish. Cover and microwave on high until heated through. Prepare sandwiches as directed above.

1 sandwich: 649 cal., 31g fat (10g sat. fat), 138mg chol., 1369mg sod., 58g carb. (17g sugars, 4g fiber), 36g pro. **Diabetic exchanges:** 1 lean meat.

CUBED BEEF &
BARLEY SOUP

"
So delicious
and easy to
make! Can't
wait to have it
again! Thanks
for sharing
the recipe.
—LACEY231
TASTEOFHOME.COM

CUBED BEEF & BARLEY SOUP

Here's a real stick-to-your-ribs soup. I've also used a chuck roast, rump roast and London broil that's been cut into bite-sized pieces with tremendous success.
—Jane Whittaker, Pensacola, FL

PREP: 20 MIN. • COOK: 8½ HOURS • MAKES: 8 SERVINGS (2 QT.)

1½ lbs. beef stew meat, cut into ½-in. cubes
1 Tbsp. canola oil
1 carton (32 oz.) beef broth
1 bottle (12 oz.) beer or nonalcoholic beer
1 small onion, chopped
½ cup medium pearl barley
3 garlic cloves, minced
1 tsp. dried oregano
1 tsp. dried parsley flakes
1 tsp. Worcestershire sauce
½ tsp. crushed red pepper flakes
½ tsp. pepper
¼ tsp. salt
1 bay leaf
2 cups frozen mixed vegetables, thawed

1. In a large skillet, brown beef in oil; drain. Transfer to a 3-qt. slow cooker.

2. Add broth, beer, onion, barley, garlic, oregano, parsley, Worcestershire sauce, pepper flakes, pepper, salt and bay leaf. Cover and cook on low 8-10 hours.

3. Stir in vegetables; cover and cook until meat is tender and vegetables are heated through, about 30 minutes longer. Discard bay leaf.

1 cup: 233 cal., 8g fat (2g sat. fat), 53mg chol., 644mg sod., 18g carb. (3g sugars, 4g fiber), 20g pro. **Diabetic exchanges:** 3 lean meat, 1 starch.

TEST KITCHEN TIP

If you'd like to enjoy this soup sooner, simply make it on the stovetop! Prepare as directed until you would add the browned beef to a slow cooker. Instead, set the beef in a large pot or Dutch oven on the stove. Proceed to Step 2 but cover and simmer for 1 hour, checking the liquid level and adding more if needed. Then add the vegetables and cook until heated through. Discard the bay leaf before serving.

CHICKEN PARMESAN STROMBOLI

I love chicken Parmesan and my family loves stromboli so one day I tried to combine the two using a few convenience products. It turned out better than I could have hoped. It's now a staple in our house.
—*Cyndy Gerken, Naples, FL*

PREP: 20 MIN. • **BAKE:** 20 MIN. • **MAKES:** 6 SERVINGS

4 frozen breaded chicken tenders (about 1½ oz. each)
1 tube (13.8 oz.) refrigerated pizza crust
8 slices part-skim mozzarella cheese
⅓ cup shredded Parmesan cheese
1 Tbsp. olive oil
½ tsp. garlic powder
¼ tsp. dried oregano
¼ tsp. pepper
   Marinara sauce, warmed

1. Prepare chicken tenders according to the package directions. Preheat oven to 400°. Unroll pizza crust onto a parchment-lined baking sheet. Layer with mozzarella, chicken tenders and Parmesan to within ½ in. of edges. Roll up jelly-roll style, starting with a short side; pinch seam to seal and tuck ends under. Combine olive oil, garlic powder, oregano and pepper; brush over top.

2. Bake until crust is dark golden brown, 18-22 minutes. Let stand 5 minutes before slicing. Serve with marinara sauce for dipping.

1 piece: 408 cal., 18g fat (7g sat. fat), 34mg chol., 859mg sod., 42g carb. (5g sugars, 2g fiber), 21g pro.

RAMEN CORN CHOWDER

This tastes so good—as if it simmered for hours, but it's ready in 15 minutes. I thought the original recipe was lacking in flavor, so I jazzed it up with extra corn and bacon bits.
—*Darlene Brenden, Salem, OR*

TAKES: 15 MIN. • **MAKES:** 4 SERVINGS

2 cups water
1 pkg. (3 oz.) chicken ramen noodles
1 can (15¼ oz.) whole kernel corn, drained
1 can (14¾ oz.) cream-style corn
1 cup 2% milk
1 tsp. dried minced onion
¼ tsp. curry powder
¾ cup shredded cheddar cheese
⅓ cup cubed cooked bacon
1 Tbsp. minced fresh parsley
1 Tbsp. minced chives

1. In a small saucepan, bring water to a boil. Break noodles into large pieces. Add noodles and contents of seasoning packet to water. Reduce heat to medium. Cook, uncovered, for 2-3 minutes or until noodles are tender.

2. Stir in the corn, cream-style corn, milk, onion and curry powder; heat through. Stir in the cheese, bacon, parsley and chives until blended. If desired, top with additional cheddar cheese and additional minced fresh chives.

1 cup: 333 cal., 9g fat (5g sat. fat), 17mg chol., 1209mg sod., 49g carb. (13g sugars, 4g fiber), 13g pro.

POZOLE

This spicy stewlike soup is traditionally served in New Mexico at holiday time to celebrate life's blessings, but it's good any time of year.
—Taste of Home *Test Kitchen*

PREP: 15 MIN. + STANDING • COOK: 65 MIN. • MAKES: 8 SERVINGS (2½ QT.)

- 4 dried ancho chiles
- 4 dried guajillo or pasilla chiles
- 2 Tbsp. canola oil, divided
- 1½ cups boiling water
- 2 lbs. boneless pork, cut into 1-in. cubes
- ½ cup chopped onion
- 4 garlic cloves, minced
- 3 cups chicken broth
- 2 cans (29 oz. each) hominy, rinsed and drained
- 1½ tsp. dried Mexican oregano
- 1 tsp. salt
  Optional toppings: Lime wedges, sliced radishes, diced avocado and sliced red onion

1. In a Dutch oven, saute chiles in 1 Tbsp. oil over medium heat until heated through, 1-2 minutes, pressing with a spatula (do not brown). Using a slotted spoon, transfer chiles to a bowl; add boiling water. Soak until softened, about 20 minutes. Remove stems and seeds, reserving water.

2. In the Dutch oven, brown the pork in remaining 1 Tbsp. oil in batches, sauteing onion and garlic with the last batch of pork. Return all pork to pan and add broth. Bring to a boil. Reduce heat; cover and simmer until meat is tender, about 30 minutes.

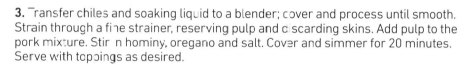

3. Transfer chiles and soaking liquid to a blender; cover and process until smooth. Strain through a fine strainer, reserving pulp and discarding skins. Add pulp to the pork mixture. Stir in hominy, oregano and salt. Cover and simmer for 20 minutes. Serve with toppings as desired.

Note: When handling chiles, disposable gloves are recommended. Avoid touching your face.

1¼ cups: 333 cal., 11g fat (3g sat. fat) 68mg chol., 1588mg sod., 29g carb. (1g sugars, 8g fiber), 27g pro.

TEST KITCHEN TIP

It's simple to customize your pozole (also spelled posole). Add color and crunch by topping with shredded cabbage, chopped green onions or crushed tortilla chips. Fresh cilantro leaves instantly add color and flavor. For a creamier texture, top servings with a dollop of sour cream.

AIR-FRYER GYRO SANDWICHES

I love gyros, but feel the meat part can be complicated! Using meatballs with
Greek seasoning and air-frying them makes things so much easier!
—DonnaMarie Ryan, Topsfield, MA

TAKES: 30 MIN. • **MAKES:** 4 SERVINGS

12 frozen fully cooked meatballs, such
    as beef or home-style
2 Tbsp. olive oil, divided
1½ tsp. Greek seasoning, divided
2 plum tomatoes, chopped
1 small red onion, chopped
1 garlic clove, minced
1 medium cucumber
½ cup plain Greek yogurt
1 Tbsp. lemon juice
½ tsp. snipped fresh dill
4 whole pita breads, warmed
½ cup crumbled feta cheese
   Lemon wedges, optional

1. Preheat air fryer to 320°. Place meatballs on greased tray in air-fryer basket. Cook until browned, 8-10 minutes. Remove to a cutting board; cool slightly. Cut meatballs in half; toss with 1 Tbsp. oil and 1 tsp. Greek seasoning. Return to air fryer. Cook 2 minutes longer. Remove and keep warm.

2. In a small bowl, combine tomatoes, red onion and garlic. Peel cucumber; chop half and add to the tomato mixture. Remove seeds and grate remaining half of cucumber; place in another small bowl. Stir in yogurt, lemon juice, dill, remaining 1 Tbsp. oil and ½ tsp. Greek seasoning.

3. Serve meatballs in pita breads with yogurt sauce, tomato mixture and feta cheese. If desired, top with additional fresh dill and serve with lemon wedges.

Note: In our testing, we find cook times vary dramatically between brands of air fryers. As a result, we give wider than normal ranges on suggested cook times. Begin checking at the first time listed and adjust as needed.

1 sandwich: 534 cal., 30g fat (12g sat. fat), 60mg chol., 1378mg sod., 44g carb. (5g sugars, 4g fiber), 21g pro.

AIR-FRYER
GYRO SANDWICHES

THAI MEATBALL SOUP

This son-approved, Thai-inspired soup—with meatballs, kale, carrots and creamy coconut milk—is warm deliciousness on a chilly day.
—*Arlene Erlbach, Morton Grove, IL*

PREP: 20 MIN. • **COOK:** 30 MIN. • **MAKES:** ABOUT 7 SERVINGS

½ cup fresh cilantro, finely chopped
⅓ cup unsweetened shredded coconut
3 Tbsp. teriyaki sauce, divided
½ tsp. salt
½ tsp. ground ginger
1½ lbs. ground chicken
¼ cup sesame oil
3 cups chicken broth
1 can (13.66 oz.) coconut milk
1½ cups julienned carrots
2 cups torn fresh kale
4½ tsp. lime juice
1 Tbsp. brown sugar
Lime wedges, optional

1. In a large bowl, combine the cilantro, coconut, 4½ tsp. teriyaki sauce, salt and ginger. Add the chicken; mix lightly but thoroughly. Shape into 1½-in. balls. In a Dutch oven, brown the meatballs in batches in sesame oil over medium-high heat; remove and keep warm. Drain any excess oil from pan. Add broth to pan; cook 1 minute, stirring to loosen browned bits from pan.

2. Return all meatballs to pan. Add coconut milk, carrots and remaining 4½ tsp. teriyaki sauce; bring to a boil. Reduce heat; simmer, covered, until the meatballs are cooked through, 5-7 minutes. Stir in kale, lime juice and brown sugar. Cook until kale just begins to wilt, about 5 minutes longer. Serve with additional chopped cilantro and lime wedges if desired.

About 1 cup: 400 cal., 32g fat (17g sat. fat), 75mg chol., 1040mg sod., 10g carb. (7g sugars, 2g fiber), 21g pro.

MUFFULETTA WELLINGTONS

This snack-sized sandwich was inspired by the muffuletta,
a New Orleans classic made with deli meat and olive salad.
—*Chelsea Madren, Anaheim, CA*

PREP: 25 MIN. • BAKE: 20 MIN. + STANDING • MAKES: 6 SERVINGS

3   Tbsp. melted butter, divided
1   Tbsp. cornmeal
1   tube (13.8 oz.) refrigerated
    pizza crust
6   Tbsp. olive bruschetta
18 slices thinly sliced hard salami
12 slices thinly sliced Black Forest
    deli ham
6   slices part-skim mozzarella cheese
6   slices provolone cheese
1   Tbsp. sesame seeds

1. Preheat oven to 425°. Grease a 12-in. cast-iron or other ovenproof skillet with 1 Tbsp. butter. Sprinkle with cornmeal.

2. Unroll pizza dough. Cut the dough into 6 portions Or a floured surface, roll each portion into a 6-in. square. Place 1 Tbsp. olive bruschetta in center of each square; top with salami, ham, mozzarella cheese and provolone cheese. Bring 4 corners of dough together above filling; pinch edges to seal.

3. Place in prepared skillet, seam side down. Brush with remaining 2 Tbsp. butter; sprinkle with sesame seeds. Bake until golden brown, 20-25 minutes. Let stand 10 minutes before serving.

1 sandwich: 562 cal., 33g fat (14g sat. fat), 93mg chol., 1815mg sod., 37g carb. (6g sugars, 1g fiber), 32g pro.

These wraps
are a super
easy and
delicious
make-ahead
supper.
—MARGERYRICHMOND820
TASTEOFHOME.COM

FIVE-SPICE CHICKEN LETTUCE WRAPS

With this lettuce wrap, I get all the satisfaction without all the carbs. The pickled carrots really make it feel special. Use them on other sandwiches and wraps for an extra pop of flavor, crunch and color.

—Stacy Schneidmiller, Beaumont, AB

PREP: 25 MIN. + MARINATING • **GRILL:** 20 MIN. • **MAKES:** 6 SERVINGS

3 Tbsp. soy sauce
4 garlic cloves, crushed
1 Tbsp. packed brown sugar
2 tsp. Chinese five-spice powder
1 tsp. salt, divided
2 lbs. boneless skinless chicken thighs
½ cup white vinegar
¼ cup water
1 Tbsp. sugar
2 medium carrots, shredded
12 Bibb lettuce leaves
¼ cup thinly sliced green onions
2 Tbsp. fresh cilantro leaves
   Sweetened shredded coconut,
   optional

1. In a bowl or shallow dish, combine the first 4 ingredients and ½ tsp. salt. Add chicken and turn to coat. Cover and refrigerate 8 hours or overnight.

2. In a small saucepan, combine vinegar, water, sugar and remaining ½ tsp. salt. Bring to a boil; whisk until sugar is dissolved. Remove from heat. Place carrots in a small bowl; pour vinegar mixture over top. Refrigerate 8 hours or overnight.

3. Drain chicken, discarding marinade. On a lightly oiled rack, grill chicken, covered, over medium heat or broil 4 in. from heat until a thermometer reads 170°, 6-8 minutes on each side. Cool slightly; slice into strips.

4. Divide chicken among lettuce leaves; top with pickled carrots, green onions and cilantro. Sprinkle with coconut if desired.

2 wraps: 236 cal., 11g fat (3g sat. fat), 101mg chol., 625mg sod., 4g carb. (2g sugars, 1g fiber), 29g pro. **Diabetic exchanges:** 4 lean meat.

Stacy Schneidmiller
Beaumont, AB

Keeping an Eye on Carbohydrates

Serving up healthy dishes is easier than you think.

What are your best tricks for cutting down on carbohydrates?
You can't go wrong with vegetables and lean meats. I think that marinades keep things interesting.

Do you have any go-to seasoning blends besides five-spice?
You could easily sub garam masala into this dish! That would be delicious.

What side dishes do you serve with these wraps?
If you want to bulk up your meal without adding carbs, serve the wraps alongside cauliflower rice with a little bit of chopped cilantro on top.

CHEESEBURGER SOUP

My mother-in-law gave me her recipe for cheeseburger soup, and I changed it a bit to make it my own. It's the perfect comfort food for a cold winter evening.
—*Christy Addison, Clarksville, OH*

PREP: 20 MIN. • **COOK:** 7 HOURS • **MAKES:** 6 SERVINGS (2¼ QT.)

1 lb. lean ground beef (90% lean)
1 small onion, chopped
1¾ lbs. potatoes (about 3-4 medium), peeled and cut into ½-in. pieces
3 cups chicken broth
1½ cups whole milk
2 medium carrots, shredded
1 celery rib, finely chopped
1 Tbsp. dried parsley flakes
½ tsp. salt
½ tsp. dried basil
¼ tsp. pepper
1 pkg. (8 oz.) Velveeta, cubed
¼ cup sour cream
Chopped fresh parsley, optional

1. In a large skillet, cook beef and onion over medium heat until meat is no longer pink, 6-8 minutes; crumble beef; drain. Transfer to a 4- or 5-qt. slow cooker. Add potatoes, broth, milk, carrots, celery and seasonings. Cook, covered, on low until vegetables are tender, 7-9 hours.

2. Stir in cheese until melted. Stir in sour cream. If desired, sprinkle with parsley.

1½ cups: 300 cal., 15g fat (8g sat. fat), 75mg chol., 949mg sod., 21g carb. (7g sugars, 2g fiber), 19g pro.

CORN QUESADILLAS

My cheesy corn quesadillas take only minutes going from skillet to table. They make craveable leftovers for brown-bag lunches, so pack some salsa too.
—*Darlene Brenden, Salem, OR*

TAKES: 15 MIN. • **MAKES:** 4 SERVINGS

1½ cups shredded Monterey Jack or pepper jack cheese
1 cup fresh or frozen corn
3 green onions, thinly sliced
¼ cup chopped fresh cilantro
2 Tbsp. sour cream
1 Tbsp. minced chipotle peppers in adobo sauce
4 flour tortillas (8 in.)
1 tsp. canola oil
Guacamole, optional

1. Place the first 6 ingredients in a large bowl; toss to combine. To assemble, lightly brush the tops of 2 tortillas with ½ tsp. oil; turn over. Top with cheese mixture and remaining tortillas. Brush tops with remaining oil.

2. Place a large nonstick skillet over medium heat. In 2 batches, cook quesadillas 1-2 minutes on each side or until golden brown and cheese is melted. Cut each quesadilla into 6 wedges. If desired, serve with guacamole.

3 wedges: 380 cal., 19g fat (10g sat. fat), 43mg chol., 524mg sod., 36g carb. (3g sugars, 3g fiber), 16g pro.

MANGO JALAPENO SLOPPY JOE SLIDERS

I've loved sloppy joes since I can remember. In an attempt to give them a makeover, I thought of this idea, which was a big hit with my family, friends and co-workers. They're fantastic appetizers or a fun meal.
—*Shea Goldstein, Royal Palm Beach, FL*

PREP: 10 MIN. • COOK: 25 MIN. • MAKES: 12 SERVINGS

1   lb. ground beef
½   cup water
1   envelope taco seasoning
2   Tbsp. hot pepper sauce
2   Tbsp. steak sauce
2   Tbsp. olive oil
1   small onion, halved and sliced
1   small green pepper, sliced
1   medium mango, peeled and chopped
1   tsp. sugar
1   jalapeno pepper, sliced
¼   tsp. salt
12 dinner or slider rolls, split
¼   cup butter, melted
1   cup mayonnaise
½   cup salsa verde
1½ cups shredded sharp white
    cheddar cheese

1. In a large cast-iron or other heavy skillet, cook beef over medium heat until no longer pink, 8-10 minutes; crumble beef; drain. Add water, taco seasoning, pepper sauce and steak sauce; cook and stir until the sauce thickens, 2-4 minutes. Remove and keep warm.

2. In another skillet, heat oil over medium-high heat. Add onion, green pepper, mango, sugar, jalapeno and salt; cook and stir until lightly browned, 8-10 minutes.

3. Meanwhile, place rolls, cut side up, on an ungreased baking sheet. Broil 3-4 in. from heat until golden brown, 2-3 minutes. Spread with melted butter. Combine mayonnaise and salsa verde; spread over roll bottoms. Top with beef mixture, pepper mixture and cheese; replace tops. Serve with extra sauce.

1 slider: 443 cal., 31g fat (10g sat. fat), 66mg chol., 870mg sod., 28g carb. (7g sugars, 2g fiber), 14g pro.

TEST KITCHEN TIP

No mango? No problem! Simply swap in pineapple for the mango. You could also leave out the mango and top the filling with a little bit of chutney before replacing the tops.

CARIBBEAN POTATO SOUP

An interesting blend of veggies that includes okra, kale and black-eyed peas goes into this bright and hearty soup. No kale on hand? Use spinach instead.
—*Crystal Jo Bruns, Iliff, CO*

TAKES: 30 MIN. • MAKES: 6 SERVINGS (2¼ QT.)

2 medium onions, chopped
2 tsp. canola oil
3 garlic cloves, minced
2 tsp. minced fresh gingerroot
2 tsp. ground coriander
1 tsp. ground turmeric
½ tsp. dried thyme
¼ tsp. ground allspice
5 cups vegetable broth
2 cups cubed peeled sweet potato
3 cups chopped fresh kale
1 cup frozen sliced okra
1 cup coconut milk
1 cup canned diced tomatoes, drained
1 cup canned black-eyed peas, rinsed
   and drained
2 Tbsp. lime juice

1. In a Dutch oven, saute onions in oil until tender. Add the garlic, ginger and spices; cook 1 minute longer.

2. Stir in the broth and potato. Bring to a boil. Reduce heat; cover and simmer for 5 minutes. Stir in the kale and okra. Return to a boil; cover and simmer 10 minutes longer or until the potato is tender. Add the milk, tomatoes, peas and lime juice; heat through.

Freeze option: Freeze cooled soup in freezer containers. To use, partially thaw in refrigerator overnight. Heat through in a saucepan, stirring occasionally; add broth or water if necessary.

1½ cups: 213 cal., 10g fat (7g sat. fat), 0 chol., 954mg sod., 28g carb. (9g sugars, 6g fiber), 5g pro.

CHICAGO-STYLE BEEF ROLLS

I have fond memories of eating these big, messy sandwiches at a neighbor's house when I was growing up. Freeze any extras and save for another meal!
—*Trisha Kruse, Eagle, ID*

PREP: 20 MIN. • COOK: 8 HOURS • MAKES: 16 SERVINGS

1 boneless beef chuck roast
   (4 to 5 lbs.)
1 Tbsp. olive oil
3 cups beef broth
1 medium onion, chopped
1 pkg. Italian salad dressing mix
3 garlic cloves, minced
1 Tbsp. Italian seasoning
½ tsp. crushed red pepper flakes
16 hoagie buns, split
   Optional: Sliced pepperoncini and
   pickled red pepper rings

1. Brown roast in oil on all sides in a large skillet; drain. Transfer beef to a 5-qt. slow cooker. Combine the broth, onion, dressing mix, garlic, Italian seasoning and pepper flakes in a large bowl; pour over roast.

2. Cover and cook on low for 8-10 hours or until tender. Remove meat; cool slightly. Skim fat from cooking juices. Shred beef with 2 forks and return to slow cooker; heat through. Using a slotted spoon, place ½ cup on each roll. Serve with pepperoncini and pepper rings if desired.

1 sandwich: 418 cal., 16g fat (5g sat. fat), 74mg chol., 771mg sod., 36g carb. (6g sugars, 1g fiber), 31g pro.

CARIBBEAN
POTATO SOUP

"
Everyone I
shared this
soup with loved
all the many
interesting
flavors.
—LIPPERTB5
TASTEOFHOME.COM

FAST REFRIED BEAN SOUP

This recipe combines the ease of canned ingredients with the heartiness of chili.
It will fill you up on cold afternoons or make a wonderful last-minute lunch.
If you like it spicier, use medium or hot green chiles instead of mild.
—*Darlene Brenden, Salem, OR*

TAKES: 25 MIN. • **MAKES:** 8 SERVINGS (2 QT.)

1 can (16 oz.) spicy fat-free refried beans
1 can (15¼ oz.) whole kernel corn, drained
1 can (15 oz.) black beans, rinsed and drained
1 can (14½ oz.) chicken broth
1 can (14½ oz.) stewed tomatoes, cut up
½ cup water
1 can (4 oz.) chopped green chiles
¼ cup salsa
Tortilla chips

In a large saucepan, combine the first 8 ingredients. Bring to a boil. Reduce heat; simmer, uncovered, until heated through, 8-10 minutes. Serve with tortilla chips.

1 cup: 117 cal., 1g fat (0 sat. fat), 1mg chol., 720mg sod., 21g carb. (6g sugars, 4g fiber), 5g pro.

APPLE & PORK BURGERS

This pork burger recipe is a favorite of ours. We had a similar burger in Hawaii and once home, I experimented and came
up with this tasty version that we actually prefer to the original. I like to serve them with a salad or fresh corn on the cob.
—*Trisha Kruse, Eagle, ID*

TAKES: 30 MIN. • **MAKES:** 2 SERVINGS

½ cup shredded peeled apple
¼ cup finely chopped onion
¼ cup drained unsweetened crushed pineapple
2 Tbsp. dry bread crumbs
1 Tbsp. reduced-sodium soy sauce
1 garlic clove, minced
½ lb. ground pork
2 slices Swiss cheese (¾ oz. each)
2 hamburger buns, split
Optional: Lettuce leaves, tomato slices, sliced ripe avocado, mustard and mayonnaise

1. In a small bowl, combine the first 6 ingredients. Crumble pork over mixture; mix lightly but thoroughly. Shape into 2 patties.

2. Grill patties, covered, over medium heat for 4-5 minutes on each side or until a thermometer reads 160°. Top with cheese. Grill 1-2 minutes longer or until cheese is melted.

3. Serve on buns with lettuce, tomato, avocado, mustard and mayonnaise as desired.

1 burger: 529 cal., 26g fat (11g sat. fat), 99mg chol., 699mg sod., 40g carb. (13g sugars, 3g fiber), 32g pro.

AIR-FRYER SHRIMP PO'BOYS

My husband loves crispy coconut shrimp and po'boys, so I combined them with a spicy remoulade and voila! This air-fryer shrimp is a big hit with family and friends and is frequently requested. For catfish po'boys, substitute cornmeal for the coconut and add a few minutes to the cooking time.
—*Marla Clark, Albuquerque, NM*

PREP: 35 MIN. • COOK: 10 MIN./BATCH • MAKES: 4 SERVINGS

½ cup mayonnaise
1 Tbsp. Creole mustard
1 Tbsp. chopped cornichons or dill pickles
1 Tbsp. minced shallot
1½ tsp. lemon juice
⅛ tsp. cayenne pepper

COCONUT SHRIMP
1 cup all-purpose flour
1 tsp. herbes de Provence
½ tsp. sea salt
½ tsp. garlic powder
½ tsp. pepper
¼ tsp. cayenne pepper
1 large egg
½ cup 2% milk
1 tsp. hot pepper sauce
2 cups sweetened shredded coconut
1 lb. uncooked shrimp (26-30 per lb.), peeled and deveined
  Cooking spray
4 hoagie buns, split
2 cups shredded lettuce
1 medium tomato, thinly sliced

1. For remoulade, in a small bowl, combine the first 6 ingredients. Refrigerate, covered, until serving.

2. Preheat air fryer to 375°. In a shallow bowl, mix flour, herbes de Provence, sea salt, garlic powder, pepper and cayenne. In a separate shallow bowl, whisk egg, milk and hot pepper sauce. Place coconut in a third shallow bowl. Dip shrimp in flour to coat both sides; shake off excess. Dip in egg mixture, then in coconut, patting to help adhere.

3. In batches, arrange shrimp in a single layer on greased tray in air-fryer basket; spritz with cooking spray. Cook until coconut is lightly browned and shrimp turn pink, 3-4 minutes on each side.

4. Spread cut side of buns with remoulade. Top with shrimp, lettuce and tomato.

1 sandwich: 716 cal., 40g fat (16g sat fat), 173mg chol., 944mg sod., 60g carb. (23g sugars, 4g fiber), 31g pro.

66
Excellent sandwich, and the mayo spread is fantastic!
—DANETTE
TASTEOFHOME.COM

STEAK SANDWICHES WITH CRISPY ONIONS

STEAK SANDWICHES WITH CRISPY ONIONS

I created this recipe for my husband. He loves a good steak sandwich, but I wanted to do something a little different. The fried crispy onions are a family favorite so I thought it would be great to put them right on the sandwich. The chimichurri-inspired mayo gives it great freshness and flavor.
—Renee Seaman, Green Township, NJ

PREP: 45 MIN. + MARINATING • GRILL: 15 MIN. • MAKES: 6 SERVINGS

1   large sweet onion
3   cups buttermilk
2   cups minced fresh cilantro
1   cup minced fresh parsley
2   garlic cloves, minced
½   tsp. plus 2 tsp. salt, divided
¼   tsp. pepper
½   cup mayonnaise
½   cup plus 3 Tbsp. olive oil, divided
1   beef flat iron steak or top sirloin steak (1½ lbs.)
1½ cups all-purpose flour
3   Tbsp. taco seasoning
    Oil for deep-fat frying
12 slices Italian bread (½ in. thick)
    Optional: Fresh arugula and sliced tomato

1. Cut onion into ¼-in. slices; separate into rings. Place in a large bowl or shallow dish. Add buttermilk; turn to coat. Refrigerate at least 4 hours or overnight. In a small bowl, combine cilantro, parsley, garlic, ½ tsp salt and pepper. Remove 2 Tbsp. herb mixture; stir into mayonnaise. Refrigerate until serving. Stir ½ cup olive oil into remaining herb mixture. Reserve 2 Tbsp. oil mixture for serving. Place remaining oil mixture in a large bowl or shallow dish. Add beef; turn to coat. Refrigerate at least 4 hours or overnight.

2. Drain the beef, discarding the marinade. Grill beef, covered, over medium heat or broil 4 in. from heat until meat reaches desired doneness, 7-9 minutes on each side (for medium-rare, a thermometer should read 135°; medium, 140°; medium-well, 145°).

3. Meanwhile, drain onion rings, discarding marinade. In a shallow dish, combine flour, taco seasoning and remaining 2 tsp. salt. Roll onion rings in flour mixture. In an electric skillet or deep-fat fryer, heat 1 in. oil to 375°. Fry the onion rings, a few at a time, until golden brown 1-1½ minutes on each side. Drain on paper towels; keep warm.

4. Remove steak to a cutting board; brush with reserved 2 Tbsp. oil mixture. Brush bread with remaining 3 Tbsp. olive oil. Grill bread over medium heat until toasted, 30-60 seconds on each side.

5. Spread mayonnaise mixture over 1 side of each toast. Thinly slice steak. Top 6 slices of toast with steak, fried onions and, if desired, arugula and tomato slices. Top with remaining toast.

1 sandwich: 930 cal., 58g fat (10g sat fat), 75mg chol., 1719mg sod., 68g carb. (6g sugars, 4g fiber), 32g pro.

GRILLED PIMIENTO CHEESE SANDWICHES

Rich and creamy pimiento cheese is a southern favorite. It makes a tasty grilled cheese sandwich, especially with sweet hot pepper jelly. Serve this with a crisp salad or tomato soup for a fantastic lunch.
—*Amy Freeze, Avon Park, FL*

TAKE 20 MIN. • MAKE 2 SERVINGS

- 4 slices sourdough bread
- ¼ cup butter, melted
- ½ cup refrigerated pimiento cheese
- 2 Tbsp. pepper jelly
- 6 cooked thick-sliced bacon strips

1. Brush 1 side of each bread slice with melted butter. In a large skillet, toast the bread, buttered side down, over medium heat until golden brown, 3-4 minutes.

2. Remove from heat; place toasted side up. Spread cheese over toasted bread slices. Top 2 slices with jelly, then with bacon. Brush outside of each sandwich with remaining melted butter. Top with remaining bread slices, cheese facing inward. Cook until bread is golden brown and cheese is melted, 3-4 minutes on each side. If desired, serve with additional jelly.

1 sandwich: 869 cal., 52g fat (28g sat. fat), 105mg chol., 1856mg sod., 70g carb. (19g sugars, 2g fiber), 27g pro.

CHIPOTLE BLT WRAPS

BLT sandwiches are so good, but they can make a lot of messy crumbs from the toasted bread. Since we also love wraps, I decided to make BLTs using tortillas instead. Warming the tortillas a little makes them easy to work with.
—*Darlene Brenden, Salem, OR*

TAKES: 15 MIN. • MAKES: 4 SERVINGS

- 3 cups chopped romaine
- 2 plum tomatoes, finely chopped
- 8 bacon strips, cooked and crumbled
- ⅓ cup reduced-fat chipotle or regular mayonnaise
- 4 flour tortillas (8 in.), warmed

1. In a large bowl, combine romaine, tomatoes and bacon. Add mayonnaise; toss to coat.

2. Spoon about 1 cup romaine mixture down center of each tortilla. Fold bottom of tortilla over filling; fold both sides to close. Serve immediately.

1 wrap: 306 cal., 15g fat (4g sat. fat), 23mg chol., 689mg sod., 32g carb. (3g sugars, 3g fiber), 11g pro.

SPICY MEATLESS CHILI

Before I retired, this recipe was a mainstay in our house. I could prepare the ingredients the night before, and then on the way out the door in the morning I could throw everything in the slow cooker.
—*Jane Whittaker, Pensacola, FL*

PREP: 25 MIN. • COOK: 8 HOURS • MAKES: 5 SERVINGS (ABOUT 2 QT.)

2 cans (14½ oz. each) Mexican diced tomatoes, undrained
1 can (15 oz.) black beans, rinsed and drained
2 cups frozen corn, thawed
1 cup salsa
1 medium zucchini, cut into ½-in. pieces
1 medium green pepper, coarsely chopped
1 small onion, coarsely chopped
1 celery rib, chopped
3 Tbsp. chili powder
1 tsp. dried oregano
2 garlic cloves, minced
¾ tsp. salt
¾ tsp. pepper
½ tsp. ground cumin
¼ tsp. cayenne pepper
Optional: Sour cream, shredded cheddar cheese and sliced jalapeno pepper

In a 4-qt. slow cooker, combine the first 15 ingredients. Cover and cook on low until vegetables are tender, 8-10 hours. If desired, top with sour cream, cheese and jalapeno pepper.

1½ cups: 224 cal., 2g fat (0 sat. fat), 0 chol., 1290mg sod., 48g carb. (15g sugars, 11g fiber), 9g pro.

DID YOU KNOW?

Mexican diced tomatoes are simply canned tomatoes with the addition of green chiles, chopped onion and cumin. They are available in different spice levels. If you don't have a can on hand, substitute a can of diced tomatoes and season the soup to taste.

PRESSURE-COOKER
SUMMER SQUASH,
PAGE 102

"
We love squash!
This was a huge
hit with the
family.
—JOAN HALLFORD
NORTH RICHLAND HILLS, TX

CHAPTER 5

POPULAR SIDES & SALADS

Need a dish to pass? How about a salad to round out a buffet? Maybe you're looking for a side to complete a weeknight dinner. No matter what the situation, you've come to the right spot! Serve up these savory sides and garden-fresh greens and get ready for compliments.

VIBRANT BLACK-EYED PEA SALAD

My black-eyed pea salad reminds me of a southern cooking class my husband and I took while visiting Savannah. People go nuts for it at picnics and potlucks, and I'm always sharing the recipe.
—*Danielle Lee, West Palm Beach, FL*

PREP: 25 MIN. + CHILLING • **MAKES:** 10 SERVINGS

2 cans (15½ oz. each) black-eyed peas, rinsed and drained
2 cups grape tomatoes, halved
1 each small green, yellow and red peppers, finely chopped
1 small red onion, chopped
1 celery rib, chopped
2 Tbsp. minced fresh basil

DRESSING
¼ cup red wine vinegar or balsamic vinegar
1 Tbsp. stone-ground mustard
1 tsp. minced fresh oregano or ¼ tsp. dried oregano
¾ tsp. salt
½ tsp. freshly ground pepper
¼ cup olive oil

1. In a large bowl, combine peas, tomatoes, peppers, onion, celery and basil.

2. For dressing, in a small bowl, whisk vinegar, mustard, oregano, salt and pepper. Gradually whisk in oil until blended. Drizzle over salad; toss to coat. Refrigerate, covered, at least 3 hours before serving.

¾ cup: 130 cal., 6g fat (1g sat. fat), 0 chol., 319mg sod., 15g carb. (3g sugars, 3g fiber), 5g pro. **Diabetic exchanges:** 1 starch, 1 fat.

TEST KITCHEN TIP

This salad makes a wonderful change-of-pace side dish, but you can also serve it as an appetizer alongside tortilla chips.

VIBRANT
BLACK-EYED
PEA SALAD

"
For my husband
and me, this
is the best
salad ever!
Definitely use
the balsamic; it
gives it a kick.
—LLOCKETTE
TASTEOFHOME.COM

ORANGE-MAPLE CRANBERRY SAUCE

During the holidays, I always have the ingredients for this cranberry sauce on hand. I serve it with turkey but also on French toast or waffles.
—*Nancy Murphy, Mount Dora, FL*

TAKES: 30 MIN. • MAKES: 8 SERVINGS

- 2 cups fresh cranberries
- ½ cup orange juice
- ½ cup maple syrup
- ¼ cup golden raisins
- ¼ cup chopped walnuts, toasted
  Optional: Orange slices and minced fresh parsley

In a large saucepan, combine all ingredients over medium-high heat. Bring mixture to a boil; reduce heat. Simmer, uncovered, until cranberries start to burst and mixture thickens, about 20 minutes, stirring occasionally. If desired, garnish with orange slices, additional chopped walnuts and minced parsley.

Note: To toast nuts, bake in a shallow pan in a 350°; oven for 5-10 minutes or cook in a skillet over low heat until lightly browned, stirring occasionally.

3 Tbsp.: 108 cal., 2g fat (0 sat. fat), 0 chol., 4mg sod., 22g carb. (17g sugars, 1g fiber), 1g pro.

PRESSURE-COOKER SUMMER SQUASH

I got tired of fixing plain old squash and cheese, so I decided to jazz it up.
—*Joan Hallford, North Richland Hills, TX*

PREP: 20 MIN. • COOK: 5 MIN. • MAKES: 8 SERVINGS

- 1 lb. medium yellow summer squash
- 1 lb. medium zucchini
- 2 medium tomatoes, chopped
- 1 cup vegetable broth
- ¼ cup thinly sliced green onions
- ½ tsp. salt
- ¼ tsp. pepper
- 1½ cups Caesar salad croutons, coarsely crushed
- ½ cup shredded cheddar cheese
- 4 bacon strips, cooked and crumbled

Cut squash and zucchini into ¼-in.-thick slices; place in a 6-qt. electric pressure cooker. Add the tomatoes, broth, green onions, salt and pepper. Lock the lid; close pressure-release valve. Adjust to pressure-cook on high for 1 minute. Quick-release pressure. Remove the vegetables with a slotted spoon. Top with croutons, cheese and bacon.

¾ cup: 111 cal., 6g fat (2g sat. fat), 12mg chol., 442mg sod., 10g carb. (4g sugars, 2g fiber), 6g pro.

CHICKEN & APPLE SALAD WITH GREENS

My favorite memory of eating this dish was when my mom
made it for lunch on weekends when we were home from school and
we could have something other than brown-bag lunches.
Happy memories of childhood days make this salad extra special.
—*Trisha Kruse, Eagle, ID*

TAKES: 30 MIN. • MAKES: 6 SERVINGS

VINAIGRETTE

- ¼ cup balsamic vinegar
- ¼ cup orange juice
- ¼ cup olive oil
- 2 Tbsp. lemon juice
- 2 Tbsp. reduced-sodium soy sauce
- 1 Tbsp. brown sugar
- 1 Tbsp. Dijon mustard
- ½ tsp. curry powder, optional
- ½ tsp. salt
- ¼ tsp. pepper
- ¼ tsp. ground ginger

SALAD

- 2 cups shredded cooked chicken
- 2 medium apples, chopped
- ½ cup thinly sliced red onion
- 10 cups torn mixed salad greens
- ½ cup chopped walnuts, toasted

In a large bowl, whisk the vinaigrette
ingredients until blended. Add chicken,
apples and onion; toss to coat. Just
before serving, place greens on a large
serving plate; top with chicken mixture.
Sprinkle with walnuts.

Note: To toast nuts, bake in a shallow
pan in a 350° oven for 5-10 minutes or
cook in a skillet over low heat until lightly browned, stirring occasionally.

1 serving: 306 cal., 19g fat (3g sat. fat), 42mg chol., 549mg sod., 20g carb.
(12g sugars, 4g fiber), 17g pro.

SCALLOPED
SWEET CORN
CASSEROLE

"Thank you, Lonnie, for sharing this recipe! I serve it with BBQ veggie-chicken strips.
—ORBS
TASTEOFHOME.COM

SCALLOPED SWEET CORN CASSEROLE

I grew up enjoying my grandmother's sweet corn casserole. She shared the recipe with me and, now a grandmother myself, I serve the comforting, delicious side dish.
—*Lonnie Hartstack, Clarinda, IA*

PREP: 25 MIN. • BAKE: 50 MIN. • MAKES: 8 SERVINGS

- 4 tsp. cornstarch
- ⅔ cup water
- ¼ cup butter, cubed
- 3 cups fresh or frozen corn
- 1 can (5 oz.) evaporated milk
- ¾ tsp. plus 1½ tsp. sugar, divided
- ½ tsp. plus ¾ tsp. salt, divided
- 3 large eggs
- ¾ cup 2% milk
- ¼ tsp. pepper
- 3 cups cubed bread
- 1 small onion, chopped
- 1 cup Rice Krispies, slightly crushed
- 3 Tbsp. butter, melted

1. Preheat oven to 350°. In a small bowl, mix cornstarch and water until smooth. In a large saucepan, heat butter over medium heat. Stir in corn, evaporated milk, ¾ tsp. sugar and ½ tsp. salt; bring just to a boil. Stir in the cornstarch mixture; return to a boil, stirring constantly. Cook and stir 1-2 minutes or until thickened; cool slightly.

2. In a large bowl, whisk eggs, milk, pepper and the remaining sugar and salt until blended. Stir in bread, onion and corn mixture. Transfer to a greased 8-in. square or 1½-qt. baking dish.

3. Bake, uncovered, 40 minutes. In a small bowl, toss Rice Krispies with melted butter; sprinkle over casserole. Bake 10-15 minutes longer or until golden brown.

Freeze option: Cool unbaked casserole, reserving Rice Krispies topping for baking; cover and freeze. To use, partially thaw in refrigerator overnight. Remove from refrigerator 30 minutes before baking. Preheat oven to 350°. Bake casserole as directed, increasing time as necessary to heat through and for a thermometer inserted in center to read 165°.

⅔ cup: 258 cal., 15g fat (8g sat fat), 104mg chol., 604mg sod., 26g carb. (9g sugars, 2g fiber), 8g pro.

MIXED FRUIT WITH LEMON-BASIL DRESSING

A slightly savory dressing really complements the sweet fruit in this recipe. I also use the dressing on salad greens.

—Dixie Terry, Goreville, IL

TAKES: 15 MIN. • **MAKES:** 8 SERVINGS

2 Tbsp. lemon juice
½ tsp. sugar
¼ tsp. salt
¼ tsp. ground mustard
⅛ tsp. onion powder
Dash pepper
6 Tbsp. olive oil
4½ tsp. minced fresh basil
1 cup cubed fresh pineapple
1 cup sliced fresh strawberries
1 cup sliced peeled kiwifruit
1 cup seedless watermelon balls
1 cup fresh blueberries
1 cup fresh raspberries

1. Place the lemon juice, sugar, salt, mustard, onion powder and pepper in a blender; cover and pulse until blended. While processing, gradually add oil in a steady stream. Stir in basil.

2. In a large bowl, combine the fruit. Drizzle with dressing and toss to coat. Refrigerate until serving.

¾ cup: 145 cal., 11g fat (1g sat. fat), 0 chol., 76mg sod., 14g carb. (9g sugars, 3g fiber), 1g pro. **Diabetic exchanges:** 2 fat, 1 fruit.

SKILLET SCALLOPED POTATOES

Our garden is a big inspiration when I'm cooking. This recipe turns produce from my husband's potato patch into a side dish we want to eat at every meal.

—Lori Daniels, Beverly, WV

TAKES: 30 MIN. • **MAKES:** 4 SERVINGS

1 Tbsp. butter
1 lb. small red potatoes, thinly sliced (about 3 cups)
1 Tbsp. dried minced onion
¾ cup chicken broth
½ cup half-and-half cream
¾ tsp. salt
¼ tsp. pepper
1 cup shredded cheddar cheese

1. In a large nonstick skillet, heat butter over medium heat. Add potatoes and onion; cook and stir 5 minutes.

2. Stir in broth, cream, salt and pepper. Bring to a boil. Reduce heat; simmer, covered, 10-12 minutes or until potatoes are tender. Sprinkle with cheese; cook, covered, 2-3 minutes longer or until cheese is melted.

¾ cup: 269 cal., 16g fat (9g sat. fat), 52mg chol., 856mg sod., 21g carb. (3g sugars, 2g fiber), 10g pro.

CLEO'S POTATO SALAD

My mom, Cleo Lightfoot, loved cooking all kinds of recipes, but her favorite meal was one she made when hosting backyard barbecues in the summer. She would make her famous ribs, baked beans and this delicious potato salad.
—*Joan Hallford, North Richland Hills, TX*

PREP: 25 MIN. • COOK: 20 MIN. + COOLING • MAKES: 12 SERVINGS

3½ lbs. red potatoes (about 12 medium), cut into 1-in. cubes
6 bacon strips, chopped
¼ cup sugar
1 Tbsp. all-purpose flour
½ cup water
1 large egg, lightly beaten
3 Tbsp. cider vinegar
1 Tbsp. grated onion
1 tsp. celery seed
1 tsp. salt
½ tsp. pepper
1 cup heavy whipping cream, whipped
4 hard-boiled large eggs, chopped
2 medium celery ribs, chopped

1. Place potatoes in a large saucepan; cover with water. Bring to a boil. Reduce the heat; cook, uncovered until tender, 10-15 minutes. Drain; cool completely.

2. Meanwhile, in a saucepan, cook bacon over medium heat until crisp. Remove with a slotted spoon; drain on paper towels. Remove all but 1 Tbsp. drippings from pan.

3. Stir sugar and flour into drippings until smooth. Gradually stir in water; cook and stir over medium-high heat until thickened and bubbly. Remove from heat. Stir a small amount of hot mixture into beaten egg; return all to pan, stirring constantly. Slowly bring to a boil, stirring constantly; remove from heat. Transfer to a large bowl; cool completely.

4. Gently stir in vinegar, onion and seasonings. Fold in whipped cream. Stir in eggs, celery, potatoes and bacon. Refrigerate, covered, until serving.

¾ **cup:** 211 cal., 11g fat (5g sat. fat), 90mg chol., 272mg sod., 23g carb. (5g sugars, 2g fiber), 6g pro.

TRA VIGNE GREEN BEANS

The title of this recipe translates to "among the vines" in Italian. I was inspired by a restaurant in the Napa Valley called, yes, you guessed it, Tra Vigne. The flavors in this dish to me represent the essence of its title.
—*Jenn Tidwell, Fair Oaks, CA*

PREP: 15 MIN. • COOK: 25 MIN. • MAKES: 9 SERVINGS

2 lbs. fresh green beans, trimmed
12 bacon strips, chopped
2 shallots, minced
4 garlic cloves, minced
½ tsp. salt
½ tsp. pepper
2 cups white grape juice
¼ cup white wine vinegar
½ cup minced chives

1. In a large saucepan, bring 4 cups water to a boil. Add green beans; cover and cook for 5 minutes. Drain and immediately place green beans in ice water. Drain and pat dry.

2. Meanwhile, in a large skillet, cook bacon over medium heat until crisp. Remove to paper towels with a slotted spoon; drain, reserving 1 Tbsp. drippings.

3. In the same skillet, saute shallots in bacon drippings until tender. Add the garlic, salt and pepper; cook 1 minute longer. Stir in juice and vinegar. Bring to a boil; cook until liquid is reduced by half.

4. Add green beans and bacon; cook until heated through. Sprinkle with chives.

¾ cup: 130 cal., 5g fat (2g sat. fat), 11mg chol., 338mg sod., 17g carb. (10g sugars, 3g fiber), 5g pro.

To make ahead: Boil the green beans, chill in ice water and drain as directed a day in advance. Store in the refrigerator.

ROASTED BALSAMIC RED POTATOES

I was intrigued when I found a potato recipe that called for vinegar, but I didn't have the seasonings on hand, so I had to improvise. I gave the recipe a whirl using Italian seasoning and balsamic vinegar, and it was fantastic!
—*Lisa Varner, El Paso, TX*

PREP: 10 MIN. • BAKE: 30 MIN. • MAKES: 6 SERVINGS

2 lbs. small red potatoes, cut into wedges
2 Tbsp. olive oil
¾ tsp. garlic pepper blend
½ tsp. Italian seasoning
¼ tsp. salt
¼ cup balsamic vinegar

1. Preheat oven to 425°. Toss potatoes with oil and seasonings; spread in a 15x10x1-in. pan.

2. Roast 25 minutes, stirring halfway. Drizzle with vinegar; roast until potatoes are tender, 5-10 minutes.

¾ cup: 159 cal., 5g fat (1g sat. fat), 0 chol., 143mg sod., 27g carb. (4g sugars, 3g fiber), 3g pro. **Diabetic exchanges:** 2 starch, 1 fat.

TRA VIGNE
GREEN BEANS

"This was a hit at Thanksgiving, with people going for seconds and thirds. A great recipe I'll serve year-round.

—EMBUNDY
TASTEOFHOME.COM

SLOW-COOKER SRIRACHA CORN

A restaurant advertised Sriracha corn on the cob, but I knew
I could make my own. The golden ears cooked up a little sweet, a little smoky
and a little hot—perfect, if you ask my three teenage boys!
—*Julie Peterson, Crofton, MD*

PREP: 15 MIN. • **COOK:** 3 HOURS • **MAKES:** 8 SERVINGS

½ cup butter, softened
2 Tbsp. honey
1 Tbsp. Sriracha chili sauce
1 tsp. smoked paprika
½ tsp. kosher salt
8 small ears sweet corn, husked
¼ cup water
   Additional smoked paprika, optional

1. Mix first 5 ingredients. Place each
ear of corn on a 12x12-in. piece of
heavy-duty foil and spread with 1 Tbsp.
butter mixture. Wrap foil around corn,
sealing tightly. Place corn in a 6-qt.
slow cooker.

2. Add water; cook, covered, on low
3-4 hours or until corn is tender. If
desired, sprinkle corn with additional
paprika before serving.

1 ear of corn: 209 cal., 13g fat (8g sat.
fat), 31mg chol., 287mg sod., 24g carb. (11g sugars, 2g fiber), 4g pro.

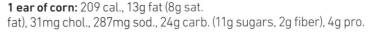

ZUCCHINI CHEDDAR SAUTE

When zucchini in your garden ripens all at once, try my
saute method and sprinkle with cheese and toppings.
We sometimes even add a few other quick-cooking veggies.
—*Margaret Drye, Plainfield, NH*

TAKES: 25 MIN. • **MAKES:** 4 SERVINGS

3 Tbsp. butter
¾ cup chopped onion
1½ tsp. dried basil
4 cups coarsely shredded zucchini
1 large garlic clove, minced
¾ tsp. salt
¼ tsp. pepper
1 cup shredded cheddar cheese
2 medium tomatoes, cut into
   ¾-in. pieces
3 Tbsp. sliced ripe olives

1. In a large skillet, heat butter over
medium heat. Add onion and basil; cook
and stir 4-5 minutes or until onion is
tender. Add zucchini and garlic; cook
and stir over medium-high heat just
until zucchini is tender, 2-3 minutes.
Stir in salt and pepper.

2. Top with cheese, tomatoes and
olives. Cook, covered, on low until
cheese is melted, about 1 minute.

¾ cup: 244 cal., 19g fat (12g sat. fat), 53mg chol., 747mg sod., 10g carb. (6g sugars, 3g
fiber), 10g pro.

SOURDOUGH, SAUSAGE & BLUEBERRY DRESSING

I was looking in my pantry for raisins to make a dressing just like my mom's.
I was out, but I spied a bag of dried blueberries and thought, *Why not?*
—Teri Rasey, Cadillac, MI

PREP: 50 MIN. • BAKE: 45 MIN. • MAKES: 20 SERVINGS

1 cup dried blueberries
½ cup blueberry schnapps liqueur
6 Tbsp. butter, divided
5 tsp. minced garlic, divided
1 loaf (14½ oz.) sourdough bread, torn
   into ½-in. pieces
1 Tbsp. avocado oil or canola oil
3 celery ribs, chopped
1 medium onion, chopped
1 large carrot, peeled and grated
2 lbs. bulk pork sausage
1 pkg. (7 oz.) blueberry white cheddar
   cheese or sharp cheddar cheese,
   shredded
½ tsp. dried rosemary, crushed
½ tsp. rubbed sage
½ tsp. pepper
2½ cups reduced-sodium chicken broth
3 large eggs, beaten
   Optional: Fresh blueberries and
   fresh sage

1. Preheat oven to 425°. In a small bowl, combine blueberries and schnapps; set aside.

2. In a small saucepan, heat 4 Tbsp. butter and 3 tsp. garlic 2-3 minutes or until butter melts and mixture is fragrant. In a large bowl, combine bread and the butter mixture; toss to coat. Spread onto a rimmed baking sheet. Bake, stirring occasionally, until golden brown, 12-15 minutes. Cool on a wire rack. Decrease oven temperature to 350°.

3. Meanwhile, in a large skillet, heat oil and remaining 2 Tbsp. butter over medium heat. Add celery ribs, onion and carrot; cook until carrot is tender, 8-10 minutes, stirring occasionally. Add remaining 2 tsp. garlic; cook 1 minute. Add sausage; cook until sausage is no longer pink, breaking up sausage into crumbles.

4. In a large bowl, combine bread, sausage mixture, cheese, rosemary, sage and pepper. Drain blueberry mixture, reserving schnapps. Add blueberries to bread mixture. In a bowl stir together the broth, beaten eggs and reserved blueberry schnapps. Pour over bread mixture; toss to combine.

5. Transfer mixture to a lightly greased 4-qt. baking dish. Bake until the top is golden brown and crispy, 45-50 minutes. If desired, garnish with fresh blueberries and sage.

¾ cup: 290 cal., 19g fat (8g sat. fat), 71mg chol., 581mg sod., 18g carb. (4g sugars, 1g fiber), 11g pro.

MINT
CHUTNEY

MINT CHUTNEY

This versatile mint chutney recipe pairs well with samosas, sandwiches and salads! Its herby, bright flavor dresses up any dish.

—Soniya Saluja, Chantilly, VA

TAKES: 10 MIN. • MAKES: ⅔ CUP

1 bunch fresh cilantro leaves, stems removed (about 2 cups)
1 bunch fresh mint leaves, stems removed (about 1 cup)
3 to 4 whole green chile peppers
3 garlic cloves, halved
Juice of 1 lemon or lime
1 Tbsp. sugar
1 tsp. cumin seeds
½ tsp. salt
1 to 2 Tbsp. water

In a blender, combine the first 8 ingredients; cover and process until smooth, adding water to reach desired consistency.

2 Tbsp.: 31 cal., 0 fat (0 sat. fat), 0 chol., 248mg sod., 7g carb. (3g sugars, 2g fiber), 1g pro. **Diabetic exchanges:** ½ starch.

TEST KITCHEN TIP

Mint chutney is very versatile. Use it as a spread inside wraps. It's also a tasty topping for your favorite Indian recipes.

The Route to Her Roots

This popular blogger re-imagines classic childhood dishes.

Soniya Saluja, Chantilly, VA

Growing up in Mumbai, Soniya Saluja relished the full-flavored foods that surrounded her daily. As co-founder of the blog *The Belly Rules the Mind*, recipe developer and *Taste of Home* Community Cook, she strives to re-create those amazing tastes for busy, health-conscious American families like her own.

Soniya's interest in food was encouraged by her mother, who instructed her in their kitchen and enrolled her in cooking and baking classes as a teenager. Later, she honed her skills as a new immigrant and a mother herself. She began posting her kitchen experiments in Facebook groups shortly after the birth of her second child.

Her most popular posts illustrated easy ways to make deep-fried Punjabi snacks. "People were really excited about my recipes," she says. "I got a lot of encouragement."

The Belly Rules the Mind soon followed, when another group member, Anvita Bhatnagar Mistry, invited Soniya to contribute to her blog. "It was all kids recipes initially," Soniya recalls. "My kids were my early critics. They tasted everything I made. If they didn't like it, it didn't go on the blog."

Today, the blog has a robust social media following and features about 400 vegetarian and vegan recipes. Although the blog highlights recipes across a variety of cuisines—including Italian and Mexican, also beloved by Soniya—she often returns to her Punjabi roots and her guiding lights, her family and their health, for inspiration.

Her creations capture the cuisine's essential flavors and textures but leave behind its heavy nature. "I try to combine modern cooking techniques with traditional tips and tricks, all simplified for the reader," she says.

"Food is an integral part of our culture and traditions," adds Soniya. "It's a great feeling to transform my mom's cooking and share it with today's home cooks."

HERBED BUTTERNUT SQUASH

This is just one of many ways I prepare butternut squash for my two girls. It's a winter staple in our house.
—*Jenn Tidwell, Fair Oaks, CA*

TAKES: 25 MIN. • **MAKES:** 6 SERVINGS

1 medium butternut squash (about 3 lbs.)
1 Tbsp. olive oil
1½ tsp. dried oregano
1 tsp. dried thyme
½ tsp. salt
¼ tsp. pepper

Peel and cut squash crosswise into ½-in.-thick slices; remove and discard seeds. In a large bowl, toss squash with remaining ingredients. Grill, covered, over medium heat or broil 4 in. from heat for 6-8 minutes on each side or until tender.

1 serving: 108 cal., 2g fat (0 sat. fat), 0 chol., 205mg sod., 23g carb. (5g sugars, 7g fiber), 2g pro. **Diabetic exchanges:** 1½ starch, ½ fat.

CRANBERRY APPLE RED CABBAGE

When I was looking for something new, I started playing with flavors and came up with this very tasty dish. My German grandmother would be impressed, I think! The colorful side is just right with pork.
—*Ann Sheehy, Lawrence, MA*

PREP: 15 MIN. • **COOK:** 5 MIN. • **MAKES:** 8 SERVINGS

1 medium head red cabbage, coarsely chopped
1 can (14 oz.) whole-berry cranberry sauce
2 medium Granny Smith apples, peeled and coarsely chopped
1 medium onion, chopped
½ cup cider vinegar
¼ cup sweet vermouth, white wine or unsweetened apple juice, optional
1 tsp. kosher salt
¾ tsp. caraway seeds
½ tsp. coarsely ground pepper

Combine all ingredients; transfer to a 6-qt. electric pressure cooker. Lock lid; close pressure-release valve. Adjust to pressure-cook on high for 3 minutes. Allow pressure to naturally release for 5 minutes. Quick-release any remaining pressure. Serve with a slotted spoon.

¾ cup: 144 cal., 0 fat (0 sat. fat), 0 chol., 296mg sod., 34g carb. (21g sugars, 4g fiber), 2g pro.

PUMPKIN GNOCCHI

We had homemade gnocchi frequently while growing up.
My mom changed the flavors with the seasons and this one was always my
favorite. They do require some time to make, but they're worth it!
—*Shawn Barto, Palmetto, FL*

PREP: 1 HOUR • COOK: 15 MINUTES • MAKES: 6 SERVINGS

1 cup mashed potatoes (without
  added milk and butter)
2 cups all-purpose flour
1 large egg, lightly beaten
1 cup canned pumpkin
2 tsp. minced fresh sage
½ cup butter, cubed

SAUCE
6 fresh sage leaves
1 garlic clove, minced
1 Tbsp. all-purpose flour
2 Tbsp. heavy whipping cream
  Shaved Parmesan cheese
¼ tsp. salt

1. In a Dutch oven, bring 6 qt. salted water to a boil. Place potatoes in a large bowl. Using a fork, make a well in the potatoes; sprinkle with flour. Mix egg, pumpkin and minced sage; pour into well. Stir vigorously until blended. On a lightly floured surface, knead 10-12 times, forming a soft dough.

2. Divide dough into 8 portions. On a floured surface, roll each portion into a ½-in.-thick rope; cut crosswise into ¾-in. pieces. Press and roll each piece with a lightly floured fork. Cook the gnocchi in batches in boiling water until they float, 3-4 minutes; remove with a slotted spoon, reserving ¾ cup pasta water.

3. In a large skillet, melt the butter over medium heat. Cook gnocchi until lightly browned, 7-8 minutes, stirring occasionally. Remove from the skillet; keep warm. For the sauce, in same skillet, discard melted butter, reserving 2 Tbsp.; add sage leaves and cook over medium heat until sage is crispy, 2-3 minutes, turning once. Remove sage and set aside. Add garlic and cook, stirring, 1 minute.

4. Stir in flour until smooth; gradually whisk in cream, salt and ¾ cup pasta water to moisten. Bring to a boil, stirring constantly; cook and stir 3-4 minutes or until thickened. Add gnocchi; toss to coat. Serve with the reserved sage leaves and Parmesan cheese.

Freeze option: Cover and freeze uncooked gnocchi in a single layer on waxed paper-lined baking sheets. Transfer to freezer containers; return to freezer. To use, cook gnocchi as directed.

¾ cup: 327 cal., 15g fat (9g sat. fat), 57mg chol., 213mg sod., 41g carb. (2g sugars, 3g fiber), 7g pro.

HARISSA SWEET POTATO FRITTERS

I had leftover sweet potatoes and had to think up a new way to use them.
We love spice, so I flavored these fun fritters with harissa—just enough for flavor but not too spicy.
If you want more heat, you can always adjust the spice to please your taste buds.

—Teri Rasey, Cadillac, MI

PREP: 20 MIN. + STANDING • **COOK:** 5 MIN./BATCH • **MAKES:** 6 SERVINGS

6 cups boiling water
3 cups shredded and peeled sweet potatoes, slightly packed (about 2 medium)
2 large eggs
¼ cup all-purpose flour
1 tsp. baking powder
1 tsp. cornstarch
1 tsp. seasoned salt
2 to 3 tsp. harissa
1 small onion, grated
¼ cup coconut oil
½ cup crumbled queso fresco
Optional: Sliced avocado, sliced tomato and minced fresh cilantro

1. Pour boiling water over sweet potatoes in a large bowl; let stand 20 minutes. Drain, squeezing to remove excess liquid. Pat dry.

2. In a large bowl, whisk the eggs, flour, baking powder, cornstarch, seasoned salt and harissa. Add the sweet potatoes and onion; toss to coat.

3. In a large nonstick skillet, heat 2 Tbsp. coconut oil over medium heat. Working in batches, drop sweet potato mixture by ¼ cupfuls into oil; press slightly to flatten. Fry for 1-2 minutes on each side until golden brown, using the remaining oil as needed. Drain on paper towels. Serve with queso fresco and, as desired, optional ingredients.

2 fritters: 217 cal., 13g fat (10g sat. fat), 69mg chol., 421mg sod., 20g carb. (3g sugars, 2g fiber), 6g pro.

TEST KITCHEN TIP

Harissa is a thick red chili paste that helps you easily spice up dishes. Look for it in ethnic aisles at the supermarket, then mix it into your family favorites. Serve it over scrambled eggs, toss it into cooked veggies or mix it with a little mayonnaise for a great dipping sauce.

"
This combo of sweet, spicy, and slightly salty flavors was delicious. Definitely will make them again!
—ANNRMS
TASTEOFHOME.COM

CAMPERS' COLESLAW

Crispy and crunchy, this no-fuss slaw makes a refreshing side dish for picnics and parties. It is an old family recipe.
—*Kimberly Wallace, Dennison, OH*

PREP: 15 MIN. + CHILLING • COOK: 5 MIN. • MAKES: 12 SERVINGS

1½ cups sugar
¾ cup white vinegar
¾ cup olive oil
1 Tbsp. salt
1 tsp. celery seed
1 medium head cabbage, shredded (about 10 cups)
1 large onion, chopped
1 medium green pepper, chopped

1. In a small saucepan, combine first 5 ingredients. Bring to a boil; cook and stir for 1-2 minutes or until sugar is dissolved. Remove from the heat; cool completely.

2. In a large bowl, toss vegetables with dressing. Refrigerate, covered, until cold. Serve with a slotted spoon.

¾ cup: 122 cal., 6g fat (1g sat. fat), 0 chol., 274mg sod., 17g carb. (14g sugars, 2g fiber), 1g pro.

Crunchy Coleslaw: To the cabbage mixture, stir in 2 julienned medium Honeycrisp apples and 1 shredded large carrot. Sprinkle ½ cup coarsely chopped peanuts over the top.

QUICK AMBROSIA FRUIT SALAD

I mix in a little coconut and just enough marshmallows so it tastes like the creamy ambrosia I grew up with. Now everyone in my home loves it too.
—*Trisha Kruse, Eagle, ID*

TAKES: 10 MIN. • MAKES: 6 SERVINGS

1 can (8¼ oz.) fruit cocktail, drained
1 can (8 oz.) unsweetened pineapple chunks, drained
1 cup green grapes
1 cup seedless red grapes
1 cup miniature marshmallows
1 medium banana, sliced
¾ cup vanilla yogurt
½ cup sweetened shredded coconut

In a large bowl, combine all ingredients. Chill until serving.

¾ cup: 191 cal., 4g fat (3g sat. fat), 2mg chol., 48mg sod., 40g carb. (34g sugars, 2g fiber), 3g pro.

LOADED STUFFED POTATO PANCAKES

When I make mashed potatoes, I always cook extra so I can prepare these over-the-top pancakes. You can also fill them with sour cream, ranch dressing or melted cheese—or all three.

—Jane Whittaker, Pensacola, FL

PREP: 25 MIN. • COOK: 5 MIN./BATCH • MAKES: 4 SERVINGS

2 cups mashed potatoes (with added milk and butter)
⅔ cup shredded cheddar cheese
⅓ cup all-purpose flour
1 large egg, lightly beaten
1 Tbsp. minced chives
½ tsp. salt
½ tsp. pepper
⅔ cup seasoned bread crumbs
1 tsp. garlic powder
1 tsp. onion powder
½ tsp. cayenne pepper
⅓ cup cream cheese, softened
Oil for deep-fat frying

1. In a large bowl, combine the first 7 ingredients. In a shallow bowl, mix bread crumbs, garlic powder, onion powder and cayenne.

2. Shape 2 tsp. cream cheese into a ball. Wrap ¼ cup potato mixture around cream cheese to cover completely. Drop into crumb mixture. Gently coat and shape into a ½-in.-thick patty. Repeat with remaining cream cheese and potato mixture.

3. In an electric skillet or deep-fat fryer, heat oil to 375°. Fry stuffed pancakes, a few at a time, until golden brown, 1-2 minutes on each side. Drain on paper towels.

2 pancakes: 491 cal., 34g fat (12g sat. fat), 96mg chol., 987mg sod., 35g carb. (3g sugars, 2g fiber), 12g pro.

TEST KITCHEN TIP

Forming the balls of cream cheese may seem cumbersome, but it's a fun way to bring kids into the kitchen. You can also speed things up by using a cookie scoop.

—MARK HAGEN, *TASTE OF HOME* CONTENT DIRECTOR

GARDEN TOMATO SALAD

For as long as I can remember, my mom made a salad of tomatoes and cucumbers. Now I make it whenever tomatoes are in reach.
—*Shannon Copley, Upper Arlington, OH*

TAKES: 15 MIN. • MAKES: 8 SERVINGS

3 large tomatoes, cut into wedges
1 large sweet onion, cut into thin wedges
1 large cucumber, sliced

DRESSING
¼ cup olive oil
2 Tbsp. cider vinegar
1 garlic clove, minced
1 tsp. minced fresh basil
1 tsp. minced chives
½ tsp. salt

In a large bowl, combine tomatoes, onion and cucumber. In a small bowl, whisk dressing ingredients until blended. Drizzle over salad; gently toss to coat. Serve immediately.

1 cup: 92 cal., 7g fat (1g sat. fat), 0 chol., 155mg sod., 7g carb. (5g sugars, 1g fiber), 1g pro. **Diabetic exchanges:** 1½ fat, 1 vegetable.

LEMON HERB QUINOA

My family is turning to quinoa more and more these days. It's a super grain that's packed with protein and vitamins. Plus, it can be paired with any kind of main course.
—*Jenn Tidwell, Fair Oaks, CA*

TAKES: 25 MIN. • MAKES: 4 SERVINGS

2 cups water
1 cup quinoa, rinsed
½ tsp. salt, divided
1 Tbsp. minced fresh basil
1 Tbsp. minced fresh cilantro
1½ tsp. minced fresh mint
1 tsp. grated lemon zest

1. In a small saucepan, bring water to a boil. Add quinoa and ¼ tsp. salt. Reduce heat; cover and simmer for 12-15 minutes or until liquid is absorbed.

2. Remove from the heat. Add the basil, cilantro, mint, lemon zest and remaining salt; fluff with a fork.

⅔ cup: 160 cal., 2g fat (0 sat. fat), 0 chol., 304mg sod., 29g carb. (0 sugars, 3g fiber), 6g pro. **Diabetic exchanges:** 2 starch.

TEST KITCHEN TIP

Not sure how to incorporate grains into your menu plans? Try serving brown rice, barley or quinoa as a side instead of potatoes or white rice. To dress them up a little, add some sauteed onion, garlic, green or sweet red pepper, or cooked beans, snow peas or peas. Use leftover cooked grains in soups or stews.

HOMEMADE ANTIPASTO SALAD

This colorful salad is a tasty crowd-pleaser. Guests love the homemade dressing, which is a nice change from bottled Italian.
—Linda Harrington, Windham, NH

PREP: 50 MINUTES + CHILLING • COOK: 10 MIN. • MAKES: 50 SERVINGS

2 pkg. (1 lb. each) spiral pasta
4 to 5 large tomatoes, chopped
3 large onions, chopped
2 large green peppers, chopped
2 cans (15 to 16 oz. each) garbanzo beans or chickpeas, rinsed and drained
1 lb. thinly sliced Genoa salami, julienned
1 lb. sliced pepperoni, julienned
½ lb. provolone cheese, cubed
1 cup pitted ripe olives, halved

DRESSING
1 cup red wine vinegar
½ cup sugar
2 Tbsp. dried oregano
2 tsp. salt
1 tsp. pepper
1½ cups olive oil

1. Cook pasta according to package directions. Drain; rinse with cold water. In several large bowls, combine pasta with next 8 ingredients.

2. For dressing, pulse vinegar, sugar, oregano, salt and pepper in a blender. While processing, gradually add oil in a steady stream. Pour over salad; toss to coat. Refrigerate, covered, 4 hours or overnight.

¾ cup: 214 cal., 15g fat (4g sat. fat), 19mg chol., 514mg sod., 13g carb. (4g sugars, 1g fiber), 7g pro.

GARLIC CREAMED SPINACH

This creamed spinach side goes with just about anything. Try it with roasted pork, baked chicken or even pasta.
—Debbie Glasscock, Conway, AR

TAKES: 20 MIN. • MAKES: 4 SERVINGS

1 Tbsp. olive oil
1 small onion, chopped
2 pkg. (10 oz. each) frozen chopped spinach, thawed and squeezed dry
2 garlic cloves, minced
8 oz. cream cheese, softened
¼ cup 2% milk
½ tsp. salt
½ tsp. pepper

In a large skillet, heat oil over medium-high heat. Add the onion; cook and stir until tender, 5-7 minutes. Add spinach and garlic; cook 2 minutes longer. Stir in remaining ingredients; cook until cream cheese is melted.

½ cup: 279 cal., 24g fat (12g sat. fat), 57mg chol., 579mg sod., 11g carb. (4g sugars, 5g fiber), 9g pro.

LEMON-ROASTED ASPARAGUS

When it comes to fixing asparagus, I think it's hard to go wrong. The springy flavors in this easy recipe burst with every bite.
—*Jenn Tidwell, Fair Oaks, CA*

TAKES: 20 MIN. • MAKES: 8 SERVINGS

2 lbs. fresh asparagus, trimmed
¼ cup olive oil
4 tsp. grated lemon zest
2 garlic cloves, minced
½ tsp. salt
½ tsp. pepper

Preheat oven to 425°. Place asparagus in a greased 15x10x1-in. baking pan. Mix remaining ingredients; drizzle over asparagus. Toss to coat. Roast until crisp-tender, 8-12 minutes.

1 serving: 75 cal., 7g fat (1g sat. fat), 0 chol., 154mg sod., 3g carb. (1g sugars, 1g fiber), 2g pro. **Diabetic exchanges:** 1½ fat, 1 vegetable.

JUICY WATERMELON SALAD

This fruit salad has such a surprising yet fabulous mix of flavors that friends often ask for the recipe. Combine seedless watermelon varieties in yellow, red and pink for a colorful twist.
—*Heidi Haight, Macomb, MI*

PREP: 20 MIN. + CHILLING • MAKES: 10 SERVINGS

8 cups cubed seedless watermelon (about 1 medium)
1 small red onion, cut into rings
1 cup coarsely chopped macadamia nuts or sliced almonds, toasted
1 cup fresh arugula or baby spinach
⅓ cup balsamic vinaigrette
3 Tbsp. canola oil
   Watermelon slices, optional
1 cup (4 oz.) crumbled blue cheese

In a large bowl, combine watermelon and onion; cover and refrigerate until cold, about 30 minutes. Just before serving, add the macadamia nuts and arugula to watermelon mixture. In a small bowl, whisk vinaigrette and oil; drizzle over salad and toss to coat. Serve over sliced watermelon if desired. Sprinkle with cheese.

Note: To toast nuts, bake in a shallow pan in a 350°; oven for 5-10 minutes or cook in a skillet over low heat until lightly browned, stirring occasionally.

1 cup: 232 cal., 20g fat (5g sat. fat), 10mg chol., 295mg sod., 15g carb. (12g sugars, 2g fiber), 4g pro.

GARLIC-ROSEMARY BRUSSELS SPROUTS

This is my go-to side dish. It is healthy and easy, and it doesn't take very much time or effort to make.
—Elisabeth Larsen, Pleasant Grove, UT

PREP: 15 MIN. • BAKE: 25 MIN. • MAKES: 8 SERVINGS

¼ cup olive oil
4 garlic cloves, minced
1 tsp. salt
½ tsp. pepper
2 lbs. Brussels sprouts (about 8 cups), trimmed and halved
1 cup panko bread crumbs
1 to 2 Tbsp. minced fresh rosemary

1. Preheat oven to 425°. Place the first 4 ingredients in a small microwave-safe bowl; microwave on high for 30 seconds.

2. Place the Brussels sprouts in a 15x10x1-in. pan; toss with 3 Tbsp. oil mixture. Roast 10 minutes.

3. Toss bread crumbs with rosemary and remaining oil mixture; sprinkle over sprouts. Bake until crumbs are browned and sprouts are tender, 12-15 minutes. Serve immediately.

¾ cup: 134 cal., 7g fat (1g sat. fat), 0 chol., 342mg sod., 15g carb. (3g sugars, 4g fiber), 5g pro. **Diabetic exchanges:** 1½ fat 1 vegetable, ½ starch.

TEST KITCHEN TIP

Heating the oil and garlic together infuses the oil with garlic flavor for even distribution over the Brussels sprouts. Remember this no-fuss trick whenever you want to jazz up veggies.

PRESSURE-COOKER
SALSA LONDON BROIL,
PAGE 132

CHAPTER 6

BEEF & POULTRY DINNERS

Hearty, comforting and oh, so satisfying, beef, chicken and turkey dinners always get thumbs-up reviews. Turn here to see which entrees today's home cooks rely on most. They'll quickly become go-to meals at your house, too.

SLOW-COOKER SPAGHETTI & MEATBALLS

I've been cooking for 50 years, and this dish is still one that guests request frequently. It is my No. 1 standby recipe and also makes amazing meatball sandwiches. The sauce works for any type of pasta.
—*Jane Whittaker, Pensacola, FL*

PREP: 50 MIN. • **COOK:** 5 HOURS • **MAKES:** 12 SERVINGS

1 cup seasoned bread crumbs
2 Tbsp. grated Parmesan and Romano cheese blend
1 tsp. pepper
½ tsp. salt
2 large eggs, lightly beaten
2 lbs. ground beef

SAUCE
1 large onion, finely chopped
1 medium green pepper, finely chopped
3 cans (15 oz. each) tomato sauce
2 cans (14½ oz. each) diced tomatoes, undrained
1 can (6 oz.) tomato paste
6 garlic cloves, minced
2 bay leaves
1 tsp. each dried basil, oregano and parsley flakes
1 tsp. salt
½ tsp. pepper
¼ tsp. crushed red pepper flakes
 Hot cooked spaghetti

1. In a large bowl, mix bread crumbs, cheese, pepper and salt; stir in eggs. Add beef; mix lightly but thoroughly. Shape into 1½-in. balls. In a large skillet, brown meatballs in batches over medium heat; drain.

2. Place the first 5 sauce ingredients in a 6-qt. slow cooker; stir in garlic and seasonings. Add meatballs, stirring gently to coat. Cook, covered, on low 5-6 hours or until meatballs are cooked through.

3. Remove bay leaves. Serve with spaghetti.

About 3 meatballs with ¾ cup sauce: 250 cal., 11g fat (4g sat. fat), 79mg chol., 1116mg sod., 20g carb. (7g sugars, 4g fiber), 20g pro.

TEST KITCHEN TIP

Generally, slow cookers cook low and slow, so meatballs like these are less likely to overcook than if you were to quickly bake them in the oven. The longer you leave meatballs in a slow cooker, however, you risk them becoming tougher and chewier. For best results, stick to the amount of time suggested in the recipe.
—MARK NEUFANG, *TASTE OF HOME* CULINARY ASSISTANT

> "This recipe got me so many compliments! For us, it's a keeper!"
> —SANDITHECAT
> TASTEOFHOME.COM

SLOW-COOKER
SPAGHETTI &
MEATBALLS

APPLESAUCE BARBECUE CHICKEN

You only need a few ingredients to create this sweet and peppery chicken. The subtle flavor of apple makes this tender barbecue dish stand out from the rest.
—*Darla Andrews, Boerne, TX*

TAKES: 20 MIN. • MAKES: 4 SERVINGS

4   boneless skinless chicken breast halves (6 oz. each)
½   tsp. pepper
1   Tbsp. olive oil
⅔   cup chunky applesauce
⅔   cup spicy barbecue sauce
2   Tbsp. brown sugar
1   tsp. chili powder

Sprinkle chicken with pepper. In a large skillet, brown chicken in oil on both sides. In a small bowl, combine the remaining ingredients; pour over chicken. Cover and cook until a thermometer reads 165°, 7-10 minutes.

Freeze option: Cool chicken; transfer to a freezer container and freeze for up to 3 months. Thaw in the refrigerator overnight. Cover and microwave on high until heated through, 8-10 minutes, stirring once.

1 chicken breast half: 308 cal., 8g fat (2g sat. fat), 94mg chol., 473mg sod., 22g carb. (19g sugars, 1g fiber), 35g pro.

PRESSURE-COOKER SALSA LONDON BROIL

SHOWN ON PAGE 128

I love using my all-in-one cooker for this recipe because it comes together so quickly but still has that long, slow-cooked flavor. The veggies semi-melt into the sauce to give it an added savory taste and the lime gives it a pleasant finish.
—*Ann Sheehy, Lawrence, MA*

PREP: 15 MIN. • COOK: 10 MIN. + RELEASING • MAKES: 4 SERVINGS

1   to 1½ lbs. beef top round steak
1   jar (16 oz.) salsa
1   medium sweet potato, peeled and chopped
1   large carrot, thinly sliced
1   garlic clove, minced
    Lime wedges
    Chopped fresh cilantro, optional

1. Cut steak into thirds; place in a 6-qt. electric pressure cooker. Add the salsa, sweet potato, carrot and garlic. Lock lid; close pressure-release valve. Adjust to pressure-cook on high for 10 minutes. Let pressure release naturally.

2. Slice roast. Serve with vegetables. Garnish with lime wedges and, if desired, chopped cilantro.

1 serving: 239 cal., 4g fat (1g sat. fat), 63mg chol., 503mg sod., 23g carb. (10g sugars, 2g fiber), 27g pro. **Diabetic exchanges:** 4 lean meat, 1½ starch.

SMOKED MEAT LOAF

Here's a new take on a family classic—smoked meat loaf. Make several loaves at once to take full advantage of the space in your smoker during the long cook time; the leftovers freeze nicely. I like to use a serrated knife when I cut this into slices because it's on the delicate side.

—*Peggy Woodward, Taste of Home Senior Food Editor*

PREP: 15 MIN. COOK: 70 MIN. + STANDING • MAKES: 8 SERVINGS

2 large eggs, lightly beaten
1 medium onion, finely chopped
¾ cup dry bread crumbs
¼ cup 2% milk
1 cup barbecue sauce, divided
1 Tbsp. Worcestershire sauce
1 tsp. salt
½ tsp. pepper
2 lbs. ground beef

RUB

2 tsp. chili powder
½ tsp. garlic salt
¼ tsp. onion powder
¼ tsp. cayenne pepper

1. Soak hickory and mesquite chips or pellets; add to smoker according to manufacturer's directions. Heat smoker to 225°.

2. In a large bowl, combine eggs, onion, bread crumbs, milk, ¼ cup barbecue sauce, Worcestershire sauce, salt and pepper. Add the beef; mix lightly but thoroughly. Shape into a 10x4-in. loaf on a greased smoker rack. Combine rub ingredients; rub over meat loaf. Place in smoker; smoke until a thermometer reads 145°, about 1 hour. Brush generously with remaining ¾ cup barbecue sauce. Smoke until a thermometer reads 160°, 10-15 minutes. Let stand 10 minutes before slicing

1 piece: 318 cal., 15g fat (6g sat. fat), 117mg chol., 937mg sod., 21g carb. (13g sugars, 1g fiber), 23g pro.

TEST KITCHEN TIP

Keep this meat loaf juicy by using a gentle touch when mixing and shaping it. Overmixing can make the loaf tough and dense. Additionally, consider replacing some of the ground beef with ground pork. The mixture of 2 different meats can help the meat loaf stay juicy.

—MARK NEUFANG, *TASTE OF HOME* CULINARY ASSISTANT

CITRUS-HERB
ROAST CHICKEN

CITRUS-HERB ROAST CHICKEN

This dish is one of my all-time favorites. The flavorful, juicy chicken combines with the aromas of spring in fresh herbs, lemon and onions to form the perfect one-pot meal. I make the gravy right in the pan.
—*Megan Fordyce, Fairchance, PA*

PREP: 25 MIN. • BAKE: 2 HOURS + STANDING • MAKES: 8 SERVINGS

6 garlic cloves
1 roasting chicken (6 to 7 lbs.)
3 lbs. baby red potatoes, halved
6 medium carrots, halved lengthwise
  and cut into 1-in. pieces
4 fresh thyme sprigs
4 fresh dill sprigs
2 fresh rosemary sprigs
1 medium lemon
1 small navel orange
1 tsp. salt
½ tsp. pepper
3 cups chicken broth, warmed
6 green onions, cut into 2-in. pieces

1. Preheat oven to 350°. Peel and cut garlic into quarters. Place chicken on a cutting board. Tuck the wings under chicken. With a sharp paring knife, cut 24 small slits in breasts, drumsticks and thighs. Insert garlic in slits. Tie the drumsticks together.

2. Place potatoes and carrots in a shallow roasting pan; top with herbs. Place chicken, breast side up, over vegetables and herbs. Cut lemon and orange in half; gently squeeze juices over chicken and vegetables. Place squeezed fruits inside chicken cavity. Sprinkle chicken with salt and pepper. Pour broth around chicken.

3. Roast until a thermometer inserted in thickest part of thigh reads 170°-175°, 2-2½ hours, sprinkling green onions over vegetables during the last 20 minutes. (Cover loosely with foil if chicken browns too quickly.)

4. Remove chicken from oven; tent with foil. Let stand 15 minutes before carving. Discard herbs. If desired, skim fat and thicken pan drippings for gravy. Serve gravy with chicken and vegetables.

7 oz. cooked chicken with 1¼ cups vegetables: 561 cal., 24g fat (7g sat. fat), 136mg chol., 826mg sod., 39g carb (5g sugars, 5g fiber), 47g pro.

SLOW-COOKED CARIBBEAN POT ROAST

This dish is definitely a year-round recipe. Sweet potatoes, orange zest and baking cocoa are my surprise ingredients.
—*Jenn Tidwell, Fair Oaks, CA*

PREP: 30 MIN. • **COOK:** 6 HOURS • **MAKES:** 10 SERVINGS

2	medium sweet potatoes, cubed
2	large carrots, sliced
¼	cup chopped celery
1	boneless beef chuck roast (2½ lbs.)
1	Tbsp. canola oil
1	large onion, chopped
2	garlic cloves, minced
1	Tbsp. all-purpose flour
1	Tbsp. sugar
1	Tbsp. brown sugar
1	tsp. ground cumin
¾	tsp. salt
¾	tsp. ground coriander
¾	tsp. chili powder
½	tsp. dried oregano
⅛	tsp. ground cinnamon
¾	tsp. grated orange zest
¾	tsp. baking cocoa
1	can (15 oz.) tomato sauce

1. Place potatoes, carrots and celery in a 5-qt. slow cooker. In a large skillet, brown meat in oil on all sides. Transfer meat to slow cooker.

2. In the same skillet, saute onion in drippings until tender. Add garlic; cook 1 minute longer. Combine the flour, sugar, brown sugar, seasonings, orange zest and cocoa. Stir in tomato sauce; add to skillet and heat through. Pour over beef.

3. Cover and cook on low until beef and vegetables are tender, 6-8 hours.

3 oz. cooked beef with ½ cup vegetable mixture :278 cal., 12g fat (4g sat. fat), 74mg chol., 453mg sod., 16g carb. (8g sugars, 3g fiber), 25g pro. **Diabetic exchanges:** 3 lean meat, 1 starch, 1 vegetable, ½ fat.

THREE-CHEESE MEATBALL MOSTACCIOLI

When my husband travels for work, I make a special dinner for my kids to help keep their minds off missing Daddy. This tasty mostaccioli is meatball magic.
—Jennifer Gilbert, Brighton, MI

PREP: 15 MIN. • BAKE: 35 MIN. • MAKES: 10 SERVINGS

1 pkg. (16 oz.) mostaccioli
2 large eggs, lightly beaten
1 carton (15 oz.) part-skim ricotta cheese
1 lb. ground beef
1 medium onion, chopped
1 Tbsp. brown sugar
1 Tbsp. Italian seasoning
1 tsp. garlic powder
¼ tsp. pepper
2 jars (24 oz. each) pasta sauce with meat
½ cup grated Romano cheese
1 pkg. (12 oz.) frozen fully cooked Italian meatballs, thawed
¾ cup shaved Parmesan cheese
Optional: Torn fresh basil or fresh oregano leaves

1. Preheat oven to 350°. Cook the mostaccioli according to package directions for al dente; drain. Meanwhile, in a small bowl, mix eggs and ricotta cheese.

2. In a 6-qt. stockpot, cook beef and onion until the beef is no longer pink, 6-8 minutes, breaking up beef into crumbles; drain. Stir in brown sugar and seasonings. Add pasta sauce and mostaccioli; toss to combine.

3. Transfer half the pasta mixture to a greased 13x9-in. baking dish. Layer with ricotta mixture and remaining pasta mixture; sprinkle with Romano cheese. Top with meatballs and Parmesan cheese.

4. Bake, uncovered, until heated through, 35-40 minutes. If desired, top with basil or oregano.

1⅓ cups: 541 cal., 23g fat (11g sat. fat), 105mg chol., 1335mg sod., 55g carb. (13g sugars, 5g fiber), 34g pro.

CHICKEN CHILES RELLENOS STRATA

This versatile bake can be made as an entree, a brunch option or a potluck dish.
It's one of the easiest meals to assemble on a busy weeknight.
—*Kallee Krong-McCreery, Escondido, CA*

PREP: 20 MIN. + CHILLING • BAKE: 35 MIN. + STANDING • MAKES: 10 SERVINGS

6 cups cubed French bread
(about 6 oz.)
2 cans (4 oz. each) chopped
green chiles
2 cups shredded Monterey Jack
cheese
2 cups shredded cooked chicken
12 large eggs
1½ cups 2% milk
2 tsp. baking powder
1 tsp. garlic salt
1 cup shredded cheddar cheese
Salsa

1. In a greased 13x9-in. baking dish, layer half of each of the following: bread cubes, chiles, Monterey Jack cheese and chicken. Repeat layers.

2. In a large bowl, whisk eggs, milk, baking powder and garlic salt until blended. Pour over layers. Sprinkle with cheddar cheese. Refrigerate, covered, overnight.

3. Preheat oven to 350°. Remove strata from refrigerator while oven heats. Bake, uncovered, until puffed and golden at edges, 35-40 minutes. Let stand 10 minutes before serving. Serve with salsa.

1 piece: 338 cal., 20g fat (9g sat. fat), 282mg chol., 820mg sod., 13g carb. (3g sugars, 1g fiber), 27g pro.

STEAK AU POIVRE FOR 2

With the punch of peppercorns and a smooth beefy sauce, this steak is everything you could want
in a celebratory meal. You'll love the hint of sweetness the bittersweet chocolate adds to the meat.
—*Crystal Jo Bruns, Iliff, CO*

TAKES: 30 MIN. • MAKES: 2 SERVINGS

2 beef tenderloin steaks (1 in. thick
and 5 oz. each)
2 Tbsp. olive oil, divided
1 Tbsp. whole white or black
peppercorns, crushed
¼ tsp. salt
1 Tbsp. finely chopped shallot
¼ cup port wine
1 Tbsp. balsamic vinegar
¼ cup condensed beef consomme,
undiluted
1 tsp. minced fresh rosemary or
¼ tsp. dried rosemary, crushed
½ oz. bittersweet chocolate, chopped

1. Rub steaks with 1 Tbsp. oil; sprinkle with peppercorns and salt. In a skillet, heat 2 tsp. oil over medium heat. Add steaks; cook 5-7 minutes on each side or until meat reaches desired doneness (for medium-rare, a thermometer should read 135°; medium, 140°; medium-well, 145°). Remove and keep warm.

2. In same pan, heat remaining oil over medium-high heat. Add shallot; cook and stir 1 minute or until tender. Add wine and vinegar, stirring to loosen browned bits from pan. Bring to a boil; cook and stir 2-3 minutes or until slightly thickened.

3. Stir in consomme and rosemary; bring to a boil. Add chocolate; cook and stir until melted and sauce is slightly thickened. Serve with steaks.

1 steak with 2 Tbsp. sauce: 425 cal., 25g fat (7g sat. fat), 62mg chol., 503mg sod., 11g carb. (6g sugars, 1g fiber), 32g pro.

CHICKEN CHILES
RELLENOS STRATA

SLOW-COOKER MONGOLIAN BEEF

This dish uses inexpensive ingredients to offer big flavor in a small amount of time. The slow cooker makes easy work of getting dinner on the table.

—Taste of Home *Test Kitchen*

PREP: 10 MIN. • COOK: 4¼ HOURS • MAKES: 4 SERVINGS

¾ cup reduced-sodium chicken broth
2 Tbsp. reduced-sodium soy sauce
1 Tbsp. hoisin sauce
2 tsp. minced fresh gingerroot
2 tsp. sesame oil
1 tsp. minced garlic
½ tsp. salt
¼ tsp. crushed red pepper flakes
1 lb. beef flank steak, cut into thin strips
2 Tbsp. cornstarch
2 Tbsp. water
2 cups hot cooked rice
5 green onions, cut into 1-in. pieces
  Sesame seeds, optional

1. In a 4- or 5-qt. slow cooker, combine first 8 ingredients. Add beef and toss to coat. Cook, covered, on low 4-5 hours or until meat is tender.

2. In a small bowl, mix cornstarch and water until smooth; gradually stir into beef. Cook, covered, on high until sauce is thickened, 15-30 minutes. Serve over hot cooked rice. Sprinkle with green onions and, if desired, sesame seeds.

1 serving: 329 cal., 11g fat (4g sat. fat), 54mg chol., 530mg sod., 30g carb. (2g sugars, 1g fiber), 26g pro.

DID YOU KNOW?

Mongolian beef got its name from a stir-fry dish from Taiwan. The recipe itself isn't from traditional Mongolian cuisine; it's named after the Mongolian barbecue cooking style.

CHICKEN WITH PUMPKIN ALFREDO

I love pumpkin and my kids love pasta, so this was a match made in heaven for us. Plus, it's an extra way to get some veggies into their diet. Use dairy-free or gluten-free ingredients if needed.
—*Courtney Stultz, Weir, KS*

PREP: 15 MIN. • COOK: 30 MIN. • MAKES: 4 SERVINGS

1 Tbsp. olive oil
2 boneless skinless chicken breast halves (6 oz. each)
1 Tbsp. Italian seasoning
¾ tsp. salt
½ tsp. pepper
8 oz. uncooked spiral pasta
2 cups fresh broccoli florets
¼ cup butter, cubed
3 garlic cloves, minced
1 cup half-and-half cream
1 cup canned pumpkin
½ cup shredded Parmesan cheese
4 bacon strips, cooked and crumbled
⅛ tsp. ground nutmeg
  Minced fresh parsley

1. In a large skillet, heat oil over medium heat. Sprinkle chicken with Italian seasoning, salt and pepper. Add to skillet cook until a thermometer reads 165°, 6-8 minutes on each side. Remove and keep warm.

2. Meanwhile, in a large saucepan cook pasta according to package directions, adding the broccoli during the last 5 minutes of cooking. In the same skillet used to cook chicken, heat the butter over medium heat. Add garlic; cook 1 minute. Stir in cream, pumpkin, Parmesan cheese and nutmeg until combined.

3. Drain the pasta and broccoli; stir into sauce. Slice chicken; serve with pasta mixture. Sprinkle with bacon, parsley and, if desired, additional Parmesan cheese.

1 serving: 631 cal., 30g fat (15g sat. fat), 123mg chol., 936mg sod., 53g carb. (6g sugars, 5g fiber), 35g pro.

Cooking Outside the Box

A little creativity goes a long way in this mom's kitchen.

What inspired you to create this change-of-pace entree?
Everyone loves pasta dishes, especially my kids, but I wanted to sneak in a little extra nutrition. Initially, they were skeptical about having pumpkin in their pasta, but it was a huge hit for everyone.

What's your favorite ingredient?
It's so hard to choose, but I think it is, indeed, pumpkin. I love roasting it for savory dishes, toasting the seeds for snacks and using fresh puree in a variety of dishes. I'm also a big lover of spices, especially cinnamon and ginger. Luckily, those two go well with pumpkin!

What tips do you have for home cooks looking to create their own recipes?
Don't be afraid to think outside the box! Literally. My mom taught me so much about cooking from scratch that we hardly used box mixes at all. Creating your own recipes can come with kitchen flubs, but it can also come with the best creations and even better memories.

Courtney Stultz
Weir, KS

EASY
SLOW-COOKER
POT ROAST

66
Absolutely
spectacular!
Quick, easy,
tender and
flavorful. A
definite keeper!
—CYNANDTOM
TASTEOFHOME.COM

EASY SLOW-COOKER POT ROAST

I love pot roast for a couple of reasons. First, it's delicious. Second, it's easy!
I can't describe the feeling of walking into my house after work and smelling
this dish that's been simmering in the slow cooker all day. There's nothing better.
—James Schend, Pleasant Prairie, WI

PREP: 10 MIN. • COOK: 10 HOURS • MAKES: 10 SERVINGS

1 boneless beef rump or chuck roast
  (3 to 3½ lbs.)
1 Tbsp. canola oil
6 medium carrots, cut into thirds
6 medium potatoes, peeled and
  quartered
1 large onion, quartered
3 tsp. Montreal steak seasoning
1 carton (32 oz.) beef broth
3 Tbsp. cornstarch
3 Tbsp. water

1. In a large skillet over medium heat, brown roast in oil on all sides. Place carrots, potatoes and onion in a 6-qt. slow cooker. Place roast on top of the vegetables; sprinkle with steak seasoning. Add broth. Cook, covered, on low 10-12 hours or until beef and vegetables are tender.

2. Remove roast and vegetables from slow cooker; keep warm.

3. Transfer cooking juices to a saucepan; skim off fat. Bring juices to a boil. In a small bowl, mix cornstarch and water until smooth; stir into juices. Return to a boil, stirring constantly; cook and stir until thickened, 1-2 minutes. Serve with the roast and vegetables.

1 serving: 354 cal., 15g fat (5g sat. fat), 88mg chol., 696mg sod., 24g carb. (4g sugars, 3g fiber), 30g pro. **Diabetic exchanges:** 4 lean meat, 1½ starch, ½ fat.

MEDITERRANEAN ORZO CHICKEN SALAD

On hot days, I pull out this recipe for a cool supper. The lemon dressing is so refreshing. If you have it, use grilled chicken.
—Susan Kieboam, Amherstburg, ON

TAKES: 25 MIN. • MAKES: 6 SERVINGS

2 cups uncooked whole wheat
  orzo pasta
2 cups shredded rotisserie chicken
10 cherry tomatoes, halved
½ cup crumbled tomato and basil feta
  cheese
1 can (2¼ oz.) sliced ripe olives,
  drained
¼ cup chopped sweet onion
¼ cup olive oil
2 Tbsp. lemon juice
½ tsp. salt
¼ tsp. dried oregano

1. Cook pasta according to package directions. Drain pasta; rinse with cold water and drain well.

2. In a large bowl, combine pasta, chicken, tomatoes, cheese, olives and onion. In a small bowl, whisk remaining ingredients until blended. Drizzle over salad; toss to coat.

1 cup: 397 cal., 16g fat (3g sat. fat), 47mg chol., 407mg sod., 40g carb. (1g sugars, 10g fiber), 22g pro. **Diabetic exchanges:** 3 lean meat, 2½ starch, 2 fat.

SHEPHERD'S PIE TWICE-BAKED POTATOES

This recipe captures the best of two classics—baked potatoes and shepherd's pie. Serve with a green salad, and satisfaction is guaranteed even for those with the heartiest appetites.
—*Cyndy Gerken, Naples, FL*

PREP: 1¾ HOURS • **BAKE:** 25 MIN. • **MAKES:** 6 SERVINGS

6	large russet potatoes
2	Tbsp. olive oil
1	lb. ground beef
1	medium onion, chopped
1	medium green pepper, chopped
1	medium sweet red pepper, chopped
4	garlic cloves, minced
1	pkg. (16 oz.) frozen mixed vegetables
3	Tbsp. Worcestershire sauce
1	Tbsp. tomato paste
1	Tbsp. steak seasoning
¼	tsp. salt
⅛	tsp. pepper
	Dash cayenne pepper
2	tsp. paprika, divided
½	cup butter, cubed
¾	cup heavy whipping cream
¼	cup sour cream
1	cup shredded Monterey Jack cheese
1	cup shredded cheddar cheese
¼	cup shredded Parmesan cheese
2	Tbsp. minced chives

TOPPINGS

½	cup shredded cheddar cheese
1	Tbsp. minced chives
1	tsp. paprika

1. Scrub and pierce potatoes; rub with oil. Bake at 375° until tender, about 1 hour.

2. In a large skillet, cook and crumble the beef with onion, peppers and garlic over medium heat until beef is no longer pink; drain. Add the mixed vegetables, Worcestershire sauce, tomato paste, steak seasoning, salt, pepper, cayenne and 1 tsp. paprika. Cook and stir until the vegetables are tender.

3. When potatoes are cool enough to handle, cut a thin slice off the top of each and discard tops. Scoop out the pulp, leaving thin shells.

4. In a large bowl, mash the pulp with butter. Add whipping cream, sour cream, cheeses and chives. Mash potatoes until combined. Spoon 1 cup of the meat mixture into each potato shell; top with ½ cup potato mixture. Sprinkle with remaining 1 tsp. paprika.

5. Place on a baking sheet. Bake at 375° for 20 minutes. Sprinkle with cheese; bake until melted, about 5 minutes longer. Sprinkle with chives and paprika.

Freeze option: Wrap unbaked stuffed potatoes and freeze in a freezer container. To use, partially thaw in refrigerator overnight. Bake as directed, adding additional time until heated through.

1 stuffed potato: 986 cal., 56g fat (32g sat. fat), 183mg chol., 1066mg sod., 86g carb. (12g sugars, 11g fiber), 37g pro.

THE BEST GRILLED SIRLOIN TIP ROAST

If you're looking for a flavorful cut of meat that's still pretty lean, give this sirloin tip roast recipe a try. I like to cook it slowly over indirect heat, mopping it frequently with red wine sauce.
—James Schend, Pleasant Prairie, WI

PREP: 40 MIN. + CHILLING • **GRILL:** 1½ HOURS + STANDING • **MAKES:** 6 SERVINGS

1 beef sirloin tip roast or beef tri-tip roast (2 to 3 lbs.)
1 Tbsp. kosher salt
2 tsp. dried thyme
2 tsp. garlic powder
1 tsp. coarsely ground pepper
1 small onion, chopped
2 Tbsp. olive oil, divided
1 bottle (750 ml) dry red wine
6 fresh thyme sprigs
1 garlic cloves, crushed
½ tsp. whole peppercorns
3 whole cloves

HORSERADISH-THYME BUTTER (OPTIONAL)
6 Tbsp. softened butter
2 Tbsp. prepared horseradish
3 Tbsp. fresh thyme leaves

1. Sprinkle the roast with salt, thyme, garlic powder and ground pepper. Cover and refrigerate at least 8 hours or up to 24 hours. Meanwhile, in a saucepan, saute the onion in 1 Tbsp. oil until tender, about 5 minutes. Add the wine, thyme, garlic, peppercorns and cloves. Simmer until reduced to ¾ cup. Cool; strain, discarding solids, and refrigerate.

2. Remove roast from the refrigerator 1 hour before grilling. Prepare grill for indirect heat, using a drip pan. Add wood chips according to manufacturer's directions.

3. Pat roast dry with paper towels. Brush with remaining 1 Tbsp. oil; place over drip pan. Grill, covered, over medium-low indirect heat, brushing with mop sauce every 20 minutes, until meat reaches desired doneness (for medium-rare, a thermometer should read 135°; medium, 140°; medium-well, 145°), 1½-2 hours. Let stand 15 minutes before slicing.

4. If desired, in a small bowl, stir together butter, horseradish and thyme. Serve on top of roast.

4 oz. cooked beef: 262 cal., 13g fat (4g sat. fat), 91mg chol., 1027mg sod., 3g carb. (1g sugars, 1g fiber), 32g pro.

TEST KITCHEN TIP

Always slice against the grain when cutting a sirloin tip roast. Cutting against the grain keeps the meat tender. You can easily find the grain by looking on the outside and then slicing it in the opposite direction.

BRAISED CORNED BEEF

You'll need a bit of time to prepare this braised corned beef, but the end results make all that time worth it. Cook this for your St. Patrick's Day celebration or for an extra-special meal.

—*Josh Rink, Taste of Home Food Stylist*

PREP: 20 MIN. + BRINING • COOK: 5 HOURS + RESTING • MAKES: 12 SERVINGS

FOR BRINE
- 2 qt. plus 2 cups water, divided
- 1 cup kosher salt
- ¾ cup packed brown sugar
- 2 Tbsp. curing salt, such as Prauge powder
- 2 Tbsp. whole peppercorns
- 1 Tbsp. mustard seed
- 1 tsp. ground ginger
- 10 whole allspice
- 10 whole cloves
- 10 whole juniper berries
- 2 bay leaves
- 2 cinnamon sticks (2-3 in.)
- 2 whole star anise
- 2 lbs. ice cubes
- 1 fresh beef brisket (4 to 5 lbs.), trimmed

FOR BRAISING
- 3 large carrots, peeled and cut into thirds
- 3 celery ribs, cut into thirds
- 2 large onions, skins removed and quartered

1. To make brine, place 2 qt. water plus the next 12 ingredients in a large 6-8 qt. stockpot; bring to a boil. Reduce heat and simmer 4-5 minutes or until the sugar and salts have dissolved, stirring occasionally. Remove from heat; add ice and stir until ice has melted. Place brine in the refrigerator and allow to cool completely. In a large bowl or shallow dish, add brisket and pour brine over beef. Cover, removing as much air as possible, ensuring brisket is completely submerged. Transfer to refrigerator; allow to rest for 10 days, agitating bowl occasionally to redistribute spices and liquid.

2. After 10 days, remove brisket from brine; rinse brisket thoroughly and discard brine. To braise brisket, preheat oven to 300°. Place carrots, celery and onions in large roasting pan; pour remaining 2 cups water into pan until water level is ½ in. high. Place brisket over vegetables and cover with aluminum foil; transfer to oven. Cook, covered, until very tender, 5-6 hours.

3. Remove brisket from roasting pan, discarding vegetables and cooking juices; tent beef with foil and allow to rest for 10 minutes before serving. Or, to slice for Reuben sandwiches, wrap corned beef well after cooling for 10 minutes; place in refrigerator and allow to cool completely overnight. Slice thinly against grain.

4 oz. cooked beef: 194 cal., 7g fat (2g sat. fat), 64mg chol., 938mg sod., 1g carb. (1g sugars, 0 fiber), 31g pro.

NENA'S PAPAS RELLENAS

A Cuban classic, these satisfying, crispy-coated potato balls are filled with a savory ground beef mixture known as picadillo.
—Marina Castle-Kelley, Canyon Country CA

PREP: 45 MIN. • COOK: 5 MIN./BATCH • MAKES: 2½ DOZEN

2½ lbs. potatoes (about 8 medium), peeled and cut into wedges
1 lb. lean ground beef (90% lean)
1 small green pepper, finely chopped
1 small onion, finely chopped
½ cup tomato sauce
½ cup sliced green olives with pimientos
½ cup raisins
1¼ tsp. salt, divided
1¼ tsp. pepper, divided
½ tsp. paprika
1 tsp. garlic powder
2 large eggs, lightly beaten
1 cup seasoned bread crumbs
Oil for deep-fat frying

1. Place the potatoes in a large saucepan and cover with water. Bring to a boil. Reduce heat; cover and cook 15-20 minutes or until tender.

2. Meanwhile, in a large skillet, cook the beef, green pepper and onion over medium heat until meat is no longer pink; drain. Stir in the tomato sauce, olives, raisins, ¼ tsp. salt, ¼ tsp. pepper and paprika; heat through.

3. Drain potatoes; mash with garlic powder and remaining salt and pepper. Shape 2 Tbsp. potatoes into a patty; place a heaping tablespoonful of filling in the center. Shape potatoes around filling, forming a ball. Repeat.

4. Place eggs and bread crumbs in separate shallow bowls. Dip potato balls in the eggs, then roll in bread crumbs. In an electric skillet or deep fryer, heat the oil to 375°. Fry potato balls, a few at a time, for 1-2 minutes or until golden brown. Drain on paper towels.

3 potato balls: 224 cal., 6g fat (2g sat. fat), 71mg chol., 615mg sod., 29g carb. (7g sugars, 2g fiber), 13g pro.

TEST KITCHEN TIP

Instead of frying the papas rellenas, you may place them on baking sheets and bake at 450° for 20 minutes or until heated through.

BRINED GRILLED
TURKEY BREAST

BRINED GRILLED TURKEY BREAST

You'll want to give thanks for this mouthwatering turkey! Moist and slightly sweet, with just a hint of spice, it's one of our best turkey recipes ever.

—Tina Mirilovich, Johnstown, PA

PREP: 20 MIN. + BRINING • GRILL: 1¼ HOURS + STANDING • MAKES: 6 SERVINGS

2 qt. cold water, divided
½ cup kosher salt
½ cup packed brown sugar
1 Tbsp. whole peppercorns
1 boneless skinless turkey breast half
   (2 to 3 lbs.)

BASTING SAUCE

¼ cup canola oil
¼ cup sesame oil
¼ cup reduced-sodium soy sauce
3 Tbsp. lemon juice
2 Tbsp. honey
3 garlic cloves, minced
¼ tsp. dried thyme
¼ tsp. crushed red pepper flakes

1. In a large saucepan, combine 1 qt. water, salt, brown sugar and peppercorns. Bring to a boil. Cook and stir until salt and sugar are dissolved. Pour into a large bowl. Add remaining 1 qt. cold water to cool the brine to room temperature. Add turkey breast; turn to coat. Cover and refrigerate 4-6 hours, turning occasionally.

2. Prepare grill for indirect medium heat, using a drip pan. Meanwhile, combine basting sauce ingredients. Grill turkey, covered, until a thermometer reads 170°, 1¼-1½ hours, basting occasionally with sauce. Remove to a cutting board. Cover and let stand 10 minutes before slicing.

5 oz. cooked turkey: 364 cal., 19g fat (2g sat. fat), 94mg chol., 553mg sod., 8g carb. (6g sugars, 0 fiber), 38g pro.

SLOW-COOKED BEEF TIPS

These slow-cooked beef tips remind me of a childhood favorite. I cook them with mushrooms and serve over brown rice, noodles or mashed potatoes.

—Amy Lents, Grand Forks, ND

PREP: 25 MIN. • COOK: 6¼ HOURS • MAKES: 2 SERVINGS

¼ lb. sliced baby portobello
   mushrooms
½ small onion, sliced
1 beef top sirloin steak (½ lb.), cubed
¼ tsp. salt
⅛ tsp. pepper
1 tsp. olive oil
3 Tbsp. dry red wine or beef broth
1 cup beef broth
1½ tsp. Worcestershire sauce
1 Tbsp. cornstarch
2 Tbsp. water
   Hot cooked mashed potatoes

1. Place mushrooms and onion in a 3-qt. slow cooker. Sprinkle beef with salt and pepper. In a large skillet, heat 1 tsp. oil over medium-high heat; brown meat in batches, adding additional oil as needed. Transfer meat to slow cooker.

2. Add wine to skillet, stirring to loosen browned bits from pan. Stir in broth and Worcestershire sauce; pour over meat. Cook, covered, on low 6-8 hours or until meat is tender.

3. In a small bowl, mix cornstarch and cold water until smooth; gradually stir into slow cooker. Cook, covered, on high 15-30 minutes or until gravy is thickened. Serve with mashed potatoes.

1 cup: 213 cal., 7g fat (2g sat. fat), 46mg chol., 836mg sod., 8g carb. (2g sugars, 1g fiber), 27g pro. **Diabetic exchanges:** 3 lean meat, 1½ fat, ½ starch.

CREAMY CHICKEN LASAGNA ROLL-UPS

The first time I made this I was at home and needed to make dinner, but I didn't want to go to the store. I used what ingredients I had to make these roll-ups. You won't believe how creamy, cheesy and delicious they are!
—Cyndy Gerken, Naples, FL

PREP: 35 MIN. • BAKE: 45 MIN. • MAKES: 10 SERVINGS

10 lasagna noodles
¾ lb. boneless skinless chicken breasts, cubed
1½ tsp. herbes de Provence
½ tsp. salt, divided
½ tsp. pepper, divided
1 Tbsp. olive oil
2 cups ricotta cheese
½ cup grated Parmesan cheese, divided
¼ cup 2% milk
2 Tbsp. minced fresh parsley
4 cups spaghetti sauce
8 oz. fresh mozzarella cheese, thinly sliced
   Additional minced fresh parsley, optional

1. Preheat oven to 375°. Cook the lasagna noodles according to the package directions.

2. Meanwhile, sprinkle chicken with herbes de Provence, ¼ tsp. salt and ¼ tsp. pepper. In a large skillet, cook chicken in oil over medium heat for 5-7 minutes or until no longer pink; set aside.

3. In a large bowl, combine ricotta, ¼ cup Parmesan cheese, milk, parsley and remaining salt and pepper. Add the chicken.

4. Drain noodles. Spread 1 cup spaghetti sauce into a greased 13x9-in. baking dish. Spread ⅓ cup chicken mixture over each noodle; carefully roll up. Place seam side down over sauce. Top with remaining sauce and Parmesan cheese.

5. Cover and bake 30 minutes. Uncover; top with the mozzarella cheese. Bake 15-20 minutes longer or until bubbly and cheese is melted. Top with additional parsley if desired.

Note: Look for herbes de Provence in the spice aisle.

1 lasagna roll-up: 378 cal., 17g fat (9g sat. fat), 63mg chol., 789mg sod., 32g carb. (11g sugars, 3g fiber), 24g pro.

TEST KITCHEN TIP

Common olive oil works better for cooking at high heat than virgin or extra-virgin oil. These higher grades have ideal flavor for cold foods, but they smoke at lower temperatures.

BUTTERY HERB ROASTED CHICKEN

Roasting chicken is always such a comforting thing, especially when you can pick the herbs right from your garden and pair them with some fresh citrus to smear across the bird. My family can't get enough of this herb-roasted chicken.
—*Jenn Tidwell, Fair Oaks, CA*

PREP: 15 MIN. • BAKE: 1½ HOURS + STANDING • MAKES: 6 SERVINGS

- 1 roasting chicken (5 to 6 lbs.)
- ½ cup unsalted butter, softened, divided
- 1 cup chicken broth
- ¾ cup orange juice
- ½ cup white wine or additional chicken broth
- 2 garlic cloves, minced
- 1 tsp. salt
- ½ tsp. pepper
- 2 fresh rosemary sprigs
- 2 fresh thyme sprigs
- 2 fresh sage sprigs

1. Preheat oven to 350°. With fingers, carefully loosen skin from chicken; rub ¼ cup butter under skin. Secure skin to underside of breast with toothpicks. Place chicken on a rack in a shallow roasting pan, breast side up. Tuck wings under chicken; tie drumsticks together. Pour broth around chicken.

2. Melt remaining ¼ cup butter; brush over chicken. Drizzle with orange juice and wine. Combine garlic, salt and pepper; rub over skin. Place rosemary, thyme and sage in roasting pan.

3. Roast until thermometer inserted in thickest part of thigh reads 170°-175°, 1½-2 hours. (Cover loosely with foil if chicken browns too quickly.) Remove chicken from oven; tent with foil. Let stand 15 minutes before carving; remove toothpicks. If desired, skim fat and thicken the pan drippings for gravy. Serve gravy with the chicken.

6 oz. cooked chicken: 599 cal., 42g fat (17g sat. fat), 191mg chol., 703mg sod., 4g carb. (3g sugars, 0 fiber), 48g pro.

POMEGRANATE SHORT RIBS

I like drizzling the pomegranate molasses sauce on top of simple roasted vegetables. It's a bit tangy and a bit sweet, and it adds a nice depth of flavor to sweet and savory dishes alike. Pomegranate molasses can be found in specialty food stores or online.

—*Shannon Sarna, South Orange, NJ*

PREP: 25 MIN. + CHILLING • **COOK:** 6 HOURS • **MAKES:** 8 SERVINGS

1   tsp. salt
½   tsp. ground cinnamon
½   tsp. pepper
¼   tsp. ground coriander
     Dash crushed red pepper flakes
8   bone-in beef short ribs (about 4 lbs.)
2   Tbsp. safflower oil
1   medium onion, chopped
3   garlic cloves, minced
1   Tbsp. tomato paste
1½   cups dry red wine or pomegranate
     juice
1½   cups chicken or beef stock
⅓   cup pomegranate molasses
3   Tbsp. soy sauce, optional
     Minced fresh parsley and
     pomegranate seeds

1. Combine the first 5 ingredients; rub over ribs. Refrigerate, covered, at least 2 hours. In a large skillet, heat oil over medium heat. Brown ribs on all sides in batches. Transfer to a 5-qt. slow cooker. Discard drippings, reserving 2 Tbsp.. Add onion to drippings; cook and stir over medium-high heat until tender, 8-10 minutes. Add garlic and tomato paste; cook 1 minute longer.

2. Add wine to pan; increase heat to medium-high. Cook 10 minutes or until slightly thickened, stirring to loosen browned bits from pan. Transfer to slow cooker. Add the stock, molasses and, if desired, soy sauce, making sure ribs are fully submerged in liquid. Cook, covered, on low 6-8 hours or until the ribs are tender. Serve ribs with fresh parsley and pomegranate seeds.

1 short rib: 267 cal., 14g fat (5g sat. fat), 55mg chol., 428mg sod., 11g carb. (7g sugars, 0 fiber), 19g pro.

AIR-FRYER BACON-WRAPPED FILETS

I got the idea for bacon-wrapped filet mignon when I saw some on sale in the grocery store. The rest was inspired by my husband, because he once made a Scotch and ginger ale sauce. I originally made this in the oven but it works equally well in the air fryer!
—*Mary Kay LaBrie, Clermont, FL*

TAKES: 30 MIN. • MAKES: 2 SERVINGS

2 bacon strips
2 beef tenderloin steaks (5 oz. each)
¼ tsp. salt
¼ tsp. coarsely ground pepper
2 cups sliced baby portobello mushrooms
¼ tsp. dried thyme
2 Tbsp. butter, divided
1½ tsp. olive oil
¼ cup Scotch whiskey
½ cup diet ginger ale
1 Tbsp. brown sugar
1½ tsp. reduced-sodium soy sauce
¼ tsp. rubbed sage

1. Place bacon strips in a single layer on tray in air-fryer basket. Cook at 350° until partially cooked but not crisp, 3-4 minutes. Remove to paper towels to drain.

2. Preheat air fryer to 375°. Sprinkle steaks with salt and pepper; wrap a strip of bacon around the side of each steak and secure with toothpicks. Place steaks in a single layer on greased tray in air-fryer basket. Cook until meat reaches desired doneness (for medium-rare, a thermometer should read 135°; medium, 140°; medium-well., 145°), 7-10 minutes, turning halfway through.

3. Meanwhile, in a large skillet, saute mushrooms and thyme in 1 Tbsp. butter and oil until tender; remove from heat. Add whiskey, stirring to loosen browned bits from pan. Stir in ginger ale, brown sugar, soy sauce and sage.

4. Bring to a boil. Reduce heat; simmer uncovered, 3-5 minutes or until reduced by half. Stir in remaining 1 Tbsp. butter. Serve with steaks.

Note: In our testing, we find cook times vary dramatically between brands of air fryers. As a result, we give wider than normal ranges on suggested cook times. Begin checking at the first time listed and adjust as needed.

1 filet with ⅓ cup mushroom mixture: 581 cal., 37g fat (15g sat. fat), 108mg chol., 729mg sod., 10g carb. (8 g sugars, 1g fiber), 35g pro.

TEST KITCHEN TIP

For a variation on this recipe, add more spices and herbs to the butter sauce. Consider garlic powder, rosemary, basil or, for a spicy kick, cayenne pepper.
—SAMMI DIVITO, *TASTE OF HOME* ASSISTANT EDITOR

EGGPLANT
ZUCCHINI
BOLOGNESE

"
This dish was
so simple to
make, and I
was wowed by
the flavors it
packed.
—RWIPPEL
TASTEOFHOME.COM

EGGPLANT ZUCCHINI BOLOGNESE

I roast the veggies while the pasta cooks, making this a quick dish.
The meal-in-one dish blends rustic comfort with fresh flavors.
—*Trisna Kruse, Eagle, ID*

PREP: 30 MIN. • COOK: 20 MIN. • MAKES: 8 SERVINGS

1 pkg. (16 oz.) penne pasta
1 small eggplant, peeled and cut into
   1-in. pieces
1 medium zucchini, cut into ¼-in.
   slices
1 medium yellow summer squash,
   cut into ¼-in. slices
1 cup chopped onion
2 Tbsp. olive oil
2 tsp. minced garlic
1 tsp. salt
½ tsp. pepper
1 lb. lean ground beef (90% lean)
1 can (28 oz.) tomato puree
1 Tbsp. Italian seasoning
1 Tbsp. brown sugar
8 tsp. grated Parmesan cheese

1. Cook pasta according to package directions.

2. In a large bowl, combine the eggplant, zucchini, squash, onion, oil, garlic, salt and pepper. Transfer to two 15x10x1-in. baking pans coated with cooking spray. Bake at 425° for 20-25 minutes or until tender.

3. Meanwhile, in a large skillet, cook and crumble beef over medium heat until no longer pink; drain. Stir in the tomato puree, Italian seasoning and brown sugar.

4. Drain pasta; stir in tomato mixture and roasted vegetables. Sprinkle with cheese.

1½ cups: 395 cal., 10g fat (3g sat. fat), 36mg chol., 378mg sod., 56g carb. (9g sugars, 5g fiber), 22g pro.

CAMPING HAYSTACKS

Try this layered dish for a satisfying meal after a busy day.
We love the easy combo of canned chili, corn chips and taco toppings.
—*Gaylene Anderson, Sandy, UT*

TAKES: 15 MIN. • MAKES: 2 SERVINGS

1 can (15 oz.) chili with beans
2 pkg. (1 oz. each) corn chips
½ cup shredded cheddar cheese
1½ cups chopped lettuce
1 small tomato, chopped
½ cup salsa
2 Tbsp. sliced ripe olives
2 Tbsp. sour cream

In a small saucepan, heat the chili. Divide corn chips between 2 plates; top with the chili. Layer with cheese, lettuce, tomato, salsa, olives and sour cream. Serve immediately.

1 serving: 620 cal., 30g fat (11g sat. fat), 61mg chol., 1654mg sod., 61g carb. (8g sugars, 10g fiber), 25g pro.

BANH MI BABY
BACK RIBS, PAGE 168

"
These are the best-tasting ribs I've ever had! Lip-smacking, fall-off-the-bone good! Great job!
—KARLA653
TASTEOFHOME.COM

CHAPTER 7

PORK & OTHER ENTREES

When it's time to mix up dinner routines, home cooks turn to pork, ham and sausage. Loaded with flavor and convenience, the following recipes are guaranteed to become staples in your house too.

SAUSAGE & BEAN SKILLET WITH CRISPY PLANTAINS

Caribbean flavors flourish in this one-pot entree topped with crushed plantain chips.
The whole family loves it—plus, it's so fast. Swap in spicy chicken sausage for the smoked links if you prefer.
—*Elisabeth Larsen, Pleasant Grove, UT*

TAKES: 30 MIN. • MAKES: 6 SERVINGS

2 Tbsp. canola oil
2 celery ribs, thinly sliced
1 medium sweet red pepper, chopped
1 small onion, chopped
1 pkg. (14 oz.) smoked sausage, cut diagonally into ½-in. slices
2 garlic cloves, minced
½ tsp. dried thyme
1 can (15 oz.) black beans, rinsed and drained
1 can (14½ oz.) diced tomatoes, undrained
¼ tsp. pepper
1 cup plantain chips, crushed
¼ cup fresh cilantro leaves, chopped
  Hot cooked rice, optional

1. In a large skillet, heat oil over medium-high heat. Add celery, red pepper and onion; cook and stir until crisp-tender, 4-5 minutes. Add sausage; cook and stir until browned, about 4 minutes longer. Add garlic and thyme; cook 1 minute longer. Stir in beans, tomatoes and pepper. Reduce heat; cook, uncovered, until sauce is slightly thickened, 4-6 minutes longer.

2. Top with plantain chips and cilantro. If desired, serve with rice.

1 cup: 379 cal., 25g fat (8g sat. fat), 44mg chol., 1017mg sod., 24g carb. (6g sugars, 5g fiber), 14g pro.

PIGS IN A PONCHO

For my pigs in a blanket, I dress things up with refried beans. Spice them up
even more with pepper jack, jalapenos and guacamole if you'd like.
—*Jennifer Stowell, Deep River, IA*

PREP: 25 MIN. • COOK: 5 MIN./BATCH • MAKES: 8 SERVINGS

8 hot dogs
1 can (16 oz.) refried beans
8 flour tortillas (10 in.)
1 can (4 oz.) chopped green chiles
1 can (2¼ oz.) sliced ripe olives, drained
2 cups shredded Monterey Jack cheese
  Oil for frying
  Optional: Sour cream and salsa

1. Heat hot dogs according to package directions. Spread beans over the center of each tortilla; layer with green chiles, olives and cheese. Place hot dog down center of tortilla. Fold bottom and sides of tortilla over filling and roll up; secure with a toothpick.

2. In a deep skillet or electric skillet, heat 1 in. oil to 375°. Fry wraps in batches, seam side down, until golden brown, 2-3 minutes on each side. Drain on paper towels. Discard toothpicks before serving. Serve with sour cream and salsa if desired.

1 serving: 726 cal., 50g fat (14g sat. fat), 50mg chol., 1494mg sod., 48g carb. (4g sugars, 5g fiber), 21g pro.

SAUSAGE & BEAN
SKILLET WITH
CRISPY PLANTAINS

HAM & SWISS BAKED PENNE

As a kid I loved the hot ham and Swiss sandwiches from a local fast-food restaurant. With its melty, gooey goodness, this bake makes me think of them.
—*Ally Billhorn, Wilton, IA*

TAKES: 30 MIN. • **MAKES:** 6 SERVINGS

2⅓ cups uncooked penne pasta
3 Tbsp. butter
3 Tbsp. all-purpose flour
2 cups 2% milk
1 cup half-and-half cream
1½ cups shredded Swiss cheese
½ cup shredded Colby cheese
2 cups cubed fully cooked ham

TOPPING
¼ cup seasoned bread crumbs
¼ cup grated Parmesan cheese
2 Tbsp. butter, melted

1. Preheat oven to 375°. Cook pasta according to package directions for al dente; drain.

2. Meanwhile, in a large saucepan, melt butter over medium heat. Stir in the flour until smooth; gradually whisk in the milk and cream. Bring to a boil, stirring constantly; cook and stir until thickened, 1-2 minutes. Gradually stir in Swiss and Colby cheeses until melted. Add ham and pasta; toss to coat.

3. Transfer to a greased 11x7-in. baking dish. In a small bowl, mix the topping ingredients; sprinkle over pasta. Bake, uncovered, until bubbly, 15-20 minutes.

1 cup: 559 cal., 30g fat (18g sat. fat), 116mg chol., 905mg sod., 41g carb. (7g sugars, 2g fiber), 31g pro.

DID YOU KNOW?

Penne pasta gets it name from the Italian word for quill, penna. *With its wide surface area and ends cut on an angle, the pasta is perfect for dishes with lots of sauce.*

SHEET-PAN PORK SUPPER

I created this recipe to suit our family's needs. It's a delicious meal in one, and so quick and easy to clean up since you use one pan for everything! You can try any variety of small potatoes—fingerlings or other colored potatoes are a fun and delicious option.

—Debbie Johnson, Centertown, MO

PREP: 10 MIN. • BAKE: 35 MIN. • MAKES: 8 SERVINGS

¼ cup butter, softened
2 tsp. minced fresh chives or
   1 tsp. dried minced chives
1 garlic clove, minced
1½ lbs. fresh green beans, trimmed
2 Tbsp. olive oil
¾ tsp. salt
½ tsp. pepper
1½ lbs. baby red potatoes, halved
2 pork tenderloins (about 1 lb. each)
½ cup teriyaki glaze or hoisin sauce
   Optional: Toasted sesame seeds and additional fresh minced chives

1. Preheat oven to 450°. In a small bowl, combine butter, chives and garlic; set aside. In a second bowl, combine green beans with 1 Tbsp. olive oil, ¼ tsp. salt and ¼ tsp. pepper. Arrange the green beans down 1 side of a 15x10x1-in. baking pan. In the same bowl, combine potatoes with remaining 1 Tbsp. olive oil, ½ tsp. salt and ¼ tsp. pepper. Arrange the potatoes on other side of pan.

2. Pat pork dry with paper towels; brush with teriyaki glaze. Place on top of green beans.

3. Bake until a thermometer inserted in pork reads 145°, 25-30 minutes. Remove tenderloins to a cutting board and top with 2 Tbsp. seasoned butter. Tent pork with aluminum foil; let stand.

4. Stir green beans and potatoes; return to oven and cook until vegetables are tender and lightly browned, about 10 minutes longer. Stir remaining seasoned butter into vegetables.

5. Slice pork; serve with roasted vegetables and pan drippings. If desired, top with sesame seeds and additional minced chives.

3 oz. cooked pork with 1¼ cups vegetables: 354 cal., 14g fat (6g sat. fat), 79mg chol., 1186mg sod., 30g carb. (9g sugars, 5g fiber), 28g pro.

SPICY PORK LOIN
ALFREDO

66
Tasty, quick
and easy.
My whole
family wanted
seconds.
—CHRIS751
TASTEOFHOME.COM

SPICY PORK LOIN ALFREDO

This recipe is so quick and easy but still has a lot of fantastic flavor. From time to time I'll add half a pound of sauteed mushrooms to the sauce just before serving.
—*Cheryl Erikson, Rock Hill, SC*

PREP: 15 MIN. • COOK: 35 MIN. • MAKES: 4 SERVINGS

1 Tbsp. chicken bouillon granules
1½ tsp. garlic powder
1 tsp. onion powder
1 tsp. salt
1 tsp. pepper
½ tsp. cayenne pepper
½ tsp. paprika
2 Tbsp. butter
1½ lbs. boneless pork loin roast, cubed
2 cups heavy whipping cream
¾ cup grated Parmesan cheese
8 oz. fettuccine

1. In a small bowl, combine first 7 ingredients; set aside. In a large skillet, heat butter over medium heat. Add pork; cook, stirring occasionally, until just starting to brown, 10-12 minutes. Stir in spice mixture; cook 1 minute. Add cream and cheese; reduce heat and simmer until sauce thickens slightly and pork is tender, about 10 minutes.

2. Meanwhile, cook pasta according to package directions for al dente. Serve pork with fettuccine.

1 serving: 942 cal., 63g fat (37g sat. fat), 249mg chol., 1638mg sod., 48g carb. (6g sugars, 3g fiber), 49g pro.

APRICOT PORK MEDALLIONS

There's nothing we love more than a tasty pork dish for supper in our house, and this recipe is up there with the best of them. I find that apricot preserves give the pork just the right amount of sweetness without being overwhelming.
—*Crystal Jo Bruns, Iliff, CO*

TAKES: 20 MIN. • MAKES: 4 SERVINGS

1 pork tenderloin (1 lb.), cut into 8 slices
1 Tbsp. plus 1 tsp. butter, divided
½ cup apricot preserves
2 green onions, sliced
1 Tbsp. cider vinegar
¼ tsp. ground mustard

1. Pound pork slices with a meat mallet to ½-in. thickness. In a large skillet, heat 1 Tbsp. butter over medium heat. Brown pork on each side. Remove pork from pan, reserving drippings.

2. Add preserves, green onions, vinegar, mustard and remaining butter to pan; bring just to a boil, stirring to loosen browned bits from pan. Reduce heat; simmer, covered, 3-4 minutes to allow flavors to blend.

3. Return pork to pan; cook until pork is tender. Let stand 5 minutes before serving.

3 oz. cooked pork with 1 Tbsp. sauce: 266 cal., 8g fat (4g sat. fat), 73mg chol., 89mg sod., 26g carb. (15g sugars, 0 fiber), 23g pro.

BANH MI BABY BACK RIBS

We love both banh mi and ribs. This creative entree has all the flavors of the beloved Vietnamese sandwich—sans bread. Sprinkle the pork with roasted peanuts and sesame seeds, in addition to the other garnishes, for a fun crunch.
—*Bonnie Geavaras-Bootz, Chandler, AZ*

PREP: 3 HOURS • GRILL: 15 MIN. • MAKES: 4 SERVINGS

- 4   lbs. pork baby back ribs
- 2   whole garlic bulbs
- 1   large navel orange, quartered
- 1   cup Korean barbecue sauce, divided
- ¾   cup rice vinegar
- ½   cup sugar
- ⅓   cup water
- ½   cup shredded carrots
- ½   cup shredded daikon radish
- ½   cup thinly sliced green onions
       Toppings: Thinly sliced cucumber, sliced fresh jalapeno pepper, cilantro leaves and lime wedges

1. Preheat oven to 325°. Place ribs in a large roasting pan. Remove papery outer skin from garlic bulbs, but do not peel or separate the cloves. Cut off top of garlic bulbs, exposing individual cloves; add to roasting pan. Add orange; cover pan with heavy-duty foil and seal tightly. Bake ribs until tender, 2-2½ hours, brushing with ½ cup Korean barbecue sauce halfway through cooking.

2. Meanwhile, in a small saucepan, combine vinegar, sugar and water. Bring mixture to a boil over high heat; cook until sugar is dissolved, about 2 minutes. Let cool completely. Place carrots, radish and green onions in a bowl; add brine. Refrigerate until serving.

3. Prepare grill for medium direct heat. Carefully remove ribs from roasting pan; discard garlic and orange. Place the ribs on grill rack; brush with some of the remaining ½ cup barbecue sauce. Grill, covered, over medium heat until browned, 15-20 minutes, turning and brushing occasionally with sauce. Cut into serving-sized portions. Serve with pickled vegetables, toppings and remaining sauce.

1 serving: 718 cal., 50g fat (16g sat. fat), 163mg chol., 1499mg sod., 23g carb. (17g sugars, 1g fiber), 45g pro.

BRATWURST & CHICKEN KABOBS

I made these lively chicken kabobs as a thank-you gift while visiting my relatives in Norway. They loved eating them almost as much as I loved cooking for them! If you prefer less heat in the chutney, you can use honey in place of pepper jelly. Also, any variety of vegetables will work with these.
—*Anna Davis, Springfield, MO*

PREP: 40 MIN. • **GRILL:** 10 MIN. • **MAKES:** 12 KABOBS

¼ cup balsamic vinegar
¼ cup cider vinegar
2 Tbsp. pepper jelly
2 Tbsp. stone-ground mustard
1 tsp. salt
½ tsp. pepper
½ cup olive oil, divided
1 can (15 oz.) peach halves in light syrup, drained and cut into ½-in. cubes
⅔ cup minced onion
1 jar (12 oz.) mango chutney
6 boneless skinless chicken breasts (6 oz. each)
1 pkg. (14 oz.) fully cooked bratwurst links
2 each medium green pepper, sweet red pepper and yellow pepper
1 large onion
3 Tbsp. brown sugar bourbon seasoning

1. Whisk together first 6 ingredients. Gradually whisk in ⅓ cup olive oil until blended. Add peaches, minced onion and chutney.

2. Cut chicken into 1-in. cubes and bratwursts into 1-in. slices. Cut the peppers into large squares and onion into cubes. Toss with brown sugar bourbon seasoning and remaining oil.

3. On 12 metal or soaked wooden skewers, alternately thread the meat and vegetables. Grill skewers, covered, on a greased grill rack over medium-high direct heat, turning occasionally, until chicken is no longer pink and vegetables are tender, 10-12 minutes. If desired, sprinkle with additional brown sugar bourbon seasoning during grilling. Serve with chutney sauce.

Note: We used McCormick brown sugar bourbon seasoning for this recipe.

1 kabob: 433 cal., 21g fat (5g sat. fat), 71mg chol., 249mg sod., 37g carb. (24g sugars, 2g fiber), 23g pro.

SAUSAGE & SWISS CHARD PASTA

I whipped up lunch with fresh produce from the farmers market, and the result was amazing.
—*Kate Stiltner, Grand Rapids, MI*

TAKES: 30 MIN. • **MAKES:** 6 SERVINGS

12 oz. uncooked orecchiette or small tube pasta (about 2½ cups)
1 Tbsp. olive oil
½ lb. bulk Italian sausage
½ cup chopped red onion
1 medium fennel bulb, chopped
½ lb. baby portobello mushrooms, chopped
3 garlic cloves, minced
1 bunch Swiss chard, trimmed and chopped
½ tsp. salt
¼ tsp. pepper
¾ cup grated Parmesan cheese, divided
½ cup pine nuts or chopped walnuts, toasted

1. Cook pasta according to the package directions for al dente. Meanwhile, in a large skillet, heat oil over medium heat. Cook sausage and red onion meat is until no longer pink, 3-4 minutes, breaking the sausage into crumbles. Add the fennel, mushrooms and garlic; cook until tender, 6-8 minutes. Add Swiss chard; cook and stir until wilted, 4-5 minutes longer.

2. Drain pasta, reserving 1 cup pasta water. In a large bowl, combine pasta, sausage mixture, salt, pepper and ½ cup Parmesan cheese, adding enough reserved pasta water to coat pasta and create a creamy texture. Serve with remaining cheese and pine nuts.

1⅓ cups: 487 cal., 25g fat (6g sat. fat), 34mg chol., 726mg sod., 51g carb. (5g sugars, 4g fiber), 19g pro.

TEST KITCHEN TIP

The pasta absorbs the cooking liquid quickly, so serve immediately for the best texture.

SAUSAGE &
SWISS CHARD PASTA

"
This pasta was absolutely delicious! Thanks for sharing the wonderful recipe.
—DONNA
TASTEOFHOME.COM

CAST-IRON SAUSAGE PEPPERONI PIZZA

Cast-iron skillets are the perfect vessel for a crisp, deep-dish pizza without needing any extra cookware. Our team developed this meaty pizza that is fabulous for any time of year.
—Taste of Home *Test Kitchen*

PREP: 30 MIN. + RISING • BAKE: 30 MIN. • MAKES: 8 SERVINGS

1   pkg. (¼ oz.) active dry yeast
½   cup warm water (110° to 115°)
½   cup butter, melted and cooled
3   large eggs, room temperature
¼   cup grated Parmesan cheese
1   tsp. salt
3   to 3½ cups bread flour
2   Tbsp. yellow cornmeal
½   lb. ground beef
½   lb. bulk Italian sausage
1   small onion, chopped
1   can (8 oz.) pizza sauce
1   jar (4½ oz.) sliced mushrooms, drained
1   pkg. (3 oz.) sliced pepperoni
½   lb. deli ham, cubed
½   cup chopped pitted green olives
1   can (4¼ oz.) chopped ripe olives, drained
1½ cups shredded part-skim mozzarella cheese
½   cup shredded Parmesan cheese
    Additional pizza sauce

1. In a small bowl, dissolve yeast in warm water. In a large bowl, combine butter, eggs, grated Parmesan, salt, yeast mixture and 2 cups flour; beat on medium speed until smooth. Stir in enough of the remaining flour to form a soft dough.

2. Turn dough onto a floured surface; knead 6-8 minutes or until smooth and elastic. Place in a greased bowl, turning once to grease the top. Cover and let rise in a warm place until doubled, about 1 hour.

3. Punch dough down; let rest for 5 minutes. Grease a 12-in. deep-dish cast-iron skillet or other ovenproof skillet; sprinkle with cornmeal. Press dough into pan; build up edge slightly.

4. Preheat oven to 400°. In a large skillet, cook beef, sausage and onion over medium heat until meat is no longer pink and onion is tender, 8-10 minutes, breaking meat into crumbles; drain. Spread pizza sauce over dough to within 1 in. of edge; sprinkle with meat mixture. Top with mushrooms, pepperoni, ham, olives, mozzarella and shredded Parmesan.

5. Bake until crust is golden brown and cheese is melted, 30-35 minutes. Serve with additional pizza sauce.

1 piece: 712 cal., 42g fat (19g sat. fat), 184mg chol., 1865mg sod., 48g carb. (3g sugars, 3g fiber), 36g pro.

ORANGE-GLAZED PORK WITH SWEET POTATOES

When it's chilly outside, I like to roast pork tenderloin with sweet potatoes, apples and an orange. The sweetness and spices make any evening cozy.
—*Danielle Lee Boyles, Weston, WI*

PREP: 20 MIN. • BAKE: 55 MIN. + STANDING • MAKES: 6 SERVINGS

1 lb. sweet potatoes (about 2 medium)
2 medium apples
1 medium orange
1 tsp. salt
½ tsp. pepper
1 cup orange juice
2 Tbsp. brown sugar
2 tsp. cornstarch
1 tsp. ground cinnamon
1 tsp. ground ginger
2 pork tenderloins (about 1 lb. each)

1. Preheat oven to 350°. Peel sweet potatoes; core apples. Cut potatoes, apples and orange crosswise into ¼-in.-thick slices. Arrange in a foil-lined 15x10x1-in. baking pan coated with cooking spray; sprinkle with salt and pepper. Roast 10 minutes.

2. Meanwhile, in a microwave-safe bowl, mix orange juice, brown sugar, cornstarch, cinnamon and ginger. Microwave, covered, on high, stirring every 30 seconds until thickened, 1-2 minutes. Stir until smooth.

3. Place pork over sweet potato mixture; drizzle with orange juice mixture. Roast until a thermometer inserted in pork reads 145° and sweet potatoes and apples are tender, 45-55 minutes longer. Remove from oven; tent with foil. Let stand 10 minutes before slicing.

4 oz. cooked pork with about 1 cup sweet potato mixture: 325 cal., 5g fat (2g sat. fat), 85mg chol., 467mg sod., 36g carb. (21g sugars, 3g fiber), 32g pro. **Diabetic exchanges:** 4 lean meat, 2 starch.

BRATWURST BURGERS WITH BRAISED ONIONS

This burger is a fun mashup of a bratwurst with onion and peppers, chicken-fried steak and a beef burger. The best of three dishes, bratwurst burgers are guaranteed to be family-pleasing.

—*Priscilla Yee, Concord, CA*

TAKES: 30 MIN. • **MAKES:** 4 SERVINGS

1 Tbsp. canola oil
1 large onion, sliced
1 medium sweet red pepper, sliced
1 medium sweet yellow pepper, sliced
1 cup dark beer or chicken broth

BURGERS
½ lb. ground beef
½ lb. uncooked bratwurst links, casings removed
1 large egg, lightly beaten
1 Tbsp. 2% milk
¾ cup seasoned bread crumbs
4 slices Muenster cheese
4 hamburger buns, split and toasted
8 tsp. spicy brown mustard

1. In a large skillet, heat the oil over medium heat. Add onion and peppers; cook and stir 5 minutes. Stir in beer. Bring to a boil. Reduce heat; simmer, uncovered, until the vegetables are tender and liquid is almost evaporated, 15-20 minutes. Remove from the heat and keep warm.

2. In a small bowl, combine the beef and bratwurst, mixing lightly but thoroughly. Shape into four ¾-in.-thick patties.

3. In a shallow bowl, mix egg and milk. Place bread crumbs in a separate shallow bowl. Dip patties in egg mixture, then roll in crumb mixture to coat.

4. In the same skillet over medium heat, cook burgers until a thermometer reads 160° for medium doneness and juices run clear, 3-4 minutes on each side; top with cheese during the last 1-2 minutes of cooking. Serve the burgers on buns with mustard and onion mixture.

1 burger: 659 cal., 36g fat (13g sat. fat), 145mg chol., 1409mg sod., 41g carb. (10g sugars, 3g fiber), 32g pro.

ASIAN PORK LINGUINE

Peanut butter, ginger and honey make an easy,
authentic-tasting sauce for noodles. If I have fresh ginger on hand,
I grate ¼ teaspoon to use in place of the ground ginger.
—Lisa Varner, El Paso, TX

TAKES: 30 MIN. • **MAKES:** 5 SERVINGS

- 6 oz. uncooked linguine
- 2 tsp. cornstarch
- ½ cup water
- ¼ cup reduced-fat creamy peanut butter
- 2 Tbsp. reduced-sodium soy sauce
- 1 Tbsp. honey
- ½ tsp. garlic powder
- ⅛ tsp. ground ginger
- 1 lb. boneless pork loin chops, cubed
- 3 tsp. sesame oil, divided
- 2 medium carrots, sliced
- 1 medium onion, halved and sliced

1. Cook linguine according to package directions. For sauce, in a small bowl, combine cornstarch and water until smooth. Whisk in the peanut butter, soy sauce, honey, garlic powder and ginger until blended; set aside.

2. In a large nonstick skillet or wok, stir-fry pork in 2 tsp. oil until no longer pink. Remove and keep warm. Stir-fry carrots and onion in remaining oil until crisp-tender. Stir the sauce and add to the pan. Bring to a boil; cook and stir until thickened, about 2 minutes.

3. Return pork to pan. Drain linguine; add to pan and stir to coat.

1 cup: 376 cal., 13g fat (3g sat fat), 44mg chol., 358mg sod., 39g carb. (9g sugars, 3g fiber), 27g pro. **Diabetic exchanges:** 3 lean meat, 2½ starch, 2 fat.

POTATO & PEPPER SAUSAGE BAKE

When my family smells this dish baking in the oven, they know they are in for a treat! If you like spice, add a pinch of red pepper flakes or switch the mild Italian sausage to hot Italian sausage.
—*Ashli Claytor, Chesapeake, VA*

PREP: 25 MIN. • **BAKE:** 30 MIN. • **MAKES:** 5 SERVINGS

- 5 large Yukon Gold potatoes, peeled and cut into 1-in. cubes
- 1 large sweet orange pepper, sliced
- 1 large sweet red pepper, sliced
- 1 shallot, chopped
- 4 garlic cloves, minced
- 1 Tbsp. olive oil
- 2 tsp. paprika
- ¾ tsp. salt
- ½ tsp. dried thyme
- ½ tsp. pepper
- 1 pkg. (19 oz.) Italian sausage links
   Minced fresh thyme, optional

1. Preheat oven to 400°. Place the potatoes, sweet peppers, shallot and garlic in a greased 15x10x1-in. baking pan. Drizzle with oil. Sprinkle with the seasonings; toss to coat. Spread evenly over pan, leaving room for the sausage. Add sausage to pan.

2. Bake, uncovered, until a thermometer inserted in sausage reads 160° and vegetables are tender, 30-35 minutes. If desired, sprinkle with minced fresh thyme before serving..

1 sausage link with ¾ cup vegetables: 446 cal., 26g fat (8g sat. fat), 58mg chol., 1021mg sod., 38g carb. (5g sugars, 4g fiber), 16g pro.

TEST KITCHEN TIP

Arrange the sausages directly on the surface of the pan instead of on top of the potatoes, so the potatoes cook evenly.

ITALIAN SAUSAGE LASAGNA ROLLS

It's the same great flavor of lasagna but in a fun and interesting shape. I often make a pan of these and pop them in the freezer for future dinners.
—*Hollie Lervold, Redding, CA*

PREP: 1 HOUR • BAKE: 45 MIN. • MAKES: 10 SERVINGS

1 Tbsp. olive oil
1 medium onion, finely chopped
2 garlic cloves, minced
1 can (28 oz.) crushed tomatoes, undrained
1 can (15 oz.) tomato sauce
1 can (6 oz.) tomato paste
1 tsp. each dried basil, marjoram, oregano, parsley flakes and thyme
½ tsp. pepper
¼ tsp. salt
1 can (2¼ oz.) sliced ripe olives, drained
10 uncooked lasagna noodles
1 pkg. (19 oz.) Italian sausage links
1 pkg. (6 oz.) fresh baby spinach
1 pkg. (8 oz.) cream cheese, softened
2 cups shredded part-skim mozzarella cheese

1. Preheat oven to 350°. In a large saucepan, heat oil over medium heat. Add onion; cook and stir 4-6 minutes or until tender. Add garlic; cook 1 minute longer. Stir in tomatoes, tomato sauce, tomato paste and seasonings; bring to a boil. Reduce heat; simmer, uncovered, 40 minutes. Stir in olives.

2. Meanwhile, cook lasagna noodles according to package directions for al dente. Cook sausages in a large skillet 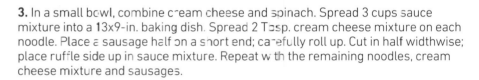 according to package directions; drain. Remove sausages and cut in half widthwise. In the same skillet, cook and stir spinach over medium-high heat 2-3 minutes or until wilted; drain spinach and squeeze dry.

3. In a small bowl, combine cream cheese and spinach. Spread 3 cups sauce mixture into a 13x9-in. baking dish. Spread 2 Tbsp. cream cheese mixture on each noodle. Place a sausage half on a short end; carefully roll up. Cut in half widthwise; place ruffle side up in sauce mixture. Repeat with the remaining noodles, cream cheese mixture and sausages.

4. Pour 1½ cups sauce mixture over rolls; sprinkle with mozzarella cheese. Bake, covered, 40 minutes. Bake, uncovered, 5-10 minutes longer or until the cheese is melted. Serve with remaining sauce mixture.

2 lasagna roll-ups: 504 cal., 32g fat (14g sat. fat) 78mg chol., 1090mg sod., 35g carb. (9g sugars, 4g fiber), 22g pro.

BARBECUE PORK
COBB SALAD

BARBECUE PORK COBB SALAD

My lunchtime salad gets way more interesting topped with barbecue pork,
cheddar cheese and creamy avocado. It's as satisfying as it is scrumptious.
—*Shawn Carleton, San Diego, CA*

PREP: 30 MIN. • COOK: 4 HOURS • MAKES: 6 SERVINGS

1¼ cups barbecue sauce
½ tsp. garlic powder
¼ tsp. paprika
1½ lbs. pork tenderloin
12 cups chopped romaine
3 plum tomatoes, chopped
2 avocados, peeled and chopped
2 small carrots, thinly sliced
1 medium sweet red or green pepper,
   chopped
3 hard-boiled large eggs, chopped
1½ cups shredded cheddar cheese
   Salad dressing of your choice

1. In a greased 3-qt. slow cooker, mix barbecue sauce, garlic powder and paprika. Add pork; turn to coat. Cook, covered, on low 4-5 hours or until pork is tender.

2. Remove pork from slow cooker; shred into bite-sized pieces. In a bowl, toss pork with 1 cup barbecue sauce mixture. Place romaine on a large serving platter; arrange pork, tomatoes, avocado, carrots, chopped pepper, eggs and cheese over romaine. Drizzle with dressing.

Freeze option: Place shredded pork in freezer containers. Cool and freeze. To use, partially thaw in refrigerator overnight. Heat through in a covered saucepan, stirring gently. Add broth or water if necessary. Continue with recipe as directed.

1 serving: 492 cal., 24g fat (9g sat. fat), 185mg chol., 868mg sod., 35g carb. (23g sugars, 7g fiber), 35g pro.

TEST KITCHEN TIP

Because this pork is just as delicious served cold, it can also be the centerpiece of a wonderful make-ahead lunch.

GERMAN BRAT SEAFOOD BOIL

Grilled bratwurst and onion add a smoky flavor to corn, potatoes and fish for a hearty meal that's always a hit.

—*Trisha Kruse, Eagle, ID*

PREP: 25 MIN. • **COOK:** 30 MIN. • **MAKES:** 6 SERVINGS

1 pkg. (19 oz.) uncooked bratwurst links
1 medium onion, quartered
2 bottles (12 oz. each) beer or 3 cups reduced-sodium chicken broth
½ cup seafood seasoning
5 medium ears sweet corn, cut into 2-in. pieces
2 lbs. small red potatoes
1 medium lemon, halved
1 lb. cod fillet, cut into 1-in. pieces
Coarsely ground pepper

1. Grill bratwurst, covered, over medium heat, turning frequently, until meat is no longer pink, 15-20 minutes. Grill the onion, covered, until lightly browned, 3-4 minutes on each side. Cut grilled bratwurst into 2-in. pieces.

2. In a stockpot, combine 2 qt. water, beer and seafood seasoning; add corn, potatoes, lemon, bratwurst and onion. Bring to a boil. Reduce heat; simmer, uncovered, until potatoes are tender, 15-20 minutes. Stir in the cod; cook for 4-6 minutes or until fish flakes easily with a fork. Drain; transfer to a large serving bowl. Sprinkle with pepper.

1 serving: 553 cal., 28g fat (9g sat. fat), 95mg chol., 1620mg sod., 46g carb. (8g sugars, 5g fiber), 30g pro.

TEST KITCHEN TIP

While half a cup of seafood seasoning may seem like a lot, keep in mind that the seasoning is ultimately dissolving into nearly 3 quarts of liquid.

SPICY PORK CHILI VERDE

My pork chili is brimming with poblano and sweet red peppers for a hearty kick.
Serve it with sour cream, Monterey Jack and tortilla chips.
—*Anthony Bolton, Bellevue, NE*

PREP: 40 MIN. + STANDING • **COOK:** 25 MIN. • **MAKES:** 6 SERVINGS

6 poblano peppers
2 Tbsp. butter
1½ lbs. pork tenderloin, cut into
   1-in. pieces
2 medium sweet red or yellow
   peppers, coarsely chopped
1 large sweet onion, coarsely chopped
1 jalapeno pepper, seeded and finely
   chopped
2 Tbsp. chili powder
2 garlic cloves, minced
1 tsp. salt
¼ tsp. ground nutmeg
2 cups chicken broth
   Optional toppings: Sour cream,
   shredded Monterey Jack cheese,
   crumbled tortilla chips and lime
   wedges

1. Place poblano peppers on a foil-lined baking sheet. Broil 4 in. from heat until skins blister, about 5 minutes. With tongs, rotate peppers a quarter turn. Broil and rotate until all sides are blistered and blackened. Immediately place peppers in a large bowl; let stand covered, 10 minutes

2. Peel off and discard charred skin. Remove and discard stems and seeds. Finely chop peppers

3. In a 6-qt. stockpot, heat butter over medium heat. Brown pork in batches. Remove with a slotted spoon.

4. In same pan, add red peppers, onion and jalapeno; cook, covered, over medium heat until tender, 8-10 minutes, stirring occasionally. Stir in chili powder, garlic, salt and nutmeg. Add broth, roasted peppers and pork; bring to a boil. Reduce heat; simmer, uncovered, until the pork is tender, 10-15 minutes. Serve with toppings as desired.

Note: Wear disposable gloves when cutting hot peppers; the oils can burn skin. Avoid touching your face.

1 cup: 235 cal., 9g fat (4g sat. fat), 75mg chol., 913mg sod., 14g carb. (8g sugars, 4g fiber), 25g pro.

AIR-FRYER LOADED PORK BURRITOS

Burritos, especially those in this quick and easy recipe, are the perfect dinner for the whole family. Keep the homemade salsa in mind for snacking, too!
—*Fiona Seels, Pittsburgh, PA*

PREP: 35 MIN. + MARINATING • **COOK:** 10 MIN./BATCH • **MAKES:** 6 SERVINGS

¾ cup thawed limeade concentrate
1 Tbsp. olive oil
2 tsp. salt, divided
1½ tsp. pepper, divided
1½ lbs. boneless pork loin, cut into thin strips
1 cup chopped seeded plum tomatoes
1 small green pepper, chopped
1 small onion, chopped
¼ cup plus ⅓ cup minced fresh cilantro, divided
1 jalapeno pepper, seeded and chopped
1 Tbsp. lime juice
¼ tsp. garlic powder
1 cup uncooked long grain rice
  Cooking spray
3 cups shredded Monterey Jack cheese
6 flour tortillas (12 in.), warmed
1 can (15 oz.) black beans, rinsed and drained
1½ cups sour cream

1. In a large shallow dish, combine the limeade concentrate, oil, 1 tsp. salt and ½ tsp. pepper; add pork. Turn to coat; cover and refrigerate at least 20 minutes.

2. For salsa, in a small bowl, combine the tomatoes, green pepper, onion, ¼ cup cilantro, jalapeno, lime juice, garlic powder, and remaining salt and pepper. Set salsa aside.

3. Meanwhile, cook rice according to package directions. Stir in remaining cilantro; keep warm.

4. Drain pork, discarding marinade. Preheat air fryer to 350°. In batches, place pork in a single layer on greased tray in air-fryer basket; spritz with cooking spray. Cook until pork is no longer pink, 8-10 minutes, turning halfway through.

5. Sprinkle ⅓ cup cheese off-center on each tortilla. Layer each with ¼ cup salsa, ½ cup rice mixture, ¼ cup black beans and ¼ cup sour cream; top with about ½ cup pork. Fold sides and ends over filling. Serve with remaining salsa.

1 burrito: 910 cal., 42g fat (22g sat. fat), 119mg chol., 1768mg sod., 82g carb. (11g sugars, 9g fiber), 50g pro.

TEST KITCHEN TIP

If you don't have an air fryer, it's easy to prepare the pork in a skillet on the stovetop.

AIR-FRYER LOADED
PORK BURRITOS

AIR-FRYER NACHO DOGS

Adults and kids alike will love these yummy Southwest-inspired hot dogs.
This is not only budget-friendly—it's also hot, cheesy and delicious
—*Joan Hallford, North Richland Hills, TX*

PREP: 25 MIN. • COOK: 10 MIN./BATCH • MAKES: 6 SERVINGS

6 hot dogs
3 cheddar cheese sticks, halved lengthwise
1¼ cups self-rising flour
1 cup plain Greek yogurt
¼ cup salsa
¼ tsp. chili powder
3 Tbsp. chopped seeded jalapeno pepper
1 cup crushed nacho-flavored tortilla chips, divided
Cooking spray
Optional: Guacamole, sour cream and additional salsa

1. Cut a slit down the length of each hot dog without cutting through; insert a halved cheese stick into the slit. Set hot dogs aside.

2. Preheat air fryer to 350°. In a large bowl, stir together flour, yogurt, salsa, chili powder, jalapenos and ¼ cup crushed tortilla chips to form a soft dough. Place dough on a lightly floured surface; divide into 6 pieces. Gently roll 1 piece of dough into a 15-in.-long strip and wrap it in a spiral around a cheese-stuffed hot dog. Repeat with remaining dough and hot dogs. Spray wrapped hot dogs with cooking spray and gently roll in remaining crushed chips. Spray air-fryer basket with cooking spray; place hot dogs in basket without touching, leaving room to expand.

3. In batches, cook until dough is slightly browned and cheese starts to melt, 8-10 minutes. If desired, serve with guacamole, sour cream and additional salsa.

1 nacho dog: 216 cal., 9g fat (5g sat. fat), 23mg chol., 513mg sod., 26g carb. (3g sugars, 1g fiber), 9g pro.

PRESSURE-COOKER MUSHROOM PORK RAGOUT

Savory, quickly made pork is luscious served in a delightful tomato gravy over noodles. It's a nice change from regular pork roast. I serve it with broccoli or green beans on the side.
—*Connie McDowell, Greenwood, DE*

PREP: 20 MIN. • COOK: 10 MIN. • MAKES: 2 SERVINGS

1 pork tenderloin (¾ lb.)
⅛ tsp. salt
⅛ tsp. pepper
1½ cups sliced fresh mushrooms
¾ cup canned crushed tomatoes
¾ cup reduced-sodium chicken broth, divided
⅓ cup sliced onion
1 Tbsp. chopped sun-dried tomatoes (not packed in oil)
1¼ tsp. dried savory
1 Tbsp. cornstarch
1½ cups hot cooked egg noodles

1. Rub pork with salt and pepper; cut in half. Place in a 6-qt. electric pressure cooker. Top with sliced mushrooms, tomatoes, ½ cup broth, the onion, sun-dried tomatoes and savory.

2. Lock lid and close pressure-release valve. Adjust to pressure-cook on high for 6 minutes. Quick-release pressure.

(A thermometer inserted in the pork should read at least 145°.) Remove pork; keep warm.

3. In a small bowl, mix cornstarch and remaining broth until smooth; stir into the pressure cooker. Select the saute setting and adjust for low heat. Simmer, stirring constantly, until thickened, 1-2 minutes. Serve pork with noodles.

5 oz. cooked pork with ¾ cup noodles: 387 cal., 8g fat (2g sat. fat), 119mg chol., 613mg sod., 37g carb. (8g sugars, 4g fiber), 43g pro. **Diabetic exchanges:** 5 lean meat, 2 vegetable, 1 starch.

COCONUT CITRUS
SAUCED COD, PAGE 197

CHAPTER 8

SEAFOOD & MEATLESS MAINS

When it's time to mix up your dinner routine, consider a fish, seafood or meatless option. Not only are the following recipes shared often by home cooks, they cook up quickly and always get requests for second helpings.

VEGETARIAN SKILLET LASAGNA

This flavorful weeknight vegetarian skillet lasagna is
sure to please any meat lover at your dinner table. Serve with
a mixed green salad to complement the meal.
—Taste of Home *Test Kitchen*

TAKES: 25 MIN. • **MAKES:** 4 SERVINGS

2   Tbsp. olive oil
2   medium zucchini, halved and sliced
½   lb. sliced fresh mushrooms
½   cup chopped onion
2   garlic cloves, minced
1   jar (24 oz.) tomato basil pasta sauce
½   cup water
¼   tsp. salt
¼   tsp. pepper
¼   tsp. crushed red pepper flakes
6   no-cook lasagna noodles, broken
½   cup shredded mozzarella cheese
     Optional: Grated Parmesan cheese
     and chopped fresh basil leaves

Heat olive oil in large cast-iron or other
ovenproof skillet over medium-high
heat. Add zucchini and mushrooms;
cook until softened, 2-3 minutes. Add
onion and garlic; cook until vegetables
are tender, 2-3 minutes. Add pasta
sauce, water and seasonings. Stir
to combine; add the broken noodles.
Bring to a boil. Reduce heat; cover and
simmer until noodles are tender, about
15 minutes. Top with mozzarella and, if
desired, Parmesan cheese. Broil until
cheese melts and starts to brown. If
desired, sprinkle with basil.

1½ cups: 355 cal., 14g fat (3g sat. fat),
11mg chol., 955mg sod., 46g carb. (18g
sugars, 7g fiber), 13g pro.

TEST KITCHEN TIP

*Vegetarian skillet lasagna lasts 3-5 days in the fridge. If you want to
enjoy this entree longer, you can freeze the lasagna for 2-3 months.*

SHEET-PAN NEW ENGLAND CLAMBAKE

This recipe transports you to hot summer nights on the beach enjoying fresh seafood, corn on the cob, spicy sausage and potatoes any time of the year! Bathed in garlicky, spicy butter, this one-pan wonder is beautiful, delicious and easy on cleanup. You could mix up the seafood and add pieces of salmon or haddock, use other quick-cooking veggies like cherry tomatoes or asparagus, or substitute kielbasa for the chorizo. It's so versatile!

—Pamela Gelsomini, Wrentham, MA

PREP: 25 MIN. • BAKE: 45 MIN. • MAKES: 6 SERVINGS

1 lb. assorted baby potatoes
2 Tbsp. olive oil
2 tsp. Italian seasoning
6 half-ears frozen corn on the cob, thawed
2 lbs. fresh mussels, scrubbed and beards removed
1½ dozen fresh littleneck clams, scrubbed
1 lb. uncooked shrimp (26-30 per lb.), peeled and deveined
½ lb. fully cooked Spanish chorizo links, cut into ½-in. pieces
¼ cup dry white wine or chicken broth
1 medium lemon, cut into wedges
½ cup butter, melted
4 garlic cloves, chopped
2 tsp. seafood seasoning
1¼ tsp. Cajun seasoning
¼ tsp. pepper
2 Tbsp. minced fresh parsley
French bread, optional

1. Preheat oven to 400°. Place potatoes in a 15x10x1-in. baking pan. Drizzle with oil and sprinkle with Italian seasoning; toss to coat. Bake 25-30 minutes or until tender. Using a potato masher, flatten potatoes to ½-in. thickness; remove and keep warm.

2. Add corn, mussels, clams, shrimp and chorizo to same pan; top with potatoes. Pour wine into pan. Squeeze lemon wedges over top; add to pan.

3. Combine butter, garlic, seafood seasoning and Cajun seasoning. Pour half the butter mixture over top. Bake until shrimp turn pink and mussels and clams open, 20-25 minutes. Discard any unopened mussels or clams.

4. Drizzle with remaining butter mixture. Sprinkle with pepper; top with parsley. If desired, serve with bread.

1 serving: 639 cal., 35g fat (15g sat fat), 214mg chol., 1302mg sod., 37g carb. (4g sugars, 3g fiber), 46g pro.

Enjoy Clambakes All Year Long

Her easy, impressive sheet-pan dinner is always a hit.

What prompted you to try this classic on a sheet pan?
One of our favorite summertime activities is having a traditional clambake over an open fire. This recipe takes us back to those warm nights during our cold winters.

What's your advice for cooking seafood?
The key? Don't overcook it. Clams and mussels are done as soon as the shells open, shrimp is done once it's pink, and fish is done when it flakes easily in the center with a fork.

Pamela Gelsomini,
Wrentham, MA

PRESSURE-COOKER
STUFFED PEPPERS

PRESSURE-COOKER STUFFED PEPPERS

Here's a good-for-you dinner that's also a meal-in-one classic.
Add a salad and, in just moments, call everyone to the table.
—Michelle Gurnsey, Lincoln, NE

PREP: 15 MIN. • COOK: 5 MIN. + RELEASING • MAKES: 4 SERVINGS

4 medium sweet red peppers
1 can (15 oz.) black beans, rinsed and drained
1 cup shredded pepper jack cheese
¾ cup salsa
1 small onion, chopped
½ cup frozen corn
⅓ cup uncooked converted long grain rice
1¼ tsp. chili powder
½ tsp. ground cumin
Reduced-fat sour cream, optional

1. Place trivet insert and 1 cup water in a 6-qt. electric pressure cooker.

2. Cut and discard tops from peppers; remove seeds. In a large bowl, mix beans, cheese, salsa, onion, corn, rice, chili powder and cumin; spoon into peppers. Set peppers on trivet.

3. Lock lid; close pressure-release valve. Adjust to pressure-cook on high for 5 minutes. Let pressure release naturally. If desired, serve with sour cream.

1 stuffed pepper: 333 cal., 10g fat (5g sat. fat), 30mg chol., 582mg sod., 45g carb. (8g sugars, 8g fiber), 15g pro. **Diabetic exchanges:** 2 starch, 2 vegetable, 2 lean meat, 1 fat.

COCONUT CITRUS SAUCED COD

SHOWN ON PAGE 190

I love to make this fusion meal on weeknights when am short on time but want something big in flavor.
—Roxanne Chan, Albany, CA

TAKES: 30 MIN. • MAKES: 4 SERVINGS

4 cod fillets (6 oz. each)
1 Tbsp. cornstarch
1 cup canned coconut milk
½ cup orange juice
2 Tbsp. sweet chili sauce
1 tsp. minced fresh gingerroot
1 tsp. soy sauce
1 can (11 oz.) mandarin oranges, drained
1 green onion, chopped
2 Tbsp. sliced almonds
1 Tbsp. sesame oil
Minced fresh cilantro

In a large saucepan, place a steamer basket over 1 in. water. Place cod in basket. Bring water to a boil. Reduce heat to maintain a low boil; steam, covered, until the fish just begins to flake easily with a fork, 8-10 minutes. Meanwhile, in a small saucepan, whisk cornstarch, coconut milk and orange juice until smooth. Add chili sauce, ginger and soy sauce. Cook and stir over medium heat until thickened, 1-2 minutes. Stir in oranges, green onion, almonds and sesame oil; heat through. Serve with cod; sprinkle with cilantro.

1 serving: 330 cal., 15g fat (10g sat. fat), 65mg chol., 316mg sod., 19g carb. (15g sugars, 1g fiber), 29g pro.

SHEET-PAN TILAPIA & VEGETABLE MEDLEY

Unlike some one-pan dinners that require precooking in
a skillet or pot, this one cooks on just the sheet pan.

—Judy Batson, Tampa, FL

PREP: 20 MIN. • **BAKE:** 20 MIN. • **MAKES:** 2 SERVINGS

2 medium Yukon Gold potatoes, cut into wedges
3 large fresh Brussels sprouts, thinly sliced
3 large radishes, thinly sliced
1 cup fresh sugar snap peas, cut into ½-in. pieces
1 small carrot, thinly sliced
2 Tbsp. butter, melted
½ tsp. garlic salt
½ tsp. pepper
2 tilapia fillets (6 oz. each)
2 tsp. minced fresh tarragon or ½ tsp. dried tarragon
⅛ tsp. salt
1 Tbsp. butter, softened
Optional: Lemon wedges and tartar sauce

1. Preheat oven to 450°. Line a 15x10x1-in. baking pan with foil; grease foil.

2. In a large bowl, combine the first 5 ingredients. Add melted butter, garlic salt and pepper; toss to coat. Place the vegetables in a single layer in prepared pan; bake until potatoes are tender, about 20 minutes.

3. Remove from oven; preheat broiler. Arrange vegetables on 1 side of sheet pan. Add fish to other side. Sprinkle fillets with tarragon and salt; dot with softened butter. Broil 4-5 in. from heat until fish flakes easily with a fork, about 5 minutes. If desired, serve with lemon wedges and tartar sauce.

1 serving: 555 cal., 20g fat (12g sat. fat), 129mg chol., 892mg sod., 56g carb. (8g sugars, 8g fiber), 41g pro.

TEST KITCHEN TIP

A quick roast softens radishes nicely and helps mellow out the sharp flavor some older radishes may have.

CREAMY PASTA PRIMAVERA

This pasta dish is a wonderful blend of crisp, colorful vegetables and a creamy Parmesan cheese sauce.

—*Darlene Brenden, Salem, OR*

TAKES: 30 MIN. • MAKES: 6 SERVINGS

- 2 cups uncooked gemelli or spiral pasta
- 1 lb. fresh asparagus, trimmed and cut into 2-in. pieces
- 3 medium carrots, shredded
- 2 tsp. canola oil
- 2 cups cherry tomatoes, halved
- 1 garlic clove, minced
- ½ cup grated Parmesan cheese
- ½ cup heavy whipping cream
- ¼ tsp. pepper

1. Cook pasta according to package directions. In a large skillet over medium-high heat, saute asparagus and carrots in oil until crisp-tender. Add the tomatoes and garlic; cook 1 minute longer.

2. Stir in the cheese, cream and pepper. Drain the pasta; gently toss with the asparagus mixture.

1⅓ cups: 275 cal., 12g fat (6g sat. fat), 33mg chol., 141mg sod., 35g carb. (5g sugars, 3g fiber), 10g pro. **Diabetic exchanges:** 2 starch, 2 fat, 1 vegetable.

TEST KITCHEN TIP

Using a small amount of a rich ingredient, like heavy cream, is a smart way keep a dish tasting indulgent while cutting calories.

PRESSURE-COOKER PAPRIKA SHRIMP & RICE

My family loves seafood, as well as rice dishes, so this was a clear winner with them! You can set your oven at its lowest temperature and use it to keep the cooked vegetables and shrimp warm, without overcooking them, as your pressure cooker cooks the rice. If serving on individual plates instead of one big platter or bowl, accompany each serving with a small sprig of basil and a lemon wedge or two for squeezing.
—*Joyce Conway, Westerville, OH*

PREP: 30 MIN. • COOK: 10 MIN. + RELEASING • MAKES: 4 SERVINGS

5 Tbsp. canola oil, divided
1 large sweet onion, chopped
1 cup chopped sweet pepper, such as yellow, orange or red
¾ lb. uncooked shrimp (16-20 per lb.), peeled and deveined
1 tsp. granulated garlic
1 tsp. paprika
½ tsp. crushed red pepper flakes
1½ cups chicken broth
1 pkg. (10 oz.) uncooked saffron rice
1 cup canned petite diced tomatoes
2 Tbsp. chopped fresh basil
  Lemon wedges

1. Select saute setting on a 6-qt. electric pressure cooker. Adjust for medium heat; add 2 Tbsp. oil. When the oil is hot, add the onion and pepper; cook and stir until crisp-tender, 4-5 minutes. Remove and keep warm.

2. Toss shrimp with granulated garlic, paprika and pepper flakes. Add remaining 3 Tbsp. oil to pan. When oil is hot, add shrimp. Cook and stir until shrimp turn pink, 5-6 minutes. Remove and keep warm. Add broth to the pressure cooker. Cook 30 seconds, stirring to loosen browned bits from pan. Press cancel. Stir in rice.

3. Lock lid; close pressure-release valve. Adjust to pressure-cook on high for 8 minutes. Allow pressure to release naturally for 10 minutes, then quick-release any remaining pressure. Stir in tomatoes, shrimp and reserved pepper mixture; heat through. Top with basil; serve with lemon wedges.

1½ cups: 525 cal., 19g fat (2g sat. fat), 103mg chol., 1455mg sod., 68g carb. (9g sugars, 3g fiber), 22g pro.

PEELING SHRIMP
Try removing shrimp legs and shell at once by starting where the head was, pulling the shell off down the back ridge of the shrimp.

PRESSURE-COOKER
PAPRIKA SHRIMP &
RICE

JACKFRUIT TACOS WITH GREEN APPLE SALSA

These easy jackfruit tacos are flavored with taco seasoning
and topped with fresh green apple salsa.

—*Henrie Marie, Marlboro, NY*

PREP: 25 MIN. • **COOK:** 10 MIN. • **MAKES:** 2 SERVINGS

3 Tbsp. olive oil, divided
1 can (20 oz.) jackfruit, rinsed, drained
   and chopped
1 envelope reduced-sodium taco
   seasoning

GREEN APPLE SALSA

½ medium ripe avocado, peeled and
   cubed
½ cup chopped baby cucumber
½ cup chopped green apple
¼ cup chopped green pepper
2 Tbsp. thinly sliced green onions
½ jalapeno pepper, seeded and minced
4 tsp. lime juice
1 Tbsp. chopped fresh cilantro
¼ tsp. sea salt

SOUR CREAM SAUCE

¼ cup sour cream
2 Tbsp. 2% milk
6 flour tortillas (6 in.), warmed
   Lime wedges, optional

1. In a large skillet, heat 2 Tbsp. oil over medium-high heat. Add the jackfruit; cook and stir for 8-10 minutes or until caramelized. Stir in taco seasoning and remaining 1 Tbsp. oil; mix well. Remove from heat; keep warm.

2. In a small bowl, mix all green salsa ingredients. For sour cream sauce, whisk together sour cream and milk until smooth. Serve jackfruit in tortillas with salsa, sour cream sauce and, if desired, lime wedges.

3 tacos: 748 cal., 39g fat (10g sat. fat), 22mg chol., 3603mg sod., 88g carb. (15g sugars, 19g fiber), 15g pro.

TEST KITCHEN TIP

Make these tacos vegan by omitting the dairy sour cream sauce or substituting vegan sour cream mixed with plant-based milk.

PORTOBELLO & CHICKPEA SHEET-PAN SUPPER

This is a fantastic meatless dinner or an amazing side dish. It works well with a variety of sheet-pan-roasted vegetables. We enjoy using zucchini or summer squash in the summer, and you can also change up the herbs in the dressing.
—*Elisabeth Larsen, Pleasant Grove, UT*

PREP: 15 MIN. • BAKE: 35 MIN. • MAKES: 4 SERVINGS

¼ cup olive oil
2 Tbsp. balsamic vinegar
1 Tbsp. minced fresh oregano
¾ tsp. garlic powder
½ tsp. salt
¼ tsp. pepper
1 can (15 oz.) chickpeas or garbanzo beans, rinsed and drained
4 large portobello mushrooms (4 to 4½ in.), stems removed
1 lb. fresh asparagus, trimmed and cut into 2-in. pieces
8 oz. cherry tomatoes

1. Preheat oven to 400°. In a small bowl, combine the first 6 ingredients. Toss chickpeas with 2 Tbsp. oil mixture. Transfer to a 15x10x1-in. baking pan. Bake 20 minutes.

2. Brush mushrooms with 1 Tbsp. oil mixture; add to pan. Toss asparagus and tomatoes with the remaining oil mixture; arrange around mushrooms. Bake until vegetables are tender, 15-20 minutes longer.

1 mushroom with 1 cup vegetables: 279 cal., 16g fat (2g sat. fat), 0 chol., 448mg sod., 28g carb. (8g sugars, 7g fiber), 8g pro. **Diabetic exchanges:** 3 fat, 2 starch.

SHRIMP WITH TOMATOES & FETA

Any recipe that is special enough for company but easy enough for a weeknight meal is a favorite in my book. All you need to finish off the meal is a side salad and crusty French bread to sop up the delicious tomato and wine juices.
—*Susan Seymour, Valatie, NY*

TAKES: 30 MIN. • MAKES: 6 SERVINGS

3 Tbsp. olive oil
2 shallots, finely chopped
2 garlic cloves, minced
6 plum tomatoes, chopped
½ cup white wine or chicken broth
1 Tbsp. dried oregano
½ tsp. salt
½ tsp. crushed red pepper flakes
¼ tsp. sweet paprika
2 lbs. uncooked large shrimp, peeled and deveined
⅔ cup crumbled feta cheese
2 tsp. minced fresh mint
    Hot cooked rice

1. In a large skillet, heat oil over medium-high heat. Add shallots and garlic; cook and stir until tender. Add tomatoes, wine, oregano, salt, pepper flakes and paprika; bring to a boil. Reduce heat; simmer, uncovered, 5 minutes.

2. Stir in shrimp and cheese; cook 5-6 minutes or until shrimp turn pink. Stir in mint. Serve with rice.

1 cup: 261 cal., 11g fat (3g sat. fat), 191mg chol., 502mg sod., 8g carb. (2g sugars, 2g fiber), 28g pro. **Diabetic exchanges:** 4 lean meat, 1 vegetable, 1 fat.

POLISH PORTOBELLO
REUBEN BURGERS

POLISH PORTOBELLO REUBEN BURGERS

These mushroom burgers are a hit every time I serve them. They are filling but not heavy.
The sauerkraut, garlic cloves and onions can be made ahead to cut down on prep time.
—*Lisa Benoit, Cookeville, TN*

PREP: 1 HOUR • BAKE: 15 MIN. • MAKES: 8 SERVINGS

5 unpeeled garlic cloves
½ tsp. plus 3 Tbsp. olive oil, divided
½ cup thinly sliced sweet onion
1 can (8 oz.) sauerkraut, rinsed and well drained
3 cups coleslaw mix
½ cup sweetened applesauce
8 large portobello mushrooms, stems removed
1 tsp. dried marjoram
1 tsp. garlic powder
8 slices Swiss cheese
8 hamburger buns, split and toasted
1 cup Thousand Island salad dressing

1. Preheat oven to 375°. Cut stem ends off unpeeled garlic cloves. Place cloves on a piece of foil. Drizzle with ½ tsp. oil; wrap in foil. Bake 20-25 minutes or until cloves are soft. Unwrap and cool to room temperature.

2. Meanwhile, in a large skillet, heat 1 Tbsp. oil over medium heat. Add onion; cook and stir until softened, 4-6 minutes. Reduce heat to medium-low; cook until deep golden brown, 30-40 minutes, stirring occasionally. Squeeze roasted garlic from skins; mash with a fork. Add to the onions. Stir in sauerkraut, coleslaw mix and applesauce. Cook and stir over medium heat until coleslaw begins to soften, about 5 minutes. Remove from the heat.

3. Place mushrooms on a baking sheet. Brush with remaining 2 Tbsp. oil. Combine seasonings; rub over mushrooms. Bake until tender, 10-15 minutes, turning once. Top with Swiss cheese; bake until cheese is melted, 2-3 minutes longer.

4. Serve mushrooms in buns with sauerkraut mixture and dressing.

1 burger: 396 cal., 22g fat (5g sat. fat), 13mg chol., 708mg sod., 38g carb. (13g sugars, 4g fiber), 10g pro.

AIR-FRYER CRUMB-TOPPED SOLE

Looking for a low-carb supper that's ready in a flash? These buttery sole fillets are covered with a rich sauce and topped with toasty bread crumbs. They're super speedy thanks to your air fryer.
—Taste of Home *Test Kitchen*

PREP: 10 MIN. • **COOK:** 10 MIN./BATCH • **MAKES:** 4 SERVINGS

3 Tbsp. reduced-fat mayonnaise
3 Tbsp. grated Parmesan cheese, divided
2 tsp. mustard seed
¼ tsp. pepper
4 sole fillets (6 oz. each)
1 cup soft bread crumbs
1 green onion, finely chopped
½ tsp. ground mustard
2 tsp. butter, melted
   Cooking spray

1. Preheat air fryer to 375°. Combine mayonnaise, 2 Tbsp. cheese, mustard seed and pepper; spread over the tops of the fillets.

2. In batches, place fish in a single layer on greased tray in air-fryer basket. Cook until fish flakes easily with a fork, 3-5 minutes.

3. Meanwhile, in a small bowl, combine bread crumbs, onion, ground mustard and remaining 1 Tbsp. cheese; stir in butter. Spoon over fillets, patting gently to adhere; spritz topping with cooking spray. Cook until golden brown, 2-3 minutes longer. If desired, sprinkle with additional green onions.

1 fillet: 233 cal., 11g fat (3g sat. fat), 89mg chol., 714mg sod., 8g carb. (1g sugars, 1g fiber), 24g pro.

TEST KITCHEN TIP

If you don't have an air fryer, you can make this recipe in an oven. Bake at 375° until fish flakes easily with a fork.

CHEESE MANICOTTI

This is the first meal I ever cooked for my husband,
and all these years later he still enjoys my manicotti!
—*Joan Hallford, North Richland Hills, TX*

PREP: 25 MIN. • BAKE: 1 HOUR • MAKES: 7 SERVINGS

1 carton (15 oz.) reduced-fat ricotta
  cheese
1 small onion, finely chopped
1 large egg, lightly beaten
2 Tbsp. minced fresh parsley
½ tsp. pepper
¼ tsp. salt
1 cup shredded part-skim mozzarella
  cheese, divided
1 cup grated Parmesan cheese,
  divided
4 cups marinara sauce
½ cup water
1 pkg. (8 oz.) manicotti shells
  Additional parsley, optional

1. Preheat oven to 350°. In a small bowl, mix the first 6 ingredients; stir in ½ cup mozzarella cheese and ½ cup Parmesan cheese. In another bowl, mix marinara sauce and water; spread ¾ cup sauce onto bottom of a 13x9-in. baking dish coated with cooking spray. Fill uncooked manicotti shells with ricotta mixture; arrange over sauce. Top with remaining sauce.

2. Bake, covered, 50 minutes or until pasta is tender. Sprinkle with remaining ½ cup mozzarella cheese and ½ cup Parmesan cheese. Bake, uncovered, 10-15 minutes longer or until cheese is melted. If desired, top with additional parsley.

2 stuffed manicotti: 361 cal., 13g fat (6g sat. fat), 64mg chol., 1124mg sod., 41g carb. (12g sugars, 4g fiber), 19g pro. **Diabetic exchanges:** 3 starch, 2 lean meat, ½ fat.

TEST KITCHEN TIP

This recipe can be assembled and refrigerated for up to 3 days; just remove from the fridge 30 minutes before baking as directed. The manicotti can also be assembled and frozen for up to 2 months. To use, partially thaw in the refrigerator overnight. Remove from the fridge 30 minutes before baking. Bake as directed, increasing the time as needed until a thermometer inserted in the center reads 165°.

BAKED FETA PASTA

There's a reason this recipe went viral on TikTok! Baked Feta Pasta is about to become a new household favorite in your home, too. It's simple to throw together and incredibly creamy and delicious.
—*Sarah Tramonte,* Taste of Home *Culinary Producer*

PREP: 15 MIN. • BAKE: 30 MIN. • MAKES: 8 SERVINGS

2 pints cherry tomatoes
3 garlic cloves, halved
½ cup olive oil
1 pkg. (8 oz.) block feta cheese
1 tsp. sea salt
¼ tsp. coarsely ground pepper
1 pkg. (16 oz.) rigatoni or other short pasta
Fresh basil leaves, coarsely chopped

1. Preheat oven to 400°. In a 13x9-in. baking dish, combine tomatoes, garlic and ¼ cup olive oil. Place the block of feta in the center, moving tomatoes so cheese is sitting on the pan bottom. Drizzle feta with remaining oil and sprinkle with salt and pepper. Bake 30-40 minutes or until tomato skins start to split and the garlic has softened.

2. Meanwhile, cook pasta according to package directions for al dente. Drain, reserving 1 cup pasta water.

3. Stir feta mixture, lightly pressing tomatoes, until combined. Add pasta and toss to combine. Stir in enough reserved pasta water to reach desired consistency. Sprinkle with basil.

1 serving: 373 cal., 16g fat (6g sat. fat), 25mg chol., 507mg sod., 46g carb. (5g sugars, 3g fiber), 12g pro.

CURRIED TOFU WITH RICE

Go meatless and give tofu a try in this bold dish. It's packed with curry and cilantro, too, so you won't even miss the meat.
—*Crystal Jo Bruns, Iliff, CO*

PREP: 15 MIN. • COOK: 20 MIN. • MAKES: 4 SERVINGS

1 pkg. (12.3 oz.) extra-firm tofu, drained and cubed
1 tsp. seasoned salt
1 Tbsp. canola oil
1 small onion, chopped
3 garlic cloves, minced
½ cup light coconut milk
¼ cup minced fresh cilantro
1 tsp. curry powder
¼ tsp. salt
¼ tsp. pepper
2 cups cooked brown rice

1. Sprinkle tofu with seasoned salt. In a large nonstick skillet, saute tofu in oil until lightly browned. Remove and keep warm.

2. In the same skillet, saute onion and garlic for 1-2 minutes or until crisp-tender. Stir in the coconut milk, cilantro, curry, salt and pepper. Bring to a boil. Reduce heat; simmer, uncovered, for 4-5 minutes or until sauce is slightly thickened. Stir in tofu; heat through. Serve with rice.

½ cup curry with ½ cup rice: 240 cal., 11g fat (3g sat. fat), 0 chol., 540mg sod., 27g carb. (2g sugars, 3g fiber), 10g pro. **Diabetic exchanges:** 1½ starch, 1 medium-fat meat, 1 fat.

BAKED
FETA PASTA

SHEET-PAN SALMON WITH SIMPLE BREAD SALAD

The fatty acids in salmon make it extremely healthy and ideal for baking. The vibrant salad, made on the same sheet pan, complements the rich fish perfectly.

—*Laura Wilhelm, West Hollywood, CA*

PREP: 20 MIN. • **BAKE:** 30 MIN. • **MAKES:** 6 SERVINGS

3 cups cubed sourdough bread
1 pint cherry tomatoes
1 medium red onion, cut into wedges
½ cup pitted Greek olives
3 Tbsp. olive oil, divided
1½ tsp. sea salt, divided
⅛ tsp. pepper
6 salmon fillets (6 oz. each)
1 tsp. paprika

DRESSING

2 Tbsp. red wine vinegar
1 Tbsp. olive oil
⅓ cup fresh Italian parsley leaves, coarsely chopped
1 Tbsp. capers, drained

1. Preheat oven to 375°. Place cubed bread, tomatoes, red onion and olives on a 15x10x1-in. pan. Drizzle with 2 Tbsp. oil and sprinkle with ½ tsp. salt and the pepper; toss to coat. Bake for 15-20 minutes or until bread cubes just begin to brown.

2. Arrange salmon fillets over crouton mixture in pan. Drizzle with remaining 1 Tbsp. oil; sprinkle with paprika and remaining 1 tsp. salt. Bake until salmon just begins to flake easily with a fork, 12-15 minutes.

3. For dressing, in a small bowl, whisk vinegar and oil. Add parsley and capers. Drizzle over salmon; sprinkle with additional parsley if desired.

1 salmon fillet with 1 cup bread salad: 442 cal., 28g fat (5g sat. fat), 85mg chol., 875mg sod., 14g carb. (3g sugars, 2g fiber), 31g pro.

COD WITH HEARTY TOMATO SAUCE

My father made up this sweet, flavorful recipe for my mother when he took over the cooking.
—Ann Marie Eberhart, Gig Harbor, WA

TAKES: 30 MIN. • MAKES: 4 SERVINGS

2 cans (14½ oz. each) diced tomatoes with basil, oregano and garlic, undrained
4 cod fillets (6 oz. each)
2 Tbsp. olive oil, divided
2 medium onions, halved and thinly sliced (about 1½ cups)
½ tsp. dried oregano
¼ tsp. pepper
¼ tsp. crushed red pepper flakes
Hot cooked whole wheat pasta
Minced fresh parsley, optional

1. Place tomatoes in a blender. Cover and process until pureed.

2. Pat fish dry with paper towels. In a large skillet, heat 1 Tbsp. oil over medium-high heat. Add cod fillets; cook until surface of fish begins to color, 2-4 minutes on each side. Remove from pan.

3. In same skillet, heat remaining oil over medium-high heat. Add onions; cook and stir until tender, 2-4 minutes. Stir in seasonings and pureed tomatoes; bring to a boil. Add cod; return just to a boil, spooning sauce over tops. Reduce heat; simmer, uncovered, 5-7 minutes or until fish just begins to flake easily with a fork. Serve with pasta. If desired, sprinkle with parsley.

1 fillet with ¾ cup sauce: 271 cal., 8g fat (1g sat. fat), 65mg chol., 746mg sod., 17g carb. (9g sugars, 4g fiber), 29g pro. **Diabetic exchanges:** 3 lean meat, 2 vegetable, 1½ fat.

ROASTED PUMPKIN
LASAGNA

"
I made this for
my pumpkin-
loving daughter
and her friends.
An excellent
recipe. Thank
you for sharing.
—JOANN740
TASTEOFHOME.COM

ROASTED PUMPKIN LASAGNA

This is a hearty meatless meal that my family enjoys.
If you prefer butternut squash, it can be used instead of pumpkin.
—*Wendy Masters, East Garafraxa, ON*

PREP: 1 HOUR. • BAKE: 1 HOUR + STANDING • MAKES: 12 SERVINGS

1 medium pie pumpkin (about 3 lbs.)
2 Tbsp. olive oil
1 tsp. salt, divided
¼ tsp. ground nutmeg
12 uncooked lasagna noodles
½ cup butter, cubed
1 cup chopped onion
3 garlic cloves, minced
½ cup all-purpose flour
4½ cups 2% milk
¼ cup chopped fresh sage
½ cup grated Parmesan cheese
2 cups shredded mozzarella cheese
Crushed red pepper flakes, optional

1. Preheat oven to 400°. Peel pumpkin; cut in half lengthwise; discard seeds or save for toasting. Cut into ¼-in. thick slices. Place in a single layer on 2 greased 15x10x1-in. baking pans. Drizzle with oil; sprinkle with ¼ tsp. salt and nutmeg. Roast until tender, 30-35 minutes. Reduce oven temperature to 350°.

2. Meanwhile, cook lasagna noodles according to package directions for al dente. In a large saucepan, melt butter over medium heat. Add onion; cook and stir until tender, 6-7 minutes. Add garlic; cook 1 minute longer. Stir in flour and remaining ¾ tsp. salt until smooth; gradually whisk in milk and sage. Bring to a boil, stirring constantly; cook and stir until thickened, 8-10 minutes. Remove from heat; stir in Parmesan cheese. Drain noodles.

3. Place 3 noodles in a greased 13x9-in. baking dish. Layer with one-third of the pumpkin, 1⅓ cups sauce and ½ cup mozzarella cheese. Repeat layers twice. Top with remaining noodles, sauce and mozzarella cheese.

4. Bake, covered, 30 minutes. Uncover and bake until golden brown and bubbly, 30-35 minutes longer. Let stand 10-15 minutes before serving. If desired, sprinkle with red pepper flakes.

1 piece: 350 cal., 17g fat (9g sat. fat), 45mg chol., 431mg sod., 37g carb. (8g sugars, 2g fiber), 13g pro.

WEEKNIGHT SKILLET SPINACH PIE

I love sneaking extra veggies into my kids' dinners. Because of this pie's flaky crust and extra cheese, the kids never know they're eating a vitamin-rich dish. Plus, I'm not hovering over an oven for hours. Put the spinach and phyllo sheets in the refrigerator the night before or early in the morning for thawing.

—*Kristyne McDougle Walter, Lorain, OH*

PREP: 35 MIN. • **BAKE:** 35 MIN. + COOLING • **MAKES:** 8 SERVINGS

2   large eggs, room temperature, lightly beaten
3   pkg. (10 oz. each) frozen chopped spinach, thawed and squeezed dry
2   cups (8 oz.) crumbled feta cheese
1½ cups shredded part-skim mozzarella cheese
¼   cup chopped walnuts, toasted
1½ tsp. dried oregano
1½ tsp. dill weed
½   tsp. pepper
¼   tsp. salt
¼   cup julienned soft sun-dried tomatoes (not packed in oil), optional
⅓   cup canola oil
12 sheets phyllo dough (14x9-in. size)

1. Preheat oven to 375°. In a large bowl, combine the eggs, spinach, cheeses, walnuts, seasonings and, if desired, tomatoes; set aside. Brush a 10-in. cast-iron or other ovenproof skillet with some of the oil; set aside.

2. Unroll phyllo dough. Place 1 sheet of phyllo dough on a work surface; brush with oil. (Keep remaining phyllo covered with a damp towel to prevent it from drying out.) Place in prepared skillet, letting edges of phyllo hang over sides. Repeat with an additional 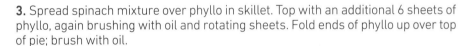 5 sheets of phyllo, again brushing with oil and rotating sheets to cover the skillet.

3. Spread spinach mixture over phyllo in skillet. Top with an additional 6 sheets of phyllo, again brushing with oil and rotating sheets. Fold ends of phyllo up over top of pie; brush with oil.

4. Using a sharp knife, cut into 8 wedges. Bake on a lower oven rack until top is golden brown, 35-40 minutes. Cool on a wire rack. Refrigerate leftovers.

1 piece: 334 cal., 23g fat (7g sat. fat), 75mg chol., 649mg sod., 17g carb. (2g sugars, 5g fiber), 18g pro.

FRIED LASAGNA

Some people go to Olive Garden for the endless breadsticks, but I'm there for the fried lasagna. After a bit of experimentation, I got the saucy crispy entree just right at home.
—*Jolene Martinelli, Fremont, NH*

PREP: 45 MIN. + FREEZING • COOK: 10 MIN./BATCH • MAKES: 10 SERVINGS

20 uncooked lasagna noodles
1 carton (32 oz.) whole-milk ricotta cheese
2½ cups shredded Italian cheese blend, divided
2 cups shredded part-skim mozzarella cheese
6 large eggs, beaten, divided use
4 tsp. Italian seasoning, divided
Oil for deep-fat frying
2½ cups panko bread crumbs
1 jar (24 oz.) marinara sauce, warmed
1 jar (15 oz.) Alfredo sauce, warmed

1. Cook lasagna noodles according to package directions for al dente. In a large bowl, combine ricotta, 1¼ cups Italian cheese blend, mozzarella, 2 eggs and 3 tsp. Italian seasoning. Drain noodles. If desired, cut off ribboned edges (discard or save for another use). Spread about ¼ cup filling on each noodle. Starting with a short side, fold each in thirds. Place all on a parchment-lined baking sheet, seam side down. Freeze just until firm, about 1 hour.

2. In an electric skillet or deep fryer, heat oil to 375°. In a shallow bowl, mix bread crumbs, ⅔ cup Italian cheese blend and 1 tsp. Italian seasoning. Place remaining 4 eggs in separate shallow bowl. Dip lasagna bundles into eggs, then into crumb mixture, patting to help coating adhere.

3. Fry bundles in batches until golden brown, 8-10 minutes, turning once. Drain on paper towels. Serve with marinara, Alfredo, the remaining Italian cheese blend and, if desired, additional Italian seasoning

2 lasagna rolls: 876 cal., 54g fat (19g sat. fat), 195mg chol., 1011mg sod., 61g carb. (11g sugars, 4g fiber), 37g pro.

KIMCHI FRIED RICE

Forget ordinary fried rice! Kimchi fried rice is just as easy, but it packs a flavorful punch. This is a fantastic use for leftovers too. You can freeze the fried rice for up to three months. When cooking your defrosted rice, add a little extra soy sauce so it doesn't dry out.
—Taste of Home *Test Kitchen*

TAKES: 20 MIN. • MAKES: 4 SERVINGS

2 Tbsp. canola oil, divided
1 small onion, chopped
1 cup kimchi, coarsely chopped
½ cup matchstick carrots
¼ cup kimchi juice
1 garlic cloves, minced
1 tsp. minced fresh gingerroot
3 cups leftover short grain rice
2 green onions, thinly sliced
3 tsp. soy sauce
1 tsp. sesame oil
4 large eggs
Optional toppings: Sliced nori, green onions and black sesame seeds

1. In large skillet, heat 1 Tbsp. canola oil over medium-high heat. Add onion; cook and stir until tender, 2-4 minutes. Add kimchi, carrots, kimchi juice, garlic and ginger; cook 2 minutes longer. Add rice, green onions, soy sauce and sesame oil; heat through, stirring frequently.

2. In another large skillet, heat remaining 1 Tbsp. canola oil over medium-high heat. Break the eggs, 1 at a time, into pan; reduce heat to low. Cook to desired doneness, turning after whites are set if desired. Serve over rice. If desired, sprinkle with nori, green onions and sesame seeds.

1 cup fried rice with 1 egg: 331 cal., 14g fat (2g sat. fat), 186mg chol., 546mg sod., 41g carb. (4g sugars, 2g fiber), 11g pro.

ITALIAN-STYLE PIZZAS

With prepared pesto and pizza crusts, these tasty pizzas come together faster than delivery! I like to serve slices with a salad and fresh fruit.
—*Trisha Kruse, Eagle, ID*

TAKES: 25 MIN. • MAKES: 2 PIZZAS

2 prebaked mini pizza crusts
½ cup prepared pesto
⅔ cup shredded part-skim mozzarella cheese
½ cup sliced sweet onion
½ cup thinly sliced fresh mushrooms
¼ cup roasted sweet red peppers, drained
2 Tbsp. grated Parmesan cheese

Place crusts on an ungreased baking sheet; spread with pesto. Layer with mozzarella cheese, onion, mushrooms and peppers; sprinkle with Parmesan cheese. Bake at 400° 10-12 minutes or until cheese is melted.

½ pizza: 429 cal., 23g fat (7g sat. fat), 23mg chol., 820mg sod., 37g carb. (3g sugars, 2g fiber), 19g pro.

KIMCHI
FRIED RICE

COMFORTING TUNA PATTIES

My grandmother and mother made these tuna patties on Fridays during Lent. I'm not the biggest fan of tuna, but it's perfect in this dish. These patties are even good cold the next day, if there are any leftovers.
—*Ann Marie Eberhart, Gig Harbor, WA*

PREP: 25 MIN. + CHILLING • **COOK:** 5 MIN./BATCH • **MAKES:** 6 SERVINGS

2 Tbsp. butter
3 Tbsp. all-purpose flour
1 cup evaporated milk
1 pouch (6.4 oz.) light tuna in water
⅓ cup plus ½ cup dry bread crumbs, divided
1 green onion, finely chopped
2 Tbsp. lemon juice
½ tsp. salt
¼ tsp. pepper
   Oil for frying

1. In a small saucepan, melt butter over medium heat. Stir in flour until smooth; gradually whisk in milk. Bring to a boil, stirring constantly; cook and stir until thickened, 2-3 minutes. Remove from heat. Transfer to a small bowl; cool.

2. Stir in tuna, ⅓ cup bread crumbs, green onion, lemon juice, salt and pepper. Refrigerate, covered, at least 30 minutes.

3. Place remaining ½ cup bread crumbs in a shallow bowl. Drop ⅓ cup tuna mixture into crumbs. Gently coat and shape into a ½-in.-thick patty. Repeat. In a large skillet, heat oil over medium heat. Add tuna patties in batches; cook until golden brown, 2-3 minutes on each side. Drain on paper towels.

Freeze option: Freeze cooled tuna patties in freezer containers, separating layers with waxed paper. To use, reheat tuna patties on a baking sheet in a preheated 325° oven until heated through.

1 tuna patty: 255 cal., 17g fat (5g sat. fat), 34mg chol., 419mg sod., 15g carb. (5g sugars, 1g fiber), 10g pro.

AIR-FRYER BLACK BEAN CHIMICHANGAS

These chimichangas get a little love from the air fryer, so they're much healthier than their deep-fried counterparts. Black beans provide protein, and this recipe is a smart way to use up leftover rice.
—*Kimberly Hammond, Kingwood, TX*

PREP: 20 MIN. • **COOK:** 5 MIN./BATCH • **MAKES:** 6 SERVINGS

2 cans (15 oz. each) black beans, rinsed and drained
1 pkg. (8.8 oz.) ready-to-serve brown rice
⅔ cup frozen corn
⅔ cup minced fresh cilantro
⅔ cup chopped green onions
½ tsp. salt
6 whole wheat tortillas (8 in.), warmed if necessary
4 tsp. olive oil
Optional: Guacamole and salsa

1. Preheat air fryer to 400°. In a large microwave-safe bowl, mix beans, rice and corn; microwave, covered, until heated through, 4-5 minutes, stirring halfway. Stir in cilantro, green onions and salt.

2. To assemble, spoon ¾ cup bean mixture across the center of each tortilla. Fold bottom and sides of tortilla over filling and roll up. Brush with olive oil.

3. In batches, place seam side down on greased tray in air-fryer basket. Cook until golden brown and crispy, 2-3 minutes. If desired, serve with guacamole and salsa.

1 chimichanga: 337 cal., 5g fat (0 sat fat), 0 chol., 602mg sod., 58g carb. (2g sugars, 10g fiber), 13g pro.

COOKIES & CREAM
BROWNIES, PAGE 241

CHAPTER 9

COOKIES, BROWNIES & BARS

For everything from after-school to late-night snacking and bake sales to family reunions, bite-sized sweets always hit the spot. Turn here the next time you need a treat that's stood the test of time. Grab a cold glass of milk or a hot cup of coffee and enjoy!

BEACH BALL COOKIES

These cookies are as colorful as beach balls and just as fun. They're delightful for kids' parties, school bake sales or when you just want a playful treat. Use bright, bold colors, or try soft pastels for springtime.

—Darlene Brenden, Salem, OR

PREP: 45 MIN. • **BAKE:** 10 MIN./BATCH • **MAKES:** 2 DOZEN

½ cup butter, softened
½ cup sugar
½ cup confectioners' sugar
1 large egg, room temperature
½ cup canola oil
1 tsp. vanilla extract
2½ cups all-purpose flour
½ tsp. baking soda
½ tsp. cream of tartar
¼ tsp. salt
   Assorted food coloring

1. Preheat oven to 350°. In a large bowl, cream butter and sugars until light and fluffy, 5-7 minutes. Beat in egg, oil and vanilla. In another bowl, whisk flour, baking soda, cream of tartar and salt; gradually beat into creamed mixture.

2. Divide dough into 5 equal portions. Tint each portion a different color with food coloring. Divide each portion into 24 equal pieces; roll each piece into a ball. Gently press together 1 ball of each color to form a larger ball; place 1 in. apart on greased baking sheets. Flatten slightly with bottom of a glass.

3. Bake until bottoms are lightly browned, 10-12 minutes. Remove from pans to wire racks to cool.

1 cookie: 152 cal., 9g fat (3g sat. fat), 18mg chol., 85mg sod., 17g carb. (7g sugars, 0 fiber), 2g pro.

BUTTERY 3-INGREDIENT SHORTBREAD COOKIES

These buttery cookies are so simple to prepare, with only a few ingredients.
—*Pattie Prescott, Manchester, NH*

PREP: 10 MIN. • **BAKE:** 30 MIN. + COOLING • **MAKES:** 16 COOKIES

1 cup unsalted butter, softened
½ cup sugar
2 cups all-purpose flour
   Confectioners' sugar, optional

1. Preheat oven to 325°. Cream butter and sugar 5-7 minutes or until light and fluffy. Gradually beat in flour. Press dough into an ungreased 9-in. square baking pan. Prick with a fork.

2. Bake 30-35 minutes or until light brown. Cut into squares while warm. Cool completely on a wire rack. If desired, dust with confectioners' sugar.

1 cookie: 183 cal., 12g fat (7g sat. fat), 31mg chol., 2mg sod., 18g carb. (6g sugars, 0 fiber), 2g pro.

FRUITY BROWNIE
PIZZA

FRUITY BROWNIE PIZZA

I start with a basic brownie mix to create this luscious treat that's sure to impress company. Sometimes I add mandarin oranges for even more color.
—Nancy Johnson, Laverne, OK

PREP: 20 MIN. + CHILLING • **BAKE:** 15 MIN. + COOLING • **MAKES:** 12 SERVINGS

1 pkg. fudge brownie mix (8-in. square pan size)
1 pkg. (8 oz.) cream cheese, softened
⅓ cup sugar
¾ cup pineapple tidbits with juice
1 small firm banana, sliced
1 medium kiwifruit, peeled and sliced
1 cup sliced fresh strawberries
¼ cup chopped pecans
1 oz. semisweet chocolate
1 Tbsp. butter

1. Preheat oven to 375°. Prepare brownie batter according to package directions. Spread onto a greased 12-in. pizza pan. Bake until a toothpick inserted in center comes out clean, 15–20 minutes. Cool completely.

2. In a large bowl, beat cream cheese and sugar until smooth. Spread over brownie crust. Drain pineapple, reserving juice. Toss banana slices with juice; drain well. Arrange banana, kiwi, strawberries and pineapple over cream cheese layer; sprinkle with pecans.

3. In a small microwave, melt chocolate and butter; stir until smooth. Drizzle over fruit. Cover and refrigerate for 1 hour.

1 piece: 366 cal., 21g fat (7g sat. fat), 38mg chol., 220mg sod., 44g carb. (30g sugars, 2g fiber), 4g pro.

TEST KITCHEN TIP

Feel free to get creative with this sweet treat. Depending on your preferences, you can try adding blueberries, raspberries, sliced peaches or even cubed melon. If you don't want a cream cheese frosting on your pizza, try a more traditional vanilla or chocolate frosting instead.
—SAMMI DIVITO, *TASTE OF HOME* ASSISTANT EDITOR

GINGERBREAD KISSES

Whether you call them kisses or hugs, these cookies show nothing but love when served warm from the oven. They're typically made with a peanut butter dough, but the ginger and spices in these thumbprints are a fun spin on an all-time favorite.
—Nancy Zimmerman, Cape May Court House, NJ

PREP: 35 MIN. + CHILLING • BAKE: 10 MIN./BATCH • MAKES: 5 DOZEN

¾ cup butter, softened
¾ cup packed brown sugar
1 large egg, room temperature
½ cup molasses
3 cups all-purpose flour
1 tsp. baking soda
¼ tsp. salt
2 tsp. ground ginger
1 tsp. ground cinnamon
¼ tsp. ground nutmeg
¼ cup sugar
60 striped chocolate kisses, unwrapped

1. Cream butter and brown sugar until light and fluffy, 5-7 minutes. Gradually beat in egg and molasses. In another bowl, whisk together flour, baking soda, salt and spices; gradually beat into creamed mixture. Refrigerate dough, covered, until firm enough to shape, about 4 hours.

2. Preheat oven to 350°. Shape dough into sixty 1-in. balls; roll in sugar. Place 1 in. apart on ungreased baking sheets. Bake until lightly browned, 8-10 minutes.

3. Press a chocolate kiss immediately into the center of each cookie. Remove from pans to wire racks to cool.

1 cookie: 88 cal., 4g fat (2g sat. fat), 10mg chol., 56mg sod., 13g carb. (8g sugars, 0 fiber), 1g pro.

LEMON ANGEL CAKE BARS

A neighbor gave me this recipe years ago and it's been in my baking rotation ever since. It can be made ahead and serves a bunch, so it's perfect for parties and potlucks.
—Marina Castle-Kelley, Canyon Country, CA

PREP: 15 MIN. + CHILLING • BAKE: 20 MIN. + COOLING • MAKES: 4 DOZEN

1 pkg. (16 oz.) angel food cake mix
1 can (15¾ oz.) lemon pie filling
1 cup unsweetened finely shredded coconut

FROSTING
1 pkg. (8 oz.) cream cheese, softened
½ cup butter, softened
1 tsp. vanilla extract
2½ cups confectioners' sugar
3 tsp. grated lemon zest

1. Preheat oven to 350°. In a large bowl, mix cake mix, pie filling and coconut until blended; spread into a greased 15x10x1-in. baking pan.

2. Bake 20-25 minutes or until toothpick inserted in center comes out clean. Cool completely in pan on a wire rack.

3. Meanwhile, in a large bowl, beat cream cheese, butter and vanilla until smooth. Gradually beat in confectioners' sugar. Spread over cooled bars; sprinkle with lemon zest. Refrigerate at least 4 hours. Cut into bars or triangles.

Note: Look for unsweetened coconut in the baking or health food section.

1 bar: 116 cal., 5g fat (3g sat. fat), 10mg chol., 135mg sod., 18g carb. (12g sugars, 0 fiber), 1g pro.

GINGERBREAD
KISSES

FLAKY CREME-FILLED COOKIES

The light, incredibly flaky base of these delightful sandwich cookies is an easy-to-make form of French puff pastry. Mix and match the flavorings, and you'll have cookies for every taste.
—*Susan Falk, Sterling Heights, MI*

PREP: 55 MIN. + CHILLING • BAKE: 10 MIN./BATCH + COOLING • MAKES: ABOUT 6½ DOZEN

2 cups all-purpose flour
¼ tsp. salt
1 cup cold butter, cubed
1 pkg. (8 oz.) cream cheese, cubed
⅔ cup marshmallow creme
⅔ cup butter, softened
1⅓ cups confectioners' sugar
Optional flavoring: 2 Tbsp. baking cocoa, ½ tsp. lemon extract or ½ tsp. peppermint extract
Optional filling: Seedless raspberry preserves, blueberry preserves or crushed peppermint candies
Additional confectioners' sugar

1. In a large bowl, combine flour and salt. Cut in cold butter and cream cheese until mixture resembles coarse crumbs. Shape into a disk; cover and refrigerate 2 hours or until easy to handle.

2. Preheat oven to 350°. On a lightly floured surface, roll dough to ⅛-in. thickness. Cut out with a floured 1½-in. cookie cutter. Place 2 in. apart on parchment-lined baking sheets. Bake 7-10 minutes or until light golden brown. Remove to wire racks to cool completely.

3. Meanwhile, in a large bowl, beat marshmallow creme and softened butter until light and fluffy. Gradually beat in confectioners' sugar. Proceed with flavored filling as desired.

1 sandwich cookie: 67 cal., 5g fat (3g sat. fat), 13mg chol., 45mg sod., 5g carb. (3g sugars, 0 fiber), 1g pro.

Chocolate-Raspberry Cookies: Beat cocoa into marshmallow creme mixture. Spread on the bottoms of half the cookies. Spread raspberry preserves on the bottoms of remaining cookies; top with creme-topped cookies. Sprinkle with confectioners' sugar.

Lemon-Blueberry Cookies: Beat lemon extract into marshmallow creme mixture. Spread on the bottoms of half the cookies. Spread blueberry preserves on the bottoms of remaining cookies; top with creme-topped cookies. Sprinkle with confectioners' sugar.

Peppermint Cookies: Beat peppermint extract into marshmallow creme mixture. (Tint with 1 drop red food coloring if desired.) Spread on the bottoms of half the cookies; top with remaining cookies. Roll sides in peppermint candies if desired. Sprinkle with confectioners' sugar.

GIANT MOLASSES COOKIES

My family always requests these soft and deliciously chewy cookies. The cookies are also perfect for shipping as holiday gifts or to troops overseas.
—*Kristine Chayes, Smithtown, NY*

PREP: 30 MIN. • BAKE: 15 MIN./BATCH • MAKES: 2 DOZEN

1½ cups butter, softened
2 cups sugar
2 large eggs, room temperature
½ cup molasses
4½ cups all-purpose flour
4 tsp. ground ginger
2 tsp. baking soda
1½ tsp. ground cinnamon
1 tsp. ground cloves
¼ tsp. salt
¼ cup chopped pecans
¾ cup coarse sugar

1. Preheat oven to 350°. In a large bowl, cream butter and sugar until light and fluffy, 5-7 minutes. Beat in eggs and molasses. Combine the flour, ginger, baking soda, cinnamon, cloves and salt; gradually add to creamed mixture and mix well. Fold in pecans.

2. Shape into 2-in. balls and roll in coarse sugar. Place 2½ in. apart on ungreased baking sheets. Bake until tops are cracked, 13-15 minutes. Remove to wire racks to cool.

1 cookie: 310 cal., 13g fat (7g sat. fat), 48mg chol., 219mg sod., 46g carb. (27g sugars, 1g fiber), 3g pro.

DID YOU KNOW?

Molasses is a byproduct of refining cane or beets into sugar. Light and dark molasses are made from the first and second refining processes, respectively. Blackstrap, made from the third procedure, is the strongest, darkest and most intensely flavored of the three. Light molasses is lightest in color, sweetest, and mildest in flavor, and also helps to make cookies softer. However, dark molasses is a great option, too, since it's what gives gingerbread cookies their distinct color and flavor. Blackstrap molasses can be quite intense in flavor, but it can work too. It really all comes down to a personal preference.
—ELLIE CROWLEY, *TASTE OF HOME* CULINARY ASSISTANT

CHEWY GERMAN
CHOCOLATE COOKIES

CHEWY GERMAN CHOCOLATE COOKIES

When I want a cookie that's as chewy as a brownie, this is the recipe I reach for.
Coffee granules add the right amount of mocha flavor.
—*Darlene Brenden, Salem, OR*

PREP: 25 MIN. • BAKE: 10 MIN./BATCH • MAKES: 4 DOZEN

12 oz. German sweet chocolate, chopped
2 Tbsp. shortening
1 tsp. instant coffee granules
3 large eggs, room temperature
1¼ cups sugar
1 tsp. vanilla extract
1 cup all-purpose flour
½ tsp. baking powder
½ tsp. salt
½ cup chopped pecans
48 pecan halves
Confectioners' sugar, optional

1. Preheat oven to 350° In a microwave, melt chocolate and shortening; stir until smooth. Stir in coffee granules; cool and set aside.

2. In a large bowl, beat eggs and sugar until light and lemon-colored. Beat in the cooled chocolate and vanilla. Combine the flour, baking powder and salt; add to chocolate mixture and mix well. Stir in chopped pecans.

3. Working quickly, drop dough by tablespoonfuls 2 in. apart onto greased baking sheets. Place a pecan half in the center of each. Bake until the cookies are set, 10-12 minutes. Cool for 1 minute before removing to wire racks. If desired, dust with confectioners' sugar.

1 cookie: 98 cal., 5g fat (2g sat. fat), 12mg chol., 34mg sod., 9g carb. (7g sugars, 1g fiber), 1g pro.

PUMPKIN CHOCOLATE CHIP COOKIES

I'm one of the cooking project leaders for my daughter's 4-H club, where these soft, delicious cookies were a huge hit with the kids.
—*Marietta Slater, Justin, TX*

PREP: 10 MIN. • BAKE: 10 MIN./BATCH • MAKES: 4 DOZEN

1 cup butter, softened
¾ cup sugar
¾ cup packed brown sugar
1 large egg, room temperature
1 tsp. vanilla extract
2 cups all-purpose flour
1 cup quick-cooking oats
1 tsp. baking soda
1 tsp. ground cinnamon
1 cup canned pumpkin
1½ cups semisweet chocolate chips

1. In a bowl, cream butter and sugars until light and fluffy, 5-7 minutes. Beat in egg and vanilla. Combine the flour, oats, baking soda and cinnamon; stir into creamed mixture alternately with pumpkin. Fold in chocolate chips.

2. Drop by tablespoonfuls onto ungreased baking sheets. Bake at 350° for 10-12 minutes or until lightly browned. Remove to wire racks to cool.

1 cookie: 112 cal., 6g fat (3g sat. fat), 15mg chol., 68mg sod., 15g carb. (10g sugars, 1g fiber), 1g pro.

APRICOT-PECAN THUMBPRINT COOKIES

I enjoy experimenting with cake mixes to make new cookie recipes. I love apricot, but feel free to fill the thumbprint in the center of these goodies with any fruit preserve you like.
—Nancy Johnson, Laverne, OK

PREP: 30 MIN. • BAKE: 15 MIN./BATCH + COOLING • MAKES: ABOUT 7 DOZEN

2 pkg. yellow cake mix (regular size)
½ cup all-purpose flour
1 cup canola oil
6 large eggs, divided use
1 tsp. ground cinnamon
½ tsp. ground ginger
3 Tbsp. water
4 cups finely chopped pecans, divided
⅔ cup apricot preserves

ICING
2 cups confectioners' sugar
3 to 5 Tbsp. water

1. Preheat oven to 350°. In a large bowl, beat cake mix, flour, oil, 4 eggs, cinnamon and ginger until well blended.

2. In a shallow bowl, whisk water and remaining eggs. Place half of the pecans in another shallow bowl. Shape dough into 1-in. balls. Dip in egg mixture, then coat with pecans, adding remaining pecans to bowl as needed. Place cookies 2 in. apart on greased baking sheets.

3. Press a deep indentation in center of each cookie with the end of a wooden spoon handle. Fill each indentation with preserves. Bake 12-14 minutes or until golden brown. Remove from pans to wire racks to cool completely.

4. In a small bowl, combine confectioners' sugar and enough water to reach a drizzling consistency. Drizzle over cookies. Let stand until set.

Freeze option: After icing is set, layer cookies between waxed paper in freezer containers. Freeze for up to 3 months. To use, thaw in covered containers.

1 cookie: 124 cal., 7g fat (1g sat. fat), 20mg chol., 88mg sod., 16g carb. (10g sugars, 0 fiber), 1g pro.

FRUITY COCONUT BALLS

My mom gave me this no-bake cookie recipe years ago when she had them on a buffet. I can't believe how simple they are to make.
—Jane Whittaker, Pensacola, FL

TAKES: 30 MIN. • MAKES: 2 DOZEN

1¼ cups sweetened shredded coconut
1 cup dried apricots, finely chopped
⅔ cup chopped pecans
½ cup fat-free sweetened condensed milk
½ cup confectioners' sugar

1. In a small bowl, combine coconut, apricots and pecans. Add condensed milk; mix well (mixture will be sticky).

2. Shape into 1¼-in. balls and roll in confectioners' sugar. Store in an airtight container in the refrigerator.

1 ball: 87 cal., 4g fat (2g sat. fat), 1mg chol., 19mg sod., 12g carb. (10g sugars, 1g fiber), 1g pro.

APRICOT-PECAN
THUMBPRINT COOKIES

MAPLE
PUMPKIN PIE

"Fabulous! I won't ever make plain pumpkin pie again. The taste is perfection!
—DAROWAN07
TASTEOFHOME.COM

MAPLE PUMPKIN PIE

Tired of traditional pumpkin pie? The maple syrup in this special pie provides a subtle but terrific enhancer.
—Lisa Varner, El Paso, TX

PREP: 25 MIN. • BAKE: 1 HOUR + CHILLING • MAKES: 8 SERVINGS

Dough for single-crust pie
2 **large eggs**
1 **can (15 oz.) pumpkin**
1 **cup evaporated milk**
¾ **cup sugar**
½ **cup maple syrup**
1 **tsp. pumpkin pie spice**
¼ **tsp. salt**

MAPLE WHIPPED CREAM
1 **cup heavy whipping cream**
2 **Tbsp. confectioners' sugar**
1 **Tbsp. maple syrup**
¼ **tsp. pumpkin pie spice**
  Chopped pecans, optional

1. Preheat oven to 425°. On a lightly floured surface, roll dough to a ⅛-in.-thick circle; transfer to a 9-in. pie plate. Trim crust to ½ in. beyond rim of plate; flute edge. Refrigerate while preparing filling.

2. In a large bowl, combine the next 7 ingredients; beat until smooth. Pour into crust. Bake for 15 minutes. Reduce heat to 350°. Bake 45-50 minutes longer or until crust is golden brown and top of pie is set (cover edge with foil during the last 15 minutes to prevent overbrowning if necessary). Cool on a wire rack for 1 hour. Refrigerate overnight or until set.

3. In a small bowl, beat the cream, confectioners' sugar, syrup and pumpkin pie spice until stiff peaks form. Pipe or dollop onto pie. Sprinkle with pecans if desired.

1 piece: 489 cal., 26g fat (16g sat. fat), 121mg chol., 290mg sod., 59g carb. (40g sugars, 2g fiber), 7g pro.

Dough for single-crust pie (9 in.): Combine 1¼ cups all-purpose flour and ¼ tsp. salt; cut in ½ cup cold butter until crumbly. Gradually add 3-5 Tbsp. ice water, tossing with a fork until dough holds together when pressed. Shape into a disk; cover and refrigerate 1 hour.

TEST KITCHEN TIP

Pure maple syrup is the way to go with this recipe, but if you are in a bind and don't have that on hand, you can use plain pancake syrup and add 4 teaspoons maple extract.

CREAMY HAZELNUT PIE

I've always been a huge fan of peanut butter. Then I tried Nutella—I was hooked! I even changed one of my favorite pie recipes by adding that ingredient.
—*Lisa Varner, El Paso, TX*

PREP: 10 MIN. + CHILLING • MAKES: 8 SERVINGS

1 pkg. (8 oz.) cream cheese, softened
1 cup confectioners' sugar
1¼ cups Nutella, divided
1 carton (8 oz.) frozen whipped topping, thawed
1 chocolate crumb crust (9 in.)

1. In a large bowl, beat cream cheese, confectioners' sugar and 1 cup Nutella until smooth. Fold in whipped topping. Spread evenly into crust.

2. Warm the remaining Nutella in a microwave for 15-20 seconds; drizzle over pie. Refrigerate at least 4 hours or overnight.

1 piece: 567 cal., 33g fat (13g sat. fat), 32mg chol., 224mg sod., 65g carb. (51g sugars, 2g fiber), 6g pro.

MARGARITA CAKE

This margarita cake is perfect for a picnic on a warm day. You'll be surprised at how closely it tastes like the real thing.
—*Dawn Lowenstein, Huntingdon Valley, PA*

PREP: 15 MIN. • BAKE: 45 MIN. + COOLING • MAKES: 16 SERVINGS

1 pkg. lemon cake mix (regular size)
1 pkg. (3.4 oz.) instant lemon pudding mix
1 can (10 oz.) frozen nonalcoholic margarita mix, thawed
4 large eggs, room temperature
½ cup butter, softened
2 Tbsp. lime juice
3 tsp. grated lime zest

GLAZE
1½ cups confectioners' sugar
3 Tbsp. lime juice

1. Preheat oven to 350°. Grease and flour a 10-in. fluted tube pan. In a large bowl, combine cake mix, pudding mix, margarita mix, eggs, butter, lime juice and zest; beat on low speed for 30 seconds. Beat on medium for 2 minutes.

2. Transfer batter to prepared pan. Bake 45-50 minutes or until a toothpick inserted in the center comes out clean. Cool in pan 10 minutes before removing to a wire rack to cool completely.

3. Meanwhile, combine glaze ingredients. Drizzle over cake.

1 piece: 284 cal., 8g fat (5g sat. fat), 62mg chol., 379mg sod., 51g carb. (37g sugars, 1g fiber), 2g pro.

FLORIDA CITRUS MERINGUE PIE

Thanks to orange and lemon, this lovely pie packs a bold sweet-tart flavor.
—*Barbara Carlucci, Orange Park, FL*

PREP: 30 MIN. • BAKE: 15 MIN. + CHILLING • MAKES: 8 SERVINGS

Dough for
single-crust pie
5 Tbsp. cornstarch
1 cup sugar
½ tsp. salt
1 cup water
1 cup orange juice
4 large egg yolks
½ cup lemon juice
2 Tbsp. butter
1 tsp. grated
   lemon zest
1 tsp. grated
   orange zest

MERINGUE
4 large egg whites
1 tsp. vanilla extract
¼ tsp. cream of tartar
½ cup sugar

1. Preheat oven to 450°. On a lightly floured surface, roll dough to a ⅛-in.-thick circle; transfer to a 9-in. pie plate. Trim to ½ in. beyond rim of plate; flute edge. Line unpricked crust with a double thickness of foil. Fill with pie weights, dried beans or uncooked rice.

2. Bake until bottom is lightly browned, 8-10 minutes. Remove foil and weights; bake until golden brown, 5-8 minutes longer. Cool on a wire rack. Reduce oven temperature to 350°.

3. Meanwhile, in a large saucepan, mix cornstarch, sugar and salt. Whisk in water and orange juice. Cook and stir over medium-high heat until thickened and bubbly. Reduce heat to low; cook and stir 2 minutes longer (mixture will be thick). Remove from heat.

4. In a small bowl, whisk a small amount of hot mixture into egg yolks; return all to pan, whisking constantly. Bring to a gentle boil; cook and stir 2 minutes. Remove from heat. Gently stir in lemon juice, butter, and lemon and orange zests.

5. For meringue, in a large bowl, beat egg whites with vanilla and cream of tartar on medium speed until foamy. Gradually add sugar, 1 Tbsp. at a time, beating on high after each addition until sugar is dissolved. Continue beating until soft glossy peaks form.

6. Transfer filling to crust. Spread meringue over filling; seal to crust edge. Swirl top with back of spoon.

7. Bake 13-16 minutes, until meringue is golden brown. Cool on a wire rack 1 hour. Chill 3 hours before serving. Refrigerate leftovers.

1 piece: 415 cal., 17g fat (10g sat. fat), 140mg chol., 318mg sod., 62g carb. (41g sugars, 1g fiber) 6g pro.

Dough for single-crust pie (9 in.): Combine 1¼ cups all-purpose flour and ¼ tsp. salt; cut in ½ cup cold butter until crumbly. Gradually add 3-5 Tbsp. ice water, tossing with a fork until dough holds together when pressed. Shape into a disk; cover and chill 1 hour.

Special Delivery

Memorable acts of cooking kindness benefit new moms.

Krystal Horudko,
Charlottetown, PE

In the small farming town of Nipawin, Saskatchewan, where I was raised, it's not uncommon for the matriarchs to prepare meals for neighbors.

When my father passed away several years ago, I walked into my mother's kitchen to find her fridge bursting with enough food to feed the entire block. In that spirit, when my co-worker had a baby, I prepared lasagna, salad, bread and chocolate cake. She was so touched by the gesture, she cried. If memory serves, I did, too.

A few months later when my childhood friend had her daughter, I repeated the meal for her family. Despite being invited in, I never stayed longer than to drop off the plates and share a brief, heartfelt hug with my friends.

Fast-forward to the birth of my second son, during the hottest week of August on Prince Edward Island. The afternoon we came home from the hospital I took a nap and did not hear my dogs bark when the doorbell rang.

When I awoke, I walked into the kitchen to a freshly baked lemon meringue pie. My next-door neighbor, Donna, made it when she saw us pull into the driveway. It was so wonderful to be blessed by her thoughtfulness. That she would bake a pie on such a hot day is a testament to what a great woman she is.

PEANUT-CASHEW MARSHMALLOW PIE

This pie appeals to kids and adults alike! The chocolate crust and caramel topping make it all the more special. I like the nice contrast of the creamy marshmallow filling with the crunchy peanuts. An added bonus is that this pie can be made ahead of time.
—Lisa Varner, El Paso, TX

PREP: 20 MIN. + CHILLING • COOK: 5 MIN. • MAKES: 8 SERVINGS

4 cups miniature marshmallows
1 cup 2% milk
1 Tbsp. butter
2 tsp. vanilla extract
1 cup cold heavy whipping cream
½ cup lightly salted dry-roasted peanuts, coarsely chopped
½ cup salted cashews, coarsely chopped
1 chocolate crumb crust (9 in.)
¼ cup hot caramel ice cream topping
2 Tbsp. chocolate syrup, optional

1. In a large saucepan, combine marshmallows and milk over medium heat, stirring often, until marshmallows are melted and mixture is smooth. Remove from heat. Transfer mixture to a bowl; stir in butter and vanilla. Place bowl in a pan of ice water. Gently stir until mixture is cool and begins to thicken, about 5 minutes.

2. In a large bowl, whip heavy cream at high speed until soft peaks form. Gently fold whipped cream into marshmallow mixture. In a small bowl, mix together peanuts and cashews; reserve ¼ cup for topping. Fold remaining nut mixture into marshmallow mixture. Spoon marshmallow mixture into crumb crust. Sprinkle reserved ¼ cup nuts over top. Refrigerate, covered, at least 6 hours or overnight. Before serving, drizzle pie with caramel topping and, if desired, chocolate syrup.

1 piece: 441 cal., 26g fat (11g sat. fat), 40mg chol., 259mg sod., 47g carb. (30g sugars, 2g fiber), 7g pro.

SPICED PEAR UPSIDE-DOWN CAKE

The flavors of fresh, sweet pears and gingerbread blend beautifully in this intriguing variation on pineapple upside-down cake. Leftovers—if there are any—taste amazing with coffee or tea the next day.
—Lisa Varner, El Paso, TX

PREP: 25 MIN. • BAKE: 35 MIN. + COOLING • MAKES: 9 SERVINGS

½ cup butter, melted
½ cup coarsely chopped walnuts
¼ cup packed brown sugar
2 large pears, peeled and sliced
½ cup butter, softened
⅓ cup sugar
1 large egg, room temperature
⅓ cup molasses
1½ cups all-purpose flour
¾ tsp. ground ginger
¾ tsp. ground cinnamon
½ tsp. salt
½ tsp. baking powder
¼ tsp. baking soda
½ cup warm water
Ice cream, optional

1. Pour melted butter into a 9-in. square baking pan; sprinkle with nuts and brown sugar. Arrange pears over nuts.

2. In a large bowl, cream softened butter and sugar until light and fluffy, 5-7 minutes. Beat in egg and molasses. Combine the flour, ginger, cinnamon, salt, baking powder and baking soda; add to creamed mixture alternately with water, beating well after each addition.

3. Spread batter over pears. Bake at 350° for 35-40 minutes or until a toothpick inserted in the center comes out clean. Cool for 10 minutes before inverting onto a serving plate. Serve warm, with ice cream if desired.

1 piece: 419 cal., 25g fat (13g sat. fat), 77mg chol., 347mg sod., 47g carb. (25g sugars, 3g fiber), 4g pro.

PEANUT-CASHEW
MARSHMALLOW PIE

"
We loved the
mix of creamy
and crunchy,
and sweet
and salty. I'll
definitely be
making this
one again.
—LINDAS_WI
TASTEOFHOME.COM

CHOCOLATE COCONUT PIE WITH COCONUT CRUST

Chewy coconut in both the fudgy filling and the homemade crust make this pie a real standout. I mix in chopped almonds for good measure!
—*Darlene Brenden, Salem, OR*

PREP: 20 MIN. + CHILLING • BAKE: 45 MIN. + COOLING • MAKES: 8 SERVINGS

1 cup all-purpose flour
½ cup sweetened shredded coconut
⅓ cup cold butter, cubed
¼ tsp. coconut extract
3 to 4 Tbsp. 2% milk

FILLING
4 oz. German sweet chocolate, chopped
¼ cup butter, melted
1 can (14 oz.) sweetened condensed milk
½ cup 2% milk
2 large eggs
1 tsp. vanilla extract
⅛ tsp. salt
1 cup sweetened shredded coconut
½ cup chopped almonds
  Whipped cream, optional

1. Place flour and coconut in a food processor; process until coconut is finely chopped. Add butter; pulse until butter is the size of peas. While pulsing, add extract and just enough milk to form moist crumbs. Shape dough into a disk; cover and refrigerate 1 hour or overnight.

2. Preheat oven to 400°. On a lightly floured surface, roll dough to a ⅛-in.-thick circle; transfer to a 9-in. pie plate. Trim crust to ½ in. beyond rim of plate; flute edge.

3. Line unpricked crust with a double thickness of foil. Fill with pie weights, dried beans or uncooked rice. Bake on a lower oven rack 10-15 minutes or until edge is light golden brown. Remove foil and weights; bake 5-7 minutes longer or until bottom is golden brown. Cool on a wire rack. Reduce oven setting to 350°.

4. For filling, in a large saucepan, melt chocolate and butter over medium heat; cool slightly. Whisk in milks, eggs, vanilla and salt. Pour into crust. Sprinkle with coconut and almonds.

5. Cover edge loosely with foil. Bake 30-35 minutes or until center is set. Remove foil. Cool on a wire rack. If desired, serve with whipped cream.

1 piece: 580 cal., 34g fat (20g sat. fat), 101mg chol., 280mg sod., 59g carb. (43g sugars, 3g fiber), 11g pro.

MACAROON CHERRY PIE

In summer, I use homegrown cherries in this amazing pie with a crunchy coconut topping. But canned tart cherries yield a dessert that's almost as delicious. I always bake this pie around Presidents Day or Valentine's Day, but it's popular with my family the whole year through.
—Lori Daniels, Beverly, WV

PREP: 25 MIN. • BAKE: 35 MIN. + CHILLING • MAKES: 8 SERVINGS

Dough for single-crust pie
3 cans (14½ oz. each) pitted tart cherries
1 cup sugar
⅓ cup cornstarch
½ tsp. ground cinnamon
¼ tsp. red food coloring, optional

TOPPING
1 large egg, room temperature, lightly beaten
2 Tbsp. 2% milk
1 Tbsp. butter, melted
¼ tsp. almond extract
¼ cup sugar
⅛ tsp. salt
1 cup sweetened shredded coconut
½ cup sliced almonds

1. Preheat oven to 400°. On a lightly floured surface, roll dough to a ⅛-in.-thick circle; transfer to a 9-in. cast-iron skillet or deep-dish pie plate. Trim to ½ in. beyond edge of plate; flute edge. Bake 6 minutes; set aside.

2. Drain cherries, reserving 1 cup juice. Set cherries aside. In a large saucepan, combine sugar and cornstarch; gradually stir in cherry juice until blended. Bring to a boil over medium heat; cook and stir until thickened, about 2 minutes.

3. Remove from heat; stir in cinnamon and, if desired, food coloring. Gently fold in cherries. Pour into crust. Cover edge loosely with foil. Bake at 400° for 20 minutes.

4. Meanwhile, in a large bowl, combine first 6 topping ingredients. Stir in coconut and almonds.

5. Remove foil from pie; spoon topping over pie. Reduce oven to 350°; bake until topping is lightly browned, 15-20 minutes. Cool on a wire rack 1 hour. Chill 4 hours or overnight before cutting.

1 piece: 434 cal., 16g fat (8g sat. fat), 36mg chol., 199mg sod., 70g carb. (48g sugars, 3g fiber), 5g pro.

Dough for single-crust pie (9 in.): Combine 1¼ cups all-purpose flour and ¼ tsp. salt; cut in ½ cup cold butter until crumbly. Gradually add 3-5 Tbsp. ice water, tossing with a fork until dough holds together when pressed. Shape into a disk; cover and refrigerate 1 hour.

Classic Crumb-Topped Cherry Pie: Preheat oven to 425°. Omit topping ingredients. Mix ½ cup all-purpose flour and ½ cup sugar; cut in ¼ cup cold butter until crumbly. Sprinkle over filling. Bake 35-45 minutes or until crust is golden brown and filling is bubbly. Cover edge loosely with foil if pie is browning too quickly.

CHERRY DREAM CAKE

CHERRY DREAM CAKE

I serve this because it's so festive and easy. No one will know that your
secret is adding a package of gelatin to a boxed cake mix!
—*Margaret McNeil, Germantown, TN*

PREP: 15 MIN. + CHILLING • BAKE: 30 MIN. + COOLING • MAKES: 20 SERVINGS

1 pkg. white cake mix (regular size)
1 pkg. (3 oz.) cherry gelatin
1½ cups boiling water
1 pkg. (8 oz.) cream cheese, softened
2 cups frozen whipped topping
1 can (21 oz.) cherry pie filling

1. Prepare cake mix according to package directions, using a greased 13x9-in. baking pan. Bake at 350° for 30-35 minutes or until a toothpick comes out clean.

2. Dissolve gelatin in boiling water. Cool cake on a wire rack for 3-5 minutes. Poke holes in cake with a meat fork or wooden skewer; gradually pour the gelatin over cake. Cool for 15 minutes. Cover and refrigerate for 30 minutes.

3. In a large bowl, beat cream cheese until fluffy. Fold in whipped topping. Carefully spread over cake. Top with pie filling. Cover and refrigerate for at least 2 hours before serving.

1 piece: 245 cal., 11g fat (5g sat. fat), 39mg chol., 242mg sod., 34g carb. (22g sugars, 1g fiber), 3g pro.

RUSTIC PEAR TART

I saw a recipe for this rustic tart in a cookbook and wanted to try my own version of it.
I changed the spices and chose my own fruits. It is a perfect dessert for fall.
—*Lisa Varner, El Paso, TX*

PREP: 20 MIN. • BAKE: 35 MIN. + COOLING • MAKES: 8 SERVINGS

1 sheet refrigerated pie crust
4 cups thinly sliced peeled fresh pears
¼ cup dried cherries
1 tsp. vanilla extract
4 Tbsp. sugar, divided
4 tsp. cornstarch
1 tsp. ground cinnamon
½ tsp. ground ginger
¼ cup chopped walnuts
1 large egg white
1 Tbsp. water

1. On a lightly floured surface, roll out crust into a 14-in. circle. Transfer to a parchment-lined baking sheet; set aside.

2. In a large bowl, combine the pears, cherries and vanilla. Combine 3 Tbsp. sugar, the cornstarch, cinnamon and ginger; sprinkle over pear mixture and stir gently to combine. Spoon over crust to within 2 in. of edge; sprinkle with walnuts. Fold edge of crust over filling, leaving center uncovered.

3. Beat egg white and water; brush over folded crust. Sprinkle with remaining sugar. Bake at 375° for 35-40 minutes or until crust is golden and filling is bubbly. Using parchment, slide tart onto a wire rack to cool.

1 piece: 239 cal., 10g fat (3g sat. fat), 5mg chol., 107mg sod., 37g carb. (18g sugars, 2g fiber), 3g pro.

Rustic Apple Tart: Substitute apples for the pears and dried cranberries for the cherries.

CHERRY PEAR PIE

Two of my family's favorite fruits appear in this splendid pie with a nutty streusel topping. I like to serve slices with cherry-vanilla frozen yogurt.
—*Trisha Kruse, Eagle, ID*

PREP: 30 MIN. • **BAKE:** 50 MIN. + COOLING • **MAKES:** 8 SERVINGS

Dough for single-crust pie

FILLING
- 6 cups sliced peeled fresh pears (about 5 large)
- ½ cup dried cherries
- 4 tsp. lemon juice
- ½ tsp. almond extract
- ¾ cup sugar
- ¼ cup cornstarch

TOPPING
- ¾ cup all-purpose flour
- ⅓ cup sugar
- ⅓ cup cold butter
- ½ cup sliced almonds

1. Preheat oven to 375°. On a lightly floured surface, roll dough to a ⅛-in.-thick circle; transfer to a 9-in. pie plate. Trim crust to ½ in. beyond rim of plate; flute edge. Refrigerate while preparing the filling.

2. In a large bowl, toss pears and cherries with lemon juice and extract. In a small bowl, mix the sugar and cornstarch; add to pear mixture, tossing to coat. Transfer to crust.

3. For topping, in a small bowl, mix flour and sugar; cut in butter until crumbly. Stir in almonds. Sprinkle over filling.

4. Bake 50-60 minutes or until golden brown and filling is bubbly. Cover edge loosely with foil during the last 15 minutes if needed to prevent overbrowning. Cool on a wire rack.

1 piece: 531 cal., 22g fat (12g sat. fat), 50mg chol., 219mg sod., 80g carb. (45g sugars, 5g fiber), 5g pro.

Dough for single-crust pie (9 in.): Combine 1¼ cups all-purpose flour and ¼ tsp. salt; cut in ½ cup cold butter until crumbly. Gradually add 3-5 Tbsp. ice water, tossing with a fork until dough holds together when pressed. Shape into a disk; cover and refrigerate 1 hour.

APRICOT ALMOND TORTE

This pretty cake takes a bit of time, so I like to make the layers in advance and assemble it the day of serving, which makes it an easier option for entertaining.
—Trisha Kruse, Eagle, ID

PREP: 45 MIN. • BAKE: 25 MIN. + COOLING • MAKES: 12 SERVINGS

- 3 large eggs, room temperature
- 1½ cups sugar
- 1 tsp. vanilla extract
- 1¾ cups all-purpose flour
- 1 cup ground almonds, toasted
- 2 tsp. baking powder
- ½ tsp. salt
- 1½ cups heavy whipping cream, whipped

FROSTING
- 1 pkg. (8 oz.) cream cheese, softened
- 1 cup sugar
- ⅛ tsp. salt
- 1 tsp. almond extract
- 1½ cups heavy whipping cream, whipped
- 1 jar (10 to 12 oz.) apricot preserves
- ½ cup slivered almonds, toasted

1. Preheat oven to 350°. In a large bowl, beat eggs, sugar and vanilla on high speed until thick and lemon-colored. Combine flour, almonds, baking powder and salt; gradually fold into egg mixture alternately with the whipped cream.

2. Transfer to 2 greased and floured 9-in. round baking pans. Bake until a toothpick inserted in the center comes out clean, 22-28 minutes. Cool 10 minutes before removing from pans to wire racks to cool completely.

3. In a large bowl, beat cream cheese, sugar and salt until smooth. Beat in extract. Fold in whipped cream.

4. Cut each cake horizontally into 2 layers. Place bottom layer on a serving plate; spread with 1 cup frosting. Top with another cake layer; spread with half the preserves. Repeat layers. Frost side of cake; decorate the top edge with remaining frosting. Sprinkle with almonds.

1 piece: 546 cal., 25g fat (12g sat. fat), 115mg chol., 284mg sod., 75g carb. (51g sugars, 2g fiber), 8g pro.

TART & TANGY LEMON TART

Our family adores lemon desserts. I like to make this lemony tart for brunch.
For extra-special events, I bake it in my heart-shaped tart pan.
—*Joyce Moynihan, Lakeville, MN*

PREP: 15 MIN. + CHILLING • BAKE: 45 MIN. + COOLING • MAKES: 14 SERVINGS

¾ cup butter, softened
½ cup confectioners' sugar
1½ cups all-purpose flour

FILLING
¾ cup sugar
1 Tbsp. grated lemon zest
¾ cup lemon juice
3 large eggs
3 large egg yolks
4 oz. cream cheese, softened
1 Tbsp. cornstarch
Sweetened whipped cream, optional

1. Preheat oven to 325°. In a large bowl, cream butter and confectioners' sugar until smooth. Gradually beat in flour. Press dough onto bottom and up side of an ungreased 11-in. fluted tart pan with removable bottom. Refrigerate 15 minutes.

2. Line the unpricked crust with a double thickness of foil. Fill with pie weights, dried beans or uncooked rice. Bake until edge is lightly browned, 18-22 minutes. Remove foil and weights; bake until bottom is golden brown, 5-7 minutes longer. Cool on a wire rack.

3. In a large bowl, beat sugar, lemon zest, lemon juice, eggs, egg yolks, cream cheese and cornstarch until blended; pour into crust. Bake until filling is set, 18-22 minutes. Cool on a wire rack. If desired, serve with whipped cream. Refrigerate leftovers.

Note: Let pie weights cool before storing. Beans and rice may be reused for pie weights, but not for cooking.

1 piece: 254 cal., 15g fat (9g sat. fat), 114mg chol., 125mg sod., 27g carb. (16g sugars, 0 fiber), 4g pro.

FROSTY MOCHA PIE

This pie is so creamy and rich-tasting that no one would guess it's light.
The added bonus is that you can make it a day or two ahead and keep it in the freezer until needed.
—*Lisa Varner, El Paso, TX*

PREP: 20 MIN. + FREEZING • MAKES: 10 SERVINGS

4 oz. reduced-fat cream cheese
¼ cup sugar
¼ cup baking cocoa
1 Tbsp. instant coffee granules
⅓ cup fat-free milk
1 tsp. vanilla extract
1 carton (12 oz.) frozen reduced-fat whipped topping, thawed
1 graham cracker crust (10 in.)
Reduced-calorie chocolate syrup, optional

1. In a large bowl, beat cream cheese, sugar and cocoa until smooth. Dissolve coffee granules in milk. Stir coffee mixture and vanilla into cream cheese mixture; fold in whipped topping.

2. Pour into crust. Cover and freeze for at least 4 hours. Remove from the freezer 10 minutes before serving. Drizzle with chocolate syrup if desired.

1 piece: 259 cal., 13g fat (7g sat. fat), 8mg chol., 198mg sod., 31g carb. (22g sugars, 1g fiber), 3g pro. **Diabetic exchanges:** 2 starch, 2 fat.

TART & TANGY
LEMON TART

66
This is an
absolute
winner! The
filling is nice
and tangy but
not too tart, and
the crust just
melts in your
mouth!
—VICTORIAPAGE
TASTEOFHOME.COM

GERMAN BUTTER POUND CAKE

Cardamom and lemon zest mix with almond and vanilla flavors
to add zip to a classic butter pound cake.
—*Kristine Chayes, Smithtown, NY*

PREP: 40 MIN. • BAKE: 1 HOUR + COOLING • MAKES: 16 SERVINGS

6 large eggs, separated
1 cup butter, softened
2 cups sugar
1 Tbsp. grated lemon zest
1 tsp. vanilla extract
½ tsp. almond extract
1½ cups all-purpose flour
2 tsp. baking powder
½ tsp. salt
½ tsp. ground cardamom
6 Tbsp. 2% milk
2 Tbsp. confectioners' sugar

1. Place egg whites in a large bowl; let stand at room temperature for 30 minutes. Generously grease and flour a 10-in. tube pan.

2. In a large bowl, cream butter and sugar until light and fluffy, 5-7 minutes. Add egg yolks, 1 at a time, beating well after each addition. Beat in lemon zest and extracts. In another bowl, mix the flour, baking powder, salt and cardamom; add to the creamed mixture alternately with milk, beating well after each addition.

3. With clean beaters, beat egg whites on medium speed until soft peaks form. Fold into batter.

4. Transfer to prepared pan. Bake at 350° for 60-70 minutes or until a toothpick inserted in center comes out clean. Cool in pan for 10 minutes before removing to a wire rack to cool. Sprinkle with confectioners' sugar.

Note: To be able to remove cakes easily, use solid shortening to grease plain and fluted tube pans.

1 piece: 275 cal., 13g fat (8g sat. fat), 110mg chol., 234mg sod., 35g carb. (27g sugars, 0 fiber), 4g pro.

STONE FRUIT PIE

This fresh, beautiful pie combines three types of fruit.
The flavor is complex, and the crust is divine.
—*Crystal Jo Bruns, Iliff, CO*

PREP: 30 MIN. • BAKE: 45 MIN. + COOLING • MAKES: 8 SERVINGS

- 2 cups fresh or frozen pitted tart cherries, thawed
- 3 medium nectarines, chopped
- 3 apricots, sliced
- ⅔ cup sugar
- 1 Tbsp. cornstarch
- 2 Tbsp. plus 2 cups all-purpose flour, divided
- ⅛ tsp. ground cinnamon
- 1 tsp. salt
- ¾ cup plus 2 Tbsp. cold butter, divided
- 6 to 7 Tbsp. ice water
- 1 large egg yolk
- 1 tsp. water

1. Preheat oven to 400°. In a small bowl, combine the cherries, nectarines, apricots, sugar, cornstarch, 2 Tbsp. flour and cinnamon; set aside.

2. In another bowl, combine salt and remaining flour; cut in ¾ cup butter until crumbly. Gradually add ice water, tossing with a fork until dough forms a ball. Divide dough into 2 portions so that 1 is slightly larger than the other. Roll out larger portion to fit a 9-in. pie plate; transfer crust to pie plate. Add filling; dot with remaining butter.

3. Roll out remaining dough; make a lattice crust. Trim, seal and flute edge. In a small bowl, whisk egg yolk and water; brush over lattice top.

4. Bake 45-50 minutes or until filling is bubbly and crust is golden brown. Cover edge with foil during the last 15 minutes to prevent overbrowning if necessary. Cool on a wire rack.

1 piece: 360 cal., 21g fat (13g sat. fat), 78mg chol., 439mg sod., 42g carb. (26g sugars, 2g fiber), 3g pro.

TEST KITCHEN TIP

You can use any type of stone fruit in this pie. Try combining white peaches with sour cherries.

> I took bananas Foster one step further and combined it with the flavors of my favorite tropical drink: a pina colada!
>
> —TRISHA KRUSE
> EAGLE, ID

SLOW-COOKER
PINA COLADA
BANANAS FOSTER,
PAGE 273

CHAPTER 11

MUST-TRY DESSERTS

When it comes to the recipes people share most, sweet treats rise to the top of the request list. Turn to this incredible collection of dinner finales the next time you need a memorable bite, then get ready to share the recipe yourself.

DOUBLE CHOCOLATE ESPRESSO CHEESECAKE

Every slice of this creamy cheesecake is a standout.
The classic pairing of chocolate and coffee always pleases partygoers.
—*Cheryl Perry, Hertford, NC*

PREP: 35 MIN. • BAKE: 1 HOUR + CHILLING • MAKES: 16 SERVINGS

1½ cups crushed vanilla wafers
    (about 45)
¼ cup butter, melted
2 Tbsp. sugar
¼ tsp. instant espresso powder

FILLING
1 cup sour cream, room temperature
¼ cup half-and-half cream, room
    temperature
1 cup 60% cacao bittersweet chocolate
    baking chips, melted
1½ tsp. instant espresso powder
1 tsp. vanilla extract
4 pkg. (8 oz. each) cream cheese,
    softened
1½ cups sugar
½ cup baking cocoa
1 Tbsp. all-purpose flour
5 large eggs, room temperature,
    lightly beaten

TOPPING
1 cup coffee liqueur
1 Tbsp. half-and-half cream
1 cup heavy whipping cream
2 Tbsp. confectioners' sugar
½ cup 60% cacao bittersweet chocolate
    baking chips, chopped
16 chocolate-covered coffee beans

1. Preheat oven to 350°. Place a greased 9-in. springform pan on a double thickness of heavy-duty foil (about 18 in. square). Securely wrap foil around pan.

2. In a large bowl, combine the wafer crumbs, butter, sugar and espresso powder. Press onto the bottom and 1 in. up the side of prepared pan.

3. In a small bowl, stir together sour cream, half-and-half and melted chocolate until blended; set aside. In second bowl, combine espresso powder and vanilla; set aside.

4. In a large bowl, beat the cream cheese and sugar; add chocolate mixture, cocoa and flour until smooth. Stir in the espresso mixture. Add eggs; beat on low speed until just combined. Pour into crust. Place springform pan in a large baking pan; add 1 in. hot water to larger pan.

5. Bake until the center is just set and top appears dull, 60-70 minutes. Remove springform pan from water bath. Cool on a wire rack for 10 minutes. Carefully run a knife around edge of pan to loosen; cool 1 hour longer. Refrigerate overnight. Remove side of pan.

6. In a small saucepan, combine liqueur and half-and-half. Bring to a boil; cook until liquid is reduced by half. Meanwhile, in a large bowl, beat whipping cream until it begins to thicken. Add confectioners' sugar; beat until stiff peaks form.

7. Drizzle cheesecake with coffee syrup; garnish with whipped cream, chocolate and coffee beans.

1 piece: 610 cal., 40g fat (23g sat. fat), 170mg chol., 259mg sod., 52g carb. (41g sugars, 2g fiber), 9g pro.

DOUBLE CHOCOLATE ESPRESSO CHEESECAKE

" The flavor is over the top delish! My guests loved it and asked for the recipe. I can hardly wait to make again.
—NUTS4COOKING
TASTEOFHOME.COM

MOLASSES-GRAHAM CRACKER PUDDINGS

When I was in college, I often had dinner with a relative after a night class.
The restaurant had Indian pudding and I always ordered it. Recently,
I adapted several recipes to re-create that pudding from years ago.
—*Joan Hallford, North Richland Hills, TX*

PREP: 25 MIN. • **BAKE:** 40 MIN. • **MAKES:** 6 SERVINGS

1   cup boiling water
½   cup raisins
2   cups 2% milk
1   cup finely crushed graham cracker
    crumbs
1   Tbsp. butter
2   large eggs, room temperature
½   cup molasses
¼   cup sugar
1   tsp. ground cinnamon
½   tsp. ground ginger
¼   tsp. salt
1½ cups vanilla ice cream

1. Preheat oven to 350°. Pour boiling water over raisins in a small bowl; let stand 5 minutes.

2. In a large saucepan, heat milk, cracker crumbs and butter until bubbles form around side of pan; remove from heat. In a large bowl, whisk the eggs, molasses, sugar, cinnamon, ginger and salt until blended but not foamy. Slowly stir in hot milk mixture. Drain raisins; stir into bowl.

3. Place six 4-oz. ramekins in a baking pan large enough to hold them without touching. Pour egg mixture into cups. Place pan on oven rack; add very hot water to pan to within ½ in. of top of cups. Bake until puffed and just set, 40-45 minutes. Remove the cups from water bath immediately to a wire rack; serve warm with ice cream.

1 serving: 369 cal., 11g fat (5g sat. fat), 88mg chol., 290mg sod., 63g carb. (51g sugars, 2g fiber), 7g pro.

BOURBON & CORNFLAKES ICE CREAM

Humphry Slocombe, a small San Francisco chain, serves scoops of Secret Breakfast—a rich and boozy vanilla-based ice cream. Ever (and especially) if the shop isn't in your corner of the country, consider giving the recipe a try!
—*Andrea Potischman, Menlo Park, CA*

PREP: 45 MIN. + CHILLING • **PROCESS:** 30 MIN. + FREEZING · **MAKES:** 1 QT.

3 Tbsp. heavy whipping cream
3 Tbsp. unsalted butter, melted
2 Tbsp. sugar
 Dash salt
1½ cups cornflakes, coarsely crushed

VANILLA BOURBON ICE CREAM
5 large egg yolks
½ cup sugar
 Dash salt
1 cup whole milk
1½ cups heavy whipping cream
1 tsp. vanilla extract
3 Tbsp. bourbon

1. Preheat oven 375°. In a small bowl combine cream, butter, sugar and salt. Stir in the cornflakes until well coated. Spread onto a parchment-lined baking sheet. Bake for 12-15 minutes or until golden brown, stirring once. Cool completely.

2. For the ice cream, in a large heavy saucepan, whisk egg yolks, sugar and salt until blended; stir in milk. Cook over low heat until mixture is just thick enough to coat a metal spoon and a thermometer reads at least 160°, stirring constantly. Do not allow to boil. Remove from heat immediately.

3. Quickly transfer to a small bowl; place bowl in a pan of ice water. Stir gently and occasionally for 2 minutes. Stir in the cream and vanilla. Press waxed paper onto surface of custard. Refrigerate several hours or overnight.

4. Stir bourbon into the custard. Fill cylinder of ice cream maker no more than two-thirds full; freeze according to manufacturer's directions, adding cornflakes during the last 2 minutes of processing. (Refrigerate any remaining mixture until ready to freeze.)

5. Transfer ice cream to freezer containers, allowing headspace for expansion. Freeze until firm, 2-4 hours.

½ cup: 353 cal., 26g fat (16g sat. fat), 187mg chol., 108mg sod., 23g carb. (19g sugars, 0 fiber), 5g pro

CHOCOLATE-
STUFFED
PEANUT BUTTER
SKILLET COOKIE

CHOCOLATE-STUFFED PEANUT BUTTER SKILLET COOKIE

A surprise chocolate filling makes this dessert extra delicious!
Serve warm from the oven with a scoop of your favorite ice cream.
—Andrea Price, Grafton, WI

PREP: 20 MIN. • BAKE: 35 MIN. + COOLING • MAKES: 12 SERVINGS

1 cup creamy peanut butter
¾ cup butter, softened
1¼ cups plus 1 Tbsp. sugar, divided
1 large egg, room temperature
1 tsp. vanilla extract
1½ cups all-purpose flour
½ tsp. baking soda
½ tsp. salt
1 cup milk chocolate chips
Vanilla ice cream, optional

1. Preheat oven to 350°. In a large bowl, cream peanut butter, butter and 1¼ cups sugar until blended. Beat in egg and vanilla. In another bowl, whisk flour, baking soda and salt; gradually beat into creamed mixture. Press half the dough into a well greased 10-in. cast-iron or other ovenproof skillet. Sprinkle chocolate chips over dough in skillet to within ½ in. of edge. Drop remaining dough over chocolate chips; spread until even. Sprinkle remaining 1 Tbsp. sugar over top.

2. Bake until a toothpick inserted in the center comes out with moist crumbs, 35-40 minutes. Cool completely on a wire rack. If desired, serve with ice cream.

1 piece: 453 cal., 27g fat (12g sat. fat), 49mg chol. 351mg sod., 47g carb. (32g sugars, 2g fiber), 8g pro.

RASPBERRY-WHITE CHOCOLATE LAVA CAKES

There is something so magical about a warm, luscious lava cake. Cutting into it and seeing the warm chocolate come rushing out always brings me joy. I wanted to see if I could do the same thing with white chocolate. Once successful, I decided to add a sprinkling of fresh raspberries.
—Margaret Knoebel, Taste of Home Associate Recipe Editor/Test Cook

TAKES: 30 MIN. • MAKES: 5 SERVINGS

⅔ cup white baking chips
½ cup butter, cubed
1 cup confectioners' sugar
2 large eggs, room temperature
2 large egg yolks, room temperature
1 tsp. vanilla extract
6 Tbsp. all-purpose flour
10 fresh raspberries

1. Preheat oven to 425°. In a microwave-safe bowl, melt baking chips and butter for 30 seconds; stir until smooth. Whisk in confectioners' sugar, eggs, egg yolks and vanilla until blended. Fold in flour.

2. Transfer to 5 generously creased 4-oz. ramekins; press 2 raspberries into center of each ramekin. Bake on a baking sheet until a thermometer reads 160° and edges of cakes are set, 14-16 minutes.

3. Remove from oven; let stand 10 minutes. Gently run a knife around sides of ramekins; invert onto dessert plates. Serve immediately. If desired, garnish with additional raspberries.

1 serving: 468 cal., 30g fat (17g sat. fat), 202mg chol., 199mg sod., 46g carb. (37g sugars, 1g fiber), 6g pro.

CHERRY PLUM SLAB PIE WITH WALNUT STREUSEL

I love to make desserts with fruit all summer! If you use store-bought crust, I recommend stacking your two pie crusts on top of each other and then rolling them to the correct size.
—*Elisabeth Larsen, Pleasant Grove, UT*

PREP: 25 MIN. • **BAKE:** 50 MIN. + COOLING • **MAKES:** 20 SERVINGS

1 lb. fresh sweet cherries, pitted
4 medium red plums, thinly sliced
½ cup sugar
¼ cup cornstarch
2 Tbsp. lemon juice
Dough for double-crust pie

TOPPING
½ cup old-fashioned oats
½ cup chopped walnuts
⅓ cup all-purpose flour
¼ cup sugar
¼ cup packed brown sugar
1 tsp. ground cinnamon
¼ tsp. salt
½ cup cold unsalted butter

1. Preheat oven to 375°. In a large bowl, combine the cherries, plums, sugar, cornstarch and lemon juice; toss to coat.

2. On a lightly floured surface, roll dough into a 16x12-in. rectangle; transfer to an ungreased 13x9-in. baking dish. Trim even with rim of dish. Add filling. For topping, in a small bowl, mix oats, walnuts, flour, sugar, brown sugar, cinnamon and salt; cut in butter until crumbly. Sprinkle over filling.

3. Bake until filling is bubbly and crust is golden brown, 50-55 minutes. Cool on a wire rack.

1 piece: 279 cal., 16g fat (9g sat. fat), 36mg chol., 155mg sod., 32g carb. (15g sugars, 2g fiber), 3g pro.

Dough for double-crust pie: Combine 2½ cups all-purpose flour and ½ tsp. salt; cut in 1 cup cold butter until crumbly. Gradually add ⅓-⅔ cup ice water, tossing with a fork until dough holds together when pressed. Divide dough in half. Shape each into a disk; wrap and refrigerate 1 hour.

SLOW-COOKER PINA COLADA BANANAS FOSTER

Make sure your bananas are not super ripe. You will want to choose ones that are still nice and firm, as they'll work best in this recipe.

—Trisha Kruse, Eagle, ID

PREP: 10 MIN. • **COOK:** 2 HOURS • **MAKES:** 6 SERVINGS (3 CUPS)

4 medium firm bananas
1 can (8 oz.) pineapple tidbits, drained
¼ cup butter, melted
1 cup packed brown sugar
¼ cup rum
½ tsp. coconut extract
½ cup sweetened shredded coconut, toasted
Optional: Coconut ice cream, vanilla wafers and cream-filled wafer cookies

Cut bananas in half lengthwise, then widthwise. Layer sliced bananas and pineapple in bottom of a 1½-qt. slow cooker. Combine butter, brown sugar, rum and coconut extract in a small bowl; pour over fruit. Cover and cook on low until heated through, about 2 hours. Sprinkle with the toasted coconut. If desired, serve with coconut ice cream, vanilla wafers or cream-filled wafer cookies.

½ **cup:** 358 cal., 11g fat (7g sat. fat), 20mg chol., 75mg sod., 63g carb. (53g sugars, 3g fiber), 1g pro.

TEST KITCHEN TIP

If you want your bananas to stay somewhat firm, add them to the slow cooker during the last 20 minutes of cooking.

ARMAGNAC CHOCOLATE ALMOND TART

I am a pecan pie lover, and this is my twist on pecan pie. I use almonds instead of pecans and golden syrup instead of corn syrup. Both chocolate and Armagnac make this tart really special. Don't skip on toasting the almonds—it brings out the nuttiness of the pie.
—*Phoebe Saad, Framingham, MA*

PREP: 30 MIN. + CHILLING • **BAKE:** 35 MIN. + COOLING • **MAKES:** 8 SERVINGS

1 cup all-purpose flour
¼ cup toasted ground almonds
1 Tbsp. sugar
   Dash salt
½ cup cold unsalted butter
2 to 4 Tbsp. ice water

FILLING
1½ cups slivered almonds, toasted
2 Tbsp. unsalted butter
1 oz. unsweetened chocolate, chopped
2 large eggs, room temperature
½ cup sugar
⅓ cup golden syrup or light corn syrup
1½ Tbsp. Armagnac or Cognac
¼ tsp. vanilla extract
⅛ tsp. salt

1. In a large bowl, mix flour, ground almonds, sugar and salt; cut in butter until crumbly. Gradually add ice water, tossing with a fork until dough holds together when pressed. Shape into a disk; wrap and refrigerate 1 hour or overnight.

2. Preheat oven to 350°. On a lightly floured surface, roll dough to a ⅛-in.-thick circle; press onto the bottom and up side of an ungreased 9-in. tart pan with removable bottom. Place on a baking sheet.

3. For filling, sprinkle slivered almonds over crust. In top of a double boiler or a metal bowl over hot water, melt butter and chocolate; stir until smooth. Remove from heat. In a large bowl, beat eggs and sugar until thick and lemon-colored. Beat in golden syrup, Armagnac, vanilla and salt until well blended. Gradually beat in chocolate mixture. Slowly spoon filling over almonds. Bake 35-40 minutes or until set. Cool completely on a wire rack.

1 piece: 462 cal., 29g fat (11g sat. fat), 85mg chol., 67mg sod., 44g carb. (27g sugars, 4g fiber), 9g pro.

ARMAGNAC CHOCOLATE
ALMOND TART

APPLE-WALNUT BREAD PUDDING

You can throw everything but the kitchen sink into bread pudding. This recipe came about because I had stale bread and apples that needed to be used. No apples? Use dried fruit, such as cranberries or apricots.
—*Debra Keil, Owasso, OK*

PREP: 30 MIN. • **BAKE:** 50 MIN. • **MAKES:** 8 SERVINGS

5 Tbsp. butter, divided
2 medium Granny Smith apples, peeled and chopped
1 cup sugar, divided
½ tsp. ground cinnamon
¼ cup brandy or unsweetened apple juice
3 cups refrigerated unsweetened vanilla almond milk
4 large eggs, beaten
½ tsp. vanilla extract
8 cups cubed day-old bread
½ cup chopped walnuts

1. Preheat oven to 350°. In a large cast-iron or other ovenproof skillet, melt 2 Tbsp. butter over medium heat. Add apples and ¼ cup sugar. Cook and stir until apples are golden brown and soft, about 6 minutes. Stir in cinnamon. Remove from heat. Stir in brandy; cook over medium heat until liquid is syrupy, 1-2 minutes. Remove from heat.

2. In a large bowl, whisk the milk, eggs, vanilla and remaining ¾ cup sugar until blended. Gently stir in the bread; let stand until bread is softened, about 5 minutes. Stir in the apple mixture and the walnuts.

3. Add 1 Tbsp. remaining butter to skillet; place in oven to heat skillet. Carefully remove hot skillet from oven once butter has melted.

4. Add bread mixture. Melt remaining 2 Tbsp. butter; drizzle over top. Bake until puffed, golden and a knife inserted in center comes out clean, 50-55 minutes. Serve warm.

1 serving: 367 cal., 17g fat (6g sat. fat), 112mg chol., 328mg sod., 48g carb. (31g sugars, 2g fiber), 8g pro.

STREUSEL SQUASH DESSERT

I call this my I Won't Tell Them It's Squash if You Don't Dessert!
This fall treat features a praline-like topping.
—*Teri Rasey, Cadillac, MI*

PREP: 1 HOUR • BAKE: 55 MIN. + CHILLING • MAKES: 18 SERVINGS

1½ cups all-purpose flour
¼ cup sugar
¼ cup confectioners' sugar
½ cup cold butter

STREUSEL TOPPING
¼ cup packed brown sugar
2 Tbsp. all-purpose flour
1 tsp. ground cinnamon
2 Tbsp. cold butter
1 cup chopped pecans

FILLING
1 medium butternut squash (4 lbs.), peeled, seeded and cubed
1 cup sugar
⅓ cup packed brown sugar
¼ cup cornstarch
3 tsp. ground cinnamon
1 tsp. salt
1 tsp. ground ginger
½ tsp. ground nutmeg
½ tsp. ground cloves
2 cans (12 oz. each) evaporated milk
4 large eggs
Optional: Whipped cream and additional cinnamon

1. In a bowl, combine flour and sugars; cut in butter until crumbly. Press into an ungreased 13x9-in. baking dish. Bake at 350° for 15-20 minutes or until edges begin to brown.

2. In a small bowl, combine brown sugar, flour and cinnamon; cut in butter until crumbly. Stir in pecans; set aside.

3. Place squash in a large saucepan and cover with water; bring to a boil. Reduce heat; cover and simmer for 15-20 minutes or until tender. Drain. Transfer to a blender or food processor; cover and process until smooth.

4. In a large bowl, combine the sugars, cornstarch and seasonings. Gradually beat in 4 cups squash, milk and eggs until smooth (save any remaining squash for another use). Pour over crust. Sprinkle with topping.

5. Bake at 350° for 55-65 minutes or until a knife inserted in center comes out clean. Cool on a wire rack. Cover and refrigerate overnight.

6. Garnish with whipped cream and additional cinnamon if desired.

1 piece: 346 cal., 14g fat (7g sat. fat), 70mg chol., 240mg sod., 50g carb. (29g sugars, 5g fiber), 7g pro.

World Travel Sparks a Love of Cooking

Creating, perfecting and sharing recipes is a much-loved hobby for this home baker.

Teri Rasey has been sharing her favorite dishes with *Taste of Home* for decades. In fact, she's had more than 40 recipes published in the magazine and on *tasteofhome.com*. Growing up in Los Angeles, traveling the world and sampling food from all over the globe truly ignited her love of cooking. Desserts and sweet snacks are her most-requested dishes—and some of her favorite things to share with friends and family. Try her Streusel Squash Dessert today and see why it's one of the recipes she's asked about most.

Teri Rasey,
Cadillac, MI

MANGO
TIRAMISU

MANGO TIRAMISU

I love tiramisu and I wanted to make one with summer flavors. I swapped the Grand Marnier and Malibu rum for the usual coffee liqueur, giving a tropical twist.
—*Carla Mendres, Winnipeg, MB*

PREP: 30 MIN. • COOK: 5 MIN. + CHILLING • MAKES: 12 SERVINGS

2 large egg yolks
1 cup confectioners' sugar, divided
2 cups heavy whipping cream, divided
1 carton (8 oz.) mascarpone cheese
2 large navel oranges
½ cup coconut rum or orange juice plus ½ tsp. coconut extract
½ cup orange liqueur or orange juice
1 tsp. vanilla extract
1 pkg. (7 oz.) crisp ladyfinger cookies
2 medium ripe mangoes, peeled and thinly sliced

1. In top of a double boiler or a metal bowl over simmering water, combine egg yolks, ½ cup confectioners' sugar and ½ cup cream. Whisking constantly, heat mixture until thick and a thermometer reads 160°. Remove from heat; whisk in mascarpone cheese until almost smooth. In another bowl, beat remaining 1½ cups cream until it begins to thicken. Add remaining ½ cup confectioners' sugar; beat until soft peaks form. Fold whipped cream into mascarpone mixture.

2. Cut oranges crosswise in half; squeeze juice from oranges into a shallow bowl. Stir in rum, orange liqueur and vanilla.

3. Quickly dip half of the ladyfingers into rum mixture and place in the bottom of a 9-in. springform pan. Top with half of the mascarpone mixture and half of the mango slices. Repeat layers. Refrigerate, covered, at least 8 hours or overnight. To serve, loosen and remove rim.

Note: This recipe was prepared with Alessi brand ladyfinger cookies.

1 piece: 413 cal., 25g fat (14g sat. fat), 117mg chol., 48mg sod., 38g carb. (31g sugars, 2g fiber), 5g pro.

EASY ALMOND JOY CHIA PUDDING

I enjoy making this recipe because it's easy and I can find all the ingredients at my local market. No baking is required, and it's served in individual jars for guests. For more flavor, add shredded coconut.
—*Ashley Altan, Hanover, MD*

PREP: 15 MIN. + CHILLING • **MAKES:** 2 SERVINGS

1 cup refrigerated unsweetened coconut milk
4 Tbsp. chia seeds
3 Tbsp. maple syrup
2 Tbsp. baking cocoa
¼ cup dairy-free semisweet chocolate chips
¼ cup slivered almonds

1. In a small bowl, mix coconut milk, chia seeds and maple syrup. Remove half the mixture to a small bowl; stir in cocoa until blended. Refrigerate both plain and chocolate mixtures, covered, until thickened, at least 6 hours.

2. In each of 2 dessert dishes, layer a fourth of the white pudding, chocolate pudding, chocolate chips and almonds. Repeat layers. Serve immediately or store in the refrigerator up to 3 days.

Note: This recipe was tested with Enjoy Life semisweet chocolate chips.

1 serving: 414 cal., 24g fat (8g sat. fat), 0 chol., 7mg sod., 50g carb. (30g sugars, 12g fiber), 9g pro.

TEST KITCHEN TIP

Feeding a bunch? This contest-winning recipe is easily doubled (or tripled) and can be made ahead.

CHERRY HAND PIES

There's nothing better than a sweet, from-scratch delight like traditional cherry pie. These precious little hand pies always go fast when I sell them at my bakery!

—Allison Cebulla, Milwaukee, WI

PREP: 45 MIN. • **BAKE:** 25 MIN. + COOLING • **MAKES:** 8 SERVINGS

- 6 Tbsp. water, divided
- 2 Tbsp. sugar
- 2 Tbsp. cherry brandy
- 4½ tsp. cornstarch
- 1½ tsp. lemon juice
- 1 tsp. quick-cooking tapioca
- ¼ tsp. grated lemon zest
  Dash salt
- 2 cups fresh or frozen pitted tart cherries, thawed and halved
- 1 cup fresh or frozen pitted dark sweet cherries, thawed and halved
- 1 Dough for double-crust pie
- 1 large egg, room temperature

ICING
- 2⅔ cups confectioners' sugar
- 3 to 4 Tbsp. hot water
- 2 Tbsp. butter, melted
- ½ tsp. almond extract
- ¼ tsp. vanilla extract
  Dash salt
  Freeze-dried strawberries, crushed, optional

1. In a large saucepan, whisk 4 Tbsp. water, sugar, brandy, cornstarch, lemon juice, tapioca, lemon zest and salt until combined. Add the cherries. Bring to a boil; cook and stir 3-5 minutes or until thickened. Remove from heat. Set aside to cool.

2. Preheat oven to 400°. On a lightly floured surface, roll half the dough to a 14x9-in. rectangle. Cut out eight 3½x4½-in. rectangles. Repeat with remaining dough.

3. Transfer 8 rectangles to parchment-lined baking sheets; spoon about 3 Tbsp. cherry mixture in center of each. Whisk egg and remaining 2 Tbsp. water. Brush edges of crust with egg wash. Top with remaining 8 rectangles; press edges with a fork to seal. Brush tops with egg wash; cut slits in tops.

4. Bake until crust is golden brown and slightly puffed, 25-30 minutes. Remove from pans to wire racks to cool. Combine confectioners' sugar, hot water, melted butter, extracts and salt; drizzle over pies. Garnish with freeze-dried strawberries if desired. Let stand until set.

1 pie: 589 cal., 27g fat (16g sat. fat), 91mg chol., 380mg sod., 83g carb. (49g sugars, 2g fiber), 6g pro.

Dough for double-crust pie: Combine 2½ cups all-purpose flour and ½ tsp. salt; cut in 1 cup cold butter until crumbly. Gradually add ⅓-⅔ cup ice water, tossing with a fork until dough holds together when pressed. Divide dough in half. Shape each into a disk; wrap and refrigerate 1 hour.

DUTCH OVEN CHERRY CHOCOLATE DUMP CAKE

Looking for a super quick dessert that will make people think you spent all day in the kitchen?
This easy dessert will wow your guests. Feel free to use your favorite pie filling in place of cherry.
—*Rashanda Cobbins, Milwaukee, WI*

PREP: 5 MIN. • **BAKE:** 35 MIN. • **MAKES:** 8 SERVINGS

1 can (21 oz.) cherry pie filling
1 can (12 oz.) evaporated milk
1 pkg. chocolate cake mix (regular size)
⅓ cup sliced almonds
¾ cup butter, melted
Vanilla ice cream, optional

Preheat oven to 350°. Line a 4-qt. Dutch oven with parchment; lightly spray with cooking spray. Combine pie filling and evaporated milk; spread filling mixture into bottom of Dutch oven. Sprinkle with cake mix (unprepared) and almonds; drizzle with butter. Bake, covered, until cake springs back when touched, 35-40 minutes. If desired, serve with ice cream.

1 cup: 515 cal., 24g fat (15g sat. fat), 61mg chol., 605mg sod., 68g carb. (44g sugars, 3g fiber), 7g pro.

TEST KITCHEN TIP

To make this cake dairy-free, use almond milk in place of evaporated milk and dairy-free margarine instead of butter.

LEMON ICEBOX CAKE

This easy cake, with subtle lemon flavor and a pleasant crunch from the cookies, is a stunning centerpiece.
—*Peggy Woodward, Taste of Home Senior Food Editor*

TAKES: 20 MIN. + CHILLING • **MAKES:** 8 SERVINGS

3 cups heavy whipping cream
3 Tbsp. sugar
3 Tbsp. grated lemon zest
63 Marie biscuits or Maria cookies
Lemon slices, optional

1. In a large bowl, beat the cream, sugar and lemon zest on high until stiff peaks form. Cut a small hole in the corner of a pastry bag. Fill with whipped cream.

2. On a serving plate, arrange 7 cookies in a circle, placing 1 cookie in the center. Pipe ⅔ cup whipped cream over the cookies. Repeat layers 8 times. Refrigerate overnight.

3. If desired, garnish with lemon slices.

1 piece: 530 cal., 37g fat (23g sat. fat), 102mg chol., 158mg sod., 44g carb. (17g sugars, 2g fiber), 6g pro.

DUTCH OVEN CHERRY
CHOCOLATE DUMP CAKE

CHAPTER 12

EASY ENTERTAINING

Whether hosting an eye-opening brunch or a holiday cocktail party, you'll easily impress with the memorable menus found here. Consider the four lineups that follow, then gather the gang for a delicious get-together that's sure to get smiles.

COZY BRUNCH

Mini Italian Frittatas

*Sweet Potato Waffles
with Nut Topping*

Brie & Sausage Brunch Bake

Wild Mushroom & Bacon Pie

Buttermilk-Beer Pancakes

MINI ITALIAN FRITTATAS

I created this recipe when my friends and I had a picnic breakfast. I wanted an egg meal that was portable and easy to make. These crowd-pleasing frittatas were the result!

—*Jess Apfe, Berkeley, CA*

PREP: 20 MIN. • BAKE: 20 MIN. • MAKES: 1 DOZEN

½ cup boiling water
¼ cup sun-dried tomatoes (not packed in oil)
¾ cup shredded part-skim mozzarella cheese, divided
½ cup chopped fresh spinach
⅓ cup water-packed artichoke hearts, rinsed, drained and chopped
⅓ cup chopped roasted sweet red peppers
¼ cup grated Parmesan cheese
¼ cup ricotta cheese
2 Tbsp. minced fresh basil
1 Tbsp. prepared pesto
2 tsp. Italian seasoning
¼ tsp. garlic powder
8 large eggs, room temperature
½ tsp. pepper
¼ tsp. salt

1. Preheat oven to 350°. Pour boiling water over tomatoes in a small bowl; let stand 5 minutes. Drain and chop tomatoes.

2. In a small bowl, combine ½ cup mozzarella cheese, spinach, artichokes hearts, red peppers, Parmesan cheese, ricotta cheese, basil, pesto, Italian seasoning, garlic powder and tomatoes. In a large bowl, whisk eggs, salt and pepper until blended; stir in cheese mixture.

3. Fill greased or foil-lined muffin cups three-fourths full. Sprinkle with remaining mozzarella cheese. Bake until set, 18-22 minutes. Cool 5 minutes before removing from pan. Serve warm with additional pesto if desired.

1 mini frittata: 95 cal., 6g fat (3g sat. fat), 149mg chol., 233mg sod., 2g carb. (1g sugars, 0 fiber), 8g pro. **Diabetic exchanges:** 1 lean meat, 1 fat.

SWEET POTATO WAFFLES WITH NUT TOPPING

Ready in just minutes, these tender waffles have a
wonderfully sweet and crunchy topping. What a mouthwatering
way to get your family out of bed in the morning!
—*Christine Keating, Norwalk, CA*

PREP: 20 MIN. • COOK: 5 MIN./BATCH • MAKES: 12 WAFFLES

2   cups biscuit/baking mix
2   Tbsp. brown sugar
½   tsp. ground cinnamon
¼   tsp. ground ginger
¼   tsp. ground nutmeg
1   large egg
1⅓ cups 2% milk
1   cup canned sweet potatoes, mashed
2   Tbsp. canola oil
1   tsp. vanilla extract

TOPPING
1   Tbsp. butter
½   cup chopped pecans
½   cup chopped walnuts
2   Tbsp. brown sugar
1   Tbsp. water
⅛   tsp. ground cinnamon
    Dash salt
    Dash ground nutmeg
    Maple syrup

1. In a large bowl, combine biscuit mix, brown sugar and spices. In another bowl, whisk egg, milk, sweet potatoes, oil and vanilla. Stir into dry ingredients just until combined.

2. Bake in a preheated waffle maker according to manufacturer's directions until golden brown.

3. Meanwhile, in a small skillet, melt butter over medium heat. Add chopped pecans and walnuts. Cook and stir for 2 minutes. Add the brown sugar, water, cinnamon, salt and nutmeg. Cook and stir until sugar is dissolved. Serve waffles with topping and syrup.

2 waffles with about 2 Tbsp. nut topping: 457 cal., 28g fat (5g sat. fat), 44mg chol., 598mg sod., 46g carb. (17g sugars, 3g fiber), 9g pro.

BRIE & SAUSAGE BRUNCH BAKE

I've made this brunch bake for holidays as well as for a weekend at a friend's cabin, and I always get requests for the recipe. It is make-ahead convenient, reheats well and even tastes great the next day.
—*Becky Hicks, Forest Lake, MN*

PREP: 30 MIN. + CHILLING • BAKE: 50 MIN. + STANDING • MAKES: 12 SERVINGS

1 lb. bulk Italian sausage
1 small onion, chopped
8 cups cubed day-old sourdough bread
½ cup chopped roasted sweet red peppers
½ lb. Brie cheese, rind removed, cubed
⅔ cup grated Parmesan cheese
2 Tbsp. minced fresh basil or 2 tsp. dried basil
8 large eggs
2 cups heavy whipping cream
1 Tbsp. Dijon mustard
1 tsp. pepper
½ tsp. salt
¾ cup shredded part-skim mozzarella cheese
3 green onions, sliced

1. In a large skillet, cook sausage and onion over medium heat until meat is no longer pink, 5-7 minutes; drain.

2. Place bread cubes in a greased 13x9-in. baking dish. Layer with the sausage mixture, red peppers, Brie and Parmesan cheeses and basil. In a large bowl, whisk eggs, cream, mustard, pepper and salt; pour over top. Cover and refrigerate overnight.

3. Remove from the refrigerator 30 minutes before baking. Preheat oven to 350°. Bake, uncovered, until a knife inserted in the center comes out clean, 45-50 minutes.

4. Sprinkle with mozzarella cheese. Bake until cheese is melted, 4-6 minutes. Let stand 10 minutes before cutting. Sprinkle with green onions.

1 piece: 451 cal., 34g fat (18g sat. fat), 217mg chol., 843mg sod., 16g carb. (3g sugars, 1g fiber), 19g pro.

WILD MUSHROOM & BACON PIE

Rustic flavors of roasted garlic and mushrooms make this savory pie a perfect option for a brunch or weeknight dinner. A mixture of mushrooms gives the pie depth of flavor—feel free to use your favorites!
—*Barbara Estabrook, Appleton, WI*

PREP: 25 MIN. • BAKE: 30 MIN. + STANDING • MAKES: 8 SERVINGS

3 garlic cloves, peeled
1 tsp. canola oil
1 sheet refrigerated pie crust
4 bacon strips, cut into ½-in. pieces
1 lb. sliced assorted fresh mushrooms
¼ cup finely chopped sweet onion
3 large eggs, room temperature
1 pkg. (8 oz.) cream cheese, softened
½ tsp. salt
¼ tsp. pepper
1 cup shredded sharp cheddar cheese
2 Tbsp. grated Parmesan cheese
⅛ tsp. paprika

1. Preheat oven to 425°. Place garlic on a double thickness of heavy-duty foil; drizzle with oil. Wrap foil around garlic. Bake until softened, 15-20 minutes. Cool. Reduce oven setting to 375°. Unroll crust into a 9-in. pie plate; flute edge.

2. In a large skillet, cook bacon over medium heat until crisp, 3-5 minutes. Remove to paper towels with a slotted spoon; drain, reserving 2 tsp. drippings. Saute the mushrooms and onion in drippings until tender, about 3 minutes; set aside.

3. In a large bowl, whisk the eggs until foamy; add cream cheese and whisk until blended. Stir in the salt, pepper and mushroom mixture. Squeeze softened garlic into mixture and mix well.

4. Sprinkle cheddar cheese over crust; top with bacon. Pour egg mixture over the top. Sprinkle with Parmesan cheese and paprika.

5. Bake until a knife inserted in the center comes out clean, 30-35 minutes. Let stand for 15 minutes before cutting.

1 piece: 468 cal., 35g fat (19g sat. fat), 181mg chol., 719mg sod., 24g carb. (3g sugars, 1g fiber), 16g pro.

BUTTERMILK-BEER PANCAKES

A friend of mine shared these pancakes with me when I was in college. His dad had made them for as long as he could remember. I love them because they are so light and fluffy!
—*Carrie Auldridge, Hudson Oaks, TX*

PREP: 10 MIN. • COOK: 5 MIN./BATCH • MAKES: 36 PANCAKES

5 cups all-purpose flour
2 Tbsp. sugar
2 tsp. salt
2 tsp. baking soda
4 large eggs, room temperature
4 cups buttermilk
¼ cup canola oil
1 bottle (12 oz.) beer

1. In a large bowl, whisk flour, sugar, salt and baking soda. In a second bowl, whisk the eggs, buttermilk and oil until blended. Add to dry ingredients, stirring just until moistened. Stir in beer.

2. Lightly grease a griddle; heat over medium heat. Pour batter by ¼ cupfuls onto griddle. Cook until bubbles on top begin to pop and bottoms are golden brown. Turn; cook until second side is golden brown.

3 pancakes: 308 cal., 7g fat (1g sat. fat), 65mg chol., 784mg sod., 47g carb. (7g sugars, 1g fiber), 10g pro.

WILD MUSHROOM &
BACON PIE

RETRO COCKTAIL PARTY

Classic Swiss Cheese Fondue

Tom Collins

Frozen Blue Lagoon Margaritas

Coconut Shrimp

Tequila Sunrise

Mai Tai

Brandy Old-Fashioned Sweet

CLASSIC SWISS CHEESE FONDUE

This rich and fancy fondue is a great appetizer that always pleases a crowd.
Don't be surprised when the pot is scraped clean!
—Taste of Home *Test Kitchen*

TAKES: 30 MIN. • MAKES: ABOUT 4 CUPS

1 garlic clove, halved
2 cups white wine, chicken broth or
  unsweetened apple juice, divided
¼ tsp. ground nutmeg
7 cups shredded Swiss cheese
2 Tbsp. cornstarch
  Optional: Cubed bread and assorted
  fresh vegetables

1. Rub garlic clove over the bottom and sides of a fondue pot; discard the garlic and set fondue pot aside. In a large saucepan over medium-low heat, bring 1¾ cups wine and nutmeg to a simmer. Gradually add cheese, stirring after each addition until cheese is melted (cheese will separate from wine).

2. Combine cornstarch and remaining wine until smooth; gradually stir into cheese mixture. Cook and stir until thickened and mixture is blended and smooth. Transfer to prepared fondue pot and keep warm. Serve with bread cubes and vegetables.

¼ cup: 214 cal. 15g fat (9g sat. fat), 44mg chol., 90mg sod., 2g carb. (0 sugars, 0 fiber), 13g pro.

TEST KITCHEN TIP

Serve this fondue with the dippers your gang likes best. Try pretzels, breadsticks, crackers, tortilla or corn chips, rye crisps or cubed bagels.

TOM COLLINS

This cocktail has been popular for a long time, but the origin of the name is still up for debate. Some think it was named after a sweet gin called Old Tom, and others believe the drink was named for the bartender who invented it.
—Taste of Home *Test Kitchen*

TAKES: 5 MIN. • **MAKES:** 1 SERVING

1½ to 2 cups ice cubes, divided
2 oz. gin
1½ oz. sour mix
½ cup club soda, chilled
Optional garnish: Orange slice and maraschino cherry

1. Fill a shaker three-fourths full with ice. Place remaining ice in a Collins or highball glass; set aside.

2. Add the gin and sour mix to shaker; cover and shake until condensation forms on outside of shaker, 10-15 seconds. Strain into prepared glass. Pour club soda into glass. If desired, garnish with orange slice and cherry.

1 serving: 213 cal., 0 fat (0 sat. fat), 0 chol., 29mg sod., 22g carb. (21g sugars, 0 fiber), 0 pro.

FROZEN BLUE LAGOON MARGARITAS

A special toast to anyone who mixes up a mysterious batch of lagoon margaritas for a summer soiree. Guests will swoon over the citrusy sweet tang and electrifying shade of blue.
—Willie DeWaard, Coralville, IA

TAKES: 15 MIN. • **MAKES:** 4 SERVINGS

4 lime slices
3 Tbsp. coarse sugar
½ cup chilled lemon-lime soda
½ cup tequila
½ cup blue curacao
⅓ cup partially thawed frozen limeade concentrate
2 cups ice cubes

1. Using lime slices, moisten the rims of 4 margarita or cocktail glasses. Set aside lime slices for garnish. Sprinkle sugar on a plate; hold each glass upside down and dip rim into sugar. Set aside. Discard remaining sugar on plate.

2. In a blender, combine the remaining ingredients; cover and process until blended. Pour into prepared glasses. Garnish with reserved lime slices. Serve immediately.

1 cup: 205 cal., 0 fat (0 sat. fat), 0 chol., 5mg sod., 26g carb. (22g sugars, 1g fiber), 0 pro.

TOM
COLLINS

66
A personal
favorite and
all-time
favorite of my
grandma's.
This recipe is
the perfect mix
ratio!
—GINA.KAPFHAMER
TASTEOFHOME.COME

COCONUT
SHRIMP

COCONUT SHRIMP

Jumbo shrimp is the perfect vehicle for crunchy, tropical coconut flakes. The fruity salsa is delightful as a dip for this island-influenced appetizer.
—Marie Hattrup, Sonoma, CA

PREP: 20 MIN. • COOK: 5 MIN./BATCH • MAKES: 1½ DOZEN

18 uncooked jumbo shrimp (about 1 lb.)
⅓ cup cornstarch
¾ tsp. salt
½ tsp. cayenne pepper
3 large egg whites
2 cups sweetened shredded coconut
Oil for deep-fat frying

APRICOT-PINEAPPLE SALSA

1 cup diced pineapple
½ cup finely chopped red onion
½ cup apricot preserves
½ cup minced fresh cilantro
2 Tbsp. lime juice
1 jalapeno pepper, seeded and chopped
Salt and pepper to taste
Lime wedges, optional

1. Peel and devein shrimp, leaving tails intact. Make a slit down inner curve of each shrimp, starting with the tail; press lightly to flatten. In a shallow dish, combine the cornstarch, salt and cayenne; set aside. In a bowl, beat egg whites until stiff peaks form. Place the coconut in another shallow dish. Coat the shrimp with cornstarch mixture; dip into egg whites, then coat with coconut.

2. In an electric skillet or deep-fat fryer, heat oil to 375°. Fry shrimp, a few at a time, 1-1½ minutes on each side or until golden brown. Drain on paper towels.

3. In a bowl, combine the salsa ingredients. Serve with shrimp and, if desired, lime wedges.

Note: Wear disposable gloves when cutting hot peppers; the oils can burn skin. Avoid touching your face.

1 shrimp with 1 Tbsp. salsa: 505 cal., 12g fat (5g sat. fat), 552mg chol., 677mg sod., 19g carb. (11g sugars, 1g fiber), 75g pro.

TEQUILA SUNRISE

Everyone loves the pretty sunset layers in this refreshing cocktail classic. It's like a mini vacation in a glass!
—Taste of Home *Test Kitchen*

TAKES: 5 MIN. • MAKES: 1 SERVING

1 to 1¼ cups ice cubes
1½ oz. tequila
4½ oz. orange juice
1½ tsp. grenadine syrup
Optional garnish:
Orange slice and maraschino cherry

1. Place ice in a Collins or highball glass. Pour the tequila and orange juice into the glass. Slowly pour grenadine over a bar spoon into the center of the drink. Garnish as desired.

¾ cup: 184 cal., 0 fat (0 sat. fat), 0 chol., 0 sod., 17g carb. (15g sugars, 0 fiber), 1g pro.

MAI TAI

This party favorite has been around for quite some time. It's not overly fruity and features a good blend of sweet and sour. For a splash of color, garnish with strawberries and lime.
—Taste of Home *Test Kitchen*

TAKES: 5 MIN. • **MAKES:** 1 SERVING

1½ to 2 cups ice cubes
2 oz. light rum
¾ oz. Triple Sec
½ oz. lemon juice
1½ tsp. lime juice
1½ tsp. amaretto
   Optional garnish: Lime slice, lime twist, edible flowers and fresh pineapple

1. Fill a shaker three-fourths full with ice. Place remaining ice in a rocks glass; set aside.

2. Add the rum, Triple Sec, juices and amaretto to shaker; cover and shake for 10-15 seconds or until condensation forms on outside of shaker. Strain into prepared glass. Garnish as desired.

⅔ cup: 241 cal., 0 fat (0 sat. fat), 0 chol., 7mg sod., 15g carb. (13g sugars, 0 fiber), 0 pro.

BRANDY OLD-FASHIONED SWEET

Here in Wisconsin, we make this old-fashioned favorite using brandy in place of whiskey and soda instead of water for a milder sweet cocktail.
—Taste of Home *Test Kitchen*

TAKES: 10 MIN. • **MAKES:** 1 SERVING

1 orange slice
1 maraschino cherry
1½ oz. maraschino cherry juice
1 tsp. bitters
¼ to ⅓ cup ice cubes
1½ oz. brandy
2 tsp. water
1 tsp. orange juice
3 oz. lemon-lime soda

In a rocks glass, muddle orange slice, cherry, cherry juice and bitters. Add ice. Pour in the brandy, water, orange juice and soda.

1 serving: 277 cal., 0 fat (0 sat. fat), 0 chol., 18mg sod., 36g carb. (17g sugars, 0 fiber), 0 pro.

TEST KITCHEN TIP

Angostura bitters are the traditional choice for old-fashioneds, but craft bitters are flooding the market today. Try orange, cherry or even smoked cinnamon for an updated twist on this classic cocktail.

—CATHERINE WARD, *TASTE OF HOME* PREP KITCHEN MANAGER

MADE FOR MUDDLING

A cocktail muddler is a narrow pestle used to lightly mash fruit and other ingredients. This method infuses drinks with a layer of flavor.

MAI TAI

IN-HOME TAKEOUT

BAKED EGG ROLLS

These egg rolls are low in fat but the crispiness from baking will fool you into thinking they were fried!
—*Barbara Lierman, Lyons, NE*

PREP: 30 MIN. • BAKE: 10 MIN. • MAKES: 16 SERVINGS

2 cups grated carrots
1 can (14 oz.) bean sprouts, drained
½ cup chopped water chestnuts
¼ cup chopped green pepper
¼ cup chopped green onions
1 garlic clove, minced
2 cups finely diced cooked chicken
4 tsp. cornstarch
1 Tbsp. water
1 Tbsp. light soy sauce
1 tsp. canola oil
1 tsp. brown sugar
  Pinch cayenne pepper
16 egg roll wrappers
  Cooking spray

1. Coat a large skillet with cooking spray; heat pan over medium heat. Add the first 6 ingredients; cook and stir until vegetables are crisp-tender, about 3 minutes. Add chicken; heat through.

2. In a small bowl, combine the cornstarch, water, soy sauce, oil, brown sugar and cayenne until smooth; stir into chicken mixture. Bring to a boil. Cook and stir for 2 minutes or until thickened remove from the heat.

3. Spoon ¼ cup chicken mixture on the bottom third of 1 egg roll wrapper; fold sides toward center and roll tightly. (Keep remaining wrappers covered with a damp paper towel until ready to use.) Place seam side down on a baking sheet coated with cooking spray. Repeat.

4. Spritz tops of egg rolls with cooking spray. Bake at 425° for 10-15 minutes or until lightly browned.

Freeze option: Freeze cooled egg rolls in a freezer container, separating layers with waxed paper. To use, reheat rolls on a baking sheet in a preheated 350° oven until crisp and heated through.

1 egg roll: 146 cal., 2g fat (0 sat. fat), 18mg chol., 250mg sod., 22g carb. (1g sugars, 1g fiber), 9g pro. **Diabetic exchanges:** 1½ starch, 1 lean meat, ½ fat.

TEST KITCHEN TIP

In a hurry? Try these effortless egg rolls. Thaw and chop 1 lb. frozen stir-fry vegetable blend; cook in a large skillet with 1 lb. bulk pork sausage until meat is no longer pink. Stir in 2 Tbsp. teriyaki sauce. Fill and bake egg rolls as directed.

> "These were delicious! My family loved them. I will definitely be making these for our next party.
> —KATEJUDY311
> TASTEOFHOME.COM

CHICKEN POT STICKERS

CHICKEN POT STICKERS

Chicken and mushrooms make up the filling in these pot stickers, which are traditional Chinese dumplings. Greasing the steamer rack makes it easy to remove them once they're steamed.

—Jacquelynne Stine, Las Vegas, NV

PREP: 50 MIN. • COOK: 5 MIN./BATCH • MAKES: 4 DOZEN

1 lb. boneless skinless chicken thighs, cut into chunks
1½ cups sliced fresh mushrooms
1 small onion, cut into wedges
2 Tbsp. hoisin sauce
2 Tbsp. prepared mustard
2 Tbsp. Sriracha chili sauce or 1 Tbsp. hot pepper sauce
1 pkg. (10 oz.) pot sticker or gyoza wrappers
1 large egg, lightly beaten

SAUCE
1 cup reduced-sodium soy sauce
1 green onion, chopped
1 tsp. ground ginger

1. In a food processor, combine chicken, mushrooms, onion, hoisin sauce, mustard and chili sauce; cover and process until blended.

2. Place 1 Tbsp. chicken mixture in the center of 1 wrapper. (Until ready to use, keep the remaining wrappers covered with a damp towel to prevent them from drying out.) Moisten entire edge with egg. Fold wrapper over filling to form a semicircle. Press edges firmly to seal, pleating the front side to form several folds.

3. Holding sealed edge, place each dumpling on an even surface; press to flatten bottom. Curve ends to form a crescent shape. Repeat with remaining wrappers and filling.

4. Working in batches, arrange pot stickers in a single layer on a large greased steamer basket rack; place in a Dutch oven over 1 in. of water. Bring to a boil; cover and steam 5-7 minutes or until filling juices run clear. Repeat with remaining pot stickers.

5. Meanwhile, in a small bowl, combine sauce ingredients. Serve with pot stickers. Refrigerate leftovers.

Freeze option: Cover and freeze uncooked pot stickers in a single layer on waxed paper-lined sheets until firm. Transfer to freezer containers; return to freezer. To use, steam as directed until heated through and juices run clear.

1 pot sticker with 1 tsp. sauce: 39 cal., 1g fat (0 sat. fat), 11mg chol., 254mg sod., 5g carb. (0 sugars, 0 fiber), 3g pro.

Around the World

An international potluck stirs up amazing flavors and a heartwarming feeling of community.

Ruth Hartunian -Alumbaugh
Willimantic, CT

I spend a lot of time around food. I enjoy making it, sharing it and planning for events that include it. Some of my favorite food memories involve the International Christian Fellowship, a group that I take part in through the University of Connecticut. The group often hosts international graduate students. I have long been involved (25 years and counting), and because of the group I've experienced wonderful things in the potluck world.

One Christmas we hosted an open house for all international graduate students at the university. For the event, I made a number of dishes, and I encouraged our international friends to bring anything they wanted to share as well. Boy, was I glad I did!

A group of women visiting from China decided to bring all the ingredients needed to make fresh dumplings, or jiaozi, from scratch.

My kitchen became a veritable assembly line of happy people using every available flat surface to fill and then cook the jiaozi. By the end of the evening, we were all absolutely stuffed—but we couldn't resist those delicious dumplings!

We also enjoyed dishes from Iran, Taiwan and Africa. These offerings brought us closer, as we learned about one another's countries and traditions through food. I didn't know half the people who showed up at my house that Christmas Day, but when it was time to part, we were all wonderful friends.

Food has a way of bringing us together, doesn't it?

SHRIMP EGG FOO YOUNG

If you love Chinese food as much as I do, you'll appreciate this shrimp egg foo young that features all the flavor without all the fat and calories. The secret lies in using just the egg white instead of the whole egg.
—*Quimberley Rice, Decatur, GA*

PREP: 25 MIN. • COOK: 5 MIN./BATCH • MAKES: 8 PATTIES (1 CUP SAUCE)

1 cup chicken broth
1 Tbsp. oyster sauce
1 Tbsp. reduced-sodium soy sauce
1 Tbsp. cornstarch
¼ cup cold water

EGG FOO YOUNG
8 oz. uncooked medium shrimp, peeled, deveined and coarsely chopped
⅔ cup coarsely chopped fresh mushrooms
½ cup bean sprouts
1 green onion, sliced
3 Tbsp. canola oil, divided
8 large egg whites
1 Tbsp. reduced-sodium soy sauce
   Black and white sesame seeds, optional

1. In a small saucepan, combine the broth, oyster sauce and soy sauce. Bring to a boil. Combine cornstarch and water until smooth; gradually stir into the pan. Bring to a boil; cook and stir until thickened, about 2 minutes. Set aside and keep warm.

2. In a large skillet, saute shrimp, mushrooms, sprouts and onion in 1 Tbsp. oil until shrimp turn pink and vegetables are crisp-tender, about 2 minutes. Remove from heat; cool slightly. In a large bowl, whisk egg whites and soy sauce. Stir in cooked shrimp mixture.

3. In a large skillet, heat remaining oil. Drop the shrimp mixture in batches by ⅓ cupfuls into oil. Cook until golden brown, 2-3 minutes on each side. Serve with sauce. If desired, sprinkle with black and white sesame seeds and additional green onions.

2 patties with ¼ cup sauce: 115 cal., 7g fat (1g sat. fat), 40mg chol., 477mg sod., 3g carb. (1g sugars, 0 fiber), 10g pro.

PRESSURE-COOKER SESAME CHICKEN

Your family will love the flavorful sauce that coats this chicken, and you'll love how quick and easy it is for a weeknight dinner! If you serve gluten-free meals, use tamari instead of soy sauce.

—Karen Kelly, Germantown, MD

PREP: 10 MIN. • COOK: 10 MIN. • MAKES: 4 SERVINGS

1 to 2 Tbsp. sesame oil
1½ lbs. boneless skinless chicken breasts, cut into 1-in. pieces
¼ cup honey
¼ cup soy sauce or gluten-free tamari soy sauce
¼ cup water
3 garlic cloves, minced
¼ tsp. crushed red pepper flakes
3 tsp. cornstarch
2 Tbsp. cold water
Hot cooked rice
1 Tbsp. sesame seeds
Thinly sliced green onions, optional

1. Select saute or browning setting on a 6-qt. electric pressure cooker. Adjust for medium heat; add 1 Tbsp. sesame oil. When oil is hot, brown chicken in batches using additional oil as necessary. Press cancel. Return all to pressure cooker. In a bowl, whisk honey, soy sauce, water, garlic and pepper flakes; stir into pressure cooker. Lock lid; close pressure-release valve. Adjust to pressure-cook on high for 4 minutes.

2. Quick-release pressure. In a small bowl, mix cornstarch and water until smooth; stir into pressure cooker. Select saute setting and adjust for low heat. Simmer, stirring constantly, until thickened, 1-2 minutes. Serve with rice. Sprinkle with sesame seeds and, if desired, green onions.

1 serving: 311 cal., 9g fat (2g sat. fat), 94mg chol., 1004mg sod., 20g carb. (17g sugars, 0 fiber), 37g pro.

TEST KITCHEN TIP

Round out this easy entree by preparing a few frozen egg rolls and picking up a box of fortune cookies from the ethnic aisle at your grocery store.

SLOW-COOKER BEEF & BROCCOLI

I love introducing my kids to all kinds of flavors. This Asian-inspired
slow-cooker meal is one of their favorites, so I serve it often.
—*Brandy Stansbury, Edna, TX*

PREP: 20 MIN. • **COOK:** 6½ HOURS • **MAKES:** 4 SERVINGS

2   cups beef broth
½   cup reduced-sodium soy sauce
⅓   cup packed brown sugar
1½   tsp. sesame oil
1   garlic cloves, minced
1   beef top sirloin steak (1½ lbs.),
     cut into ½-in.-thick strips
2   Tbsp. cornstarch
¼   cup cold water
4   cups fresh broccoli florets
     Hot cooked rice
     Optional: Sesame seeds and thinly
     sliced green onions

1. In a 5-qt. slow cooker, combine the first 5 ingredients. Add beef; stir to coat. Cover and cook on low until tender, about 6 hours.

2. In a small bowl, whisk cornstarch and cold water until smooth; stir into slow cooker. Cover and cook on high until thickened, about 30 minutes. Meanwhile, in a large saucepan, place a steamer basket over 1 in. of water. Place broccoli in basket. Bring water to a boil. Reduce heat to maintain a simmer; steam, covered, until crisp-tender, 3-4 minutes. Stir broccoli into slow cooker. Serve over rice. If desired, garnish with sesame seeds and green onions.

1 cup: 366 cal., 9g fat (3g sat. fat), 69mg chol., 1696mg sod., 28g carb. (19g sugars, 2g fiber), 42g pro.

TEST KITCHEN TIP

To make this slow-cooked dish healthier, try adding more veggies and serving over hot cooked brown rice, quinoa or even cauliflower rice.

SLOW-COOKER
BEEF & BROCCOLI

"This was so easy for a weeknight meal. My family just loved it. Thank you for sharing.
—KATECRID47
TASTEOFHOME.COM

BONFIRE GET-TOGETHER

Cheese & Pimiento Spread

Favorite Hot Chocolate

Watermelon & Cucumber Salsa

Mac & Cheese Cups

Grandma's Classic Potato Salad

S'mores Cupcakes

CHEESE & PIMIENTO SPREAD

My mother made delicious pimiento cheese, but this is a spicy, modern version of her recipe.
Serve it stuffed in celery or spread on crackers or a sandwich.
—Elizabeth Hester, Elizabethtown, NC

TAKES: 15 MIN. • MAKES: 2¾ CUPS

12 oz. sharp white cheddar cheese
8 oz. reduced-fat cream cheese, softened
2 tsp. Worcestershire sauce
2 tsp. white vinegar
¼ tsp. white pepper
¼ tsp. garlic powder
¼ tsp. cayenne pepper
1 jar (4 oz.) diced pimientos, undrained
   Assorted crackers and vegetables

Shred the white cheddar cheese; transfer to a large bowl. Add cream cheese, Worcestershire sauce, vinegar, pepper, garlic powder and cayenne; beat on low speed until blended. Drain pimientos, reserving 2 Tbsp. juice. Stir in pimientos and reserved juice. Serve with crackers and vegetables.

2 Tbsp.: 90 cal., 7g fat (4g sat. fat), 23mg chol., 150mg sod., 1g carb. (1g sugars, 0 fiber), 5g pro.

FAVORITE HOT CHOCOLATE

You need just a few basic ingredients to stir up this spirit-warming sipper. The comforting beverage is smooth and not too sweet, making t just right for cozy chilly night.
—Flo Snodderly, North Vernon, IN

TAKES: 15 MIN. • MAKES: 8 SERVINGS

1 can (14 oz.) sweetened condensed milk
½ cup baking cocoa
6½ cups water
2 tsp. vanilla extract
   Optional: Sweetened whipped cream, marshmallows, chocolate syrup and Pirouette cookies

1. Place milk and baking cocoa in a large saucepan; cook and stir over medium heat until blended. Gradually stir in water; heat through, stirring occasionally.

2. Remove from heat; stir in vanilla. Add toppings as desired.

1 cup: 177 cal., 5g fat (3g sat. fat), 17mg chol., 63mg sod., 30g carb. (27g sugars, 1g fiber), 5g pro.

WATERMELON & CUCUMBER SALSA

The combo of watermelon and cucumber may sound unusual—it tastes anything but!
Eat the salsa with chips, or serve it as a topper with hot dogs or chicken tacos for a refreshing change of pace.
—*Suzanne Curletto, Walnut Creek, CA*

TAKES: 15 MIN. • MAKES: 3 CUPS

1½ cups seeded chopped watermelon
¾ cup finely chopped cucumber
½ cup finely chopped sweet onion
¼ cup minced fresh cilantro
1 jalapeno pepper, seeded and minced
2 Tbsp. lime juice
¼ tsp. salt

In a small bowl, combine all ingredients; refrigerate until serving.

Note: Wear disposable gloves when cutting hot peppers; the oils can burn skin. Avoid touching your face.

¼ cup: 10 cal., 0 fat (0 sat. fat), 0 chol., 50mg sod., 3g carb. (2g sugars, 0 fiber), 0 pro.
Diabetic exchanges: Free food.

MAC & CHEESE CUPS

I started making these for a close friend's daughter when she started eating solid food.
She loves mac and cheese and could hold these in her tiny hands to feed herself.
Now the adults like them more than the kids! They're always requested at potlucks.
—*Karen Lambert, Weaverville, NC*

PREP: 20 MIN. • BAKE: 25 MIN. • MAKES: 24 SERVINGS

1 lb. uncooked elbow macaroni
3 cups sharp cheddar cheese, finely shredded
5 Tbsp. butter, softened
3 large eggs
1 cup half-and-half cream
½ cup sour cream
1 tsp. salt
½ tsp. pepper

1. Preheat oven to 350°. Cook macaroni according to package directions, drain. Transfer to a large bowl. Stir in cheese and butter until melted.

2. In another bowl, whisk the eggs, cream, sour cream, salt and pepper until blended. Add to macaroni mixture; stir until well blended. Spoon macaroni into 24 well-greased muffin cups. Bake until golden brown, 25-30 minutes.

1 piece: 178 cal., 10g fat (6g sat. fat), 50mg chol., 226mg sod., 15g carb. (1g sugars, 1g fiber), 7g pro.

WATERMELON &
CUCUMBER SALSA

GRANDMA'S CLASSIC
POTATO SALAD

GRANDMA'S CLASSIC POTATO SALAD

When I asked my grandmother how old this recipe was, she told me that her mom used to make it when she was a little girl. It has definitely stood the test of time.
—*Kimberly Wallace, Dennison, OH*

PREP: 25 MIN. • COOK: 20 MIN. + CHILLING • MAKES: 10 SERVINGS

6   medium potatoes, peeled and cubed
¼   cup all-purpose flour
1   Tbsp. sugar
1½   tsp. salt
1   tsp. ground mustard
1   tsp. pepper
¾   cup water
2   large eggs, beaten
¼   cup white vinegar
4   hard-boiled large eggs, divided use
2   celery ribs, chopped
1   medium onion, chopped
    Sliced green onions, optional

1. Place potatoes in a large saucepan and cover with water. Bring to a boil. Reduce heat; cover and cook until tender, 15-20 minutes. Drain and cool to room temperature.

2. Meanwhile, in a small heavy saucepan, combine flour, sugar, salt, mustard and pepper. Gradually stir in water until smooth. Cook and stir over medium-high heat until thickened and bubbly. Reduce heat; cook and stir 2 minutes longer.

3. Remove from the heat. Stir a small amount of hot mixture into beaten eggs; return all to the pan, stirring constantly. Bring to a gentle boil; cook and stir 2 minutes longer. Remove from the heat and cool completely. Gently stir in vinegar.

4. Chop and refrigerate 1 hard-boiled egg; chop the remaining 3 hard-boiled eggs. In a large bowl, combine the potatoes, celery, chopped onion and eggs; add dressing and stir until blended. Refrigerate until chilled. Garnish with reserved chopped egg and, if desired, sliced green onions.

¾ cup: 144 cal., 3g fat (1g sat. fat), 112mg chol., 402mg sod., 23g carb. (3g sugars, 2g fiber), 6g pro. **Diabetic exchanges:** 1½ starch, ½ fat.

S'MORES CUPCAKES

Marshmallow frosting puts these cupcakes over the top. Chocolate bar pieces and graham cracker crumbs on top make them extra indulgent and even more like the real thing—but better!
—*Erin Rachwal, Hartland, WI*

PREP: 30 MIN. • BAKE: 20 MIN. + COOLING • MAKES: 2 DOZEN

¾ cup water
¾ cup buttermilk
2 large eggs, room temperature
3 Tbsp. canola oil
1 tsp. vanilla extract
1½ cups all-purpose flour
1½ cups sugar
¾ cup baking cocoa
1½ tsp. baking soda
¾ tsp. salt
¾ tsp. baking powder

FROSTING
1½ cups butter, softened
2 cups confectioners' sugar
½ tsp. vanilla extract
2 jars (7 oz. each) marshmallow creme
2 Tbsp. graham cracker crumbs
2 milk chocolate candy bars
 (1.55 oz. each)
 Optional: Toasted marshmallows
 and graham cracker pieces

1. Preheat oven to 350°. In a large bowl, beat water, buttermilk, eggs, oil and vanilla until well blended. Combine flour, sugar, cocoa, baking soda, salt and baking powder; gradually beat into water mixture until blended.

2. Fill paper-lined muffin cups half full with batter. Bake until a toothpick comes out clean, 16-20 minutes. Cool in pans 10 minutes before removing from pans to wire racks to cool completely.

3. For frosting, in a large bowl, beat butter until fluffy; beat in confectioners' sugar and vanilla until smooth. Add the marshmallow creme; beat until light and fluffy. Spread or pipe frosting over cupcakes. Sprinkle with the cracker crumbs. Break each candy bar into 12 pieces; garnish cupcakes. If desired, top with toasted marshmallows and graham cracker pieces.

1 cupcake: 330 cal., 15g fat (8g sat. fat), 47mg chol., 298mg sod., 43g carb. (35g sugars, 1g fiber), 3g pro.

S'MORES
CUPCAKES

RECIPE INDEX